MQQQ2Q49Q6

"For Eleanor and Roy Roseda ⸺ -it is practice. No other book I ⸺ ⸺ ⸺ ⸺ e way, contains so many authentic, breathtaking, and productive stories of how effective spiritual warfare opens door after door for the spread of the Gospel worldwide."

—DR. C. PETER WAGNER
FORMER PROFESSOR AT THE FULLER THEOLOGICAL
SEMINARY'S SCHOOL OF WORLD MISSIONS,
PROFESSOR EMERITUS, SCHOOL OF WORLD MISSIONS

"After reading *God Wins* by Roy and Eleanor Rosedale, I felt refreshed and incredibly encouraged. The real-life experiences portrayed in this book read like an instruction manual on how to trust God when nothing else makes sense. I came away from these stories hoping that I will have the same simple faith to ask God to step in and win again as He always does."

—DR. WALTER LINN
PRESIDENT OF GENESIS COUNSELING SERVICE

"In *God Wins* the Rosedales have given us a 'credible witness' that models by example how Christians are to live their lives 'by the faith of the Son of God' (Gal. 2:20). They have invited us to 'come and see' (John 1:46) God at work in overcoming evil with good with real life miraculous encounters that are happening all over the world. Christians need to read this as an antidote for overcoming the pollution of oppressive secularism that is making the western church spiritually impotent. Secularists need to read it to honestly try to understand why their naturalistic worldview makes them look naïve and not credible to the majority of the human family. I recommend *God Wins* to everyone because whatever your worldview all of us at times need to be aroused from our 'dogmatic slumber.'"

—RANDY W. RODDEN
PROFESSOR OF PHILOSOPHY AND CHRISTIAN WORLDVIEW STUDIES
COMMUNITY CHRISTIAN COLLEGE
PRESIDENT OF ANSWERS INTERNATIONAL MINISTRIES

GOD
WINS!

GOD WINS!

130 TRUE STORIES *of* VICTORY OVER EVIL *in* JESUS' NAME *plus* ANGELIC HELP *and* MIRACLES

ELEANOR B. ROSEDALE
DR. ROY S. ROSEDALE

CREATION HOUSE

GOD WINS! by Eleanor B. Rosedale and Roy S. Rosedale
Published by Creation House
A Charisma Media Company
600 Rinehart Road
Lake Mary, Florida 32746
www.charismamedia.com

Unless otherwise indicated, Bible quotations are taken from *The King James Version* (KJV).

Scripture quotations marked NAS are from the New American Standard Bible. Copyright © 1960, 1962, 1963, 1968, 1971, 1972, 1973, 1975, 1977, 1995 by the Lockman Foundation. Used by permission. (www.Lockman.org)

Scripture quotations marked NIV are from the Holy Bible, New International Version. Copyright © 1973, 1978, 1984, International Bible Society. Used by permission.

Design Director: Bill Johnson
Cover design by Terry Clifton

Library of Congress Cataloging-in-Publication Data: 2013941265
International Standard Book Number: 978-1-62136-402-3
E-book International Standard Book Number: 978-1-62136-403-0

While the author has made every effort to provide accurate telephone numbers and Internet addresses at the time of publication, neither the publisher nor the author assumes any responsibility for errors or for changes that occur after publication.

This book was previously published as *God Wins*, ISBN 978-1612153865, by Xulon Press, copyright © 2011.

14 15 16 17 18 — 9 8 7 6 5 4 3 2
Printed in the United States of America

DEDICATION TREE

We
Dedicate
God Wins to
Eleanor's mother,
Rose Marie Boehringer,
Who loved Jesus and was
Always kind.
She loved people
And wanted to help them know
Jesus
Personally and live forever.
Mom is now in Heaven, rejoicing with
People she led to Him.
And to our beloved children: Karen, Michael,
And Robin, who are faithful to Christ
And continually inspire us.
And to their dear spouses and our six wonderful
Grandchildren, all of whom are delightful and interesting,
Talented and kind. They love Jesus and tell others about Him.
And with special heartfelt thanks
We also dedicate this book to our faithful ministry partners.
Every victory is *your victory too,*
Because we have been a team. We thank God for each
Of you; for your love and friendship, financial support and prayer.
We pray that all of you will feel blessed and encouraged by
these true stories of victory in Christ.

TABLE OF CONTENTS

SECTION TWO:
GOD'S ANGELS: HELPERS OF HIS PEOPLE

SECTION THREE:
GOD'S HATRED OF WITCHCRAFT

ACKNOWLEDGMENTS

W E ARE INDEBTED to all the authors listed in the bibliography, and especially Drs. C. Peter Wagner, Timothy M. Warner, and Gregory A. Boyd.

Dr. Wagner was one of Roy's very valued professors and mentors at the Fuller School of World Mission as Roy sought to learn more about the power of Christ in overcoming evil. For many years Dr. Wagner has been a courageous pioneer in educating Christians about the reality of spiritual war and its affect in hindering the spread of the Gospel. He also teaches the victory that Christians can gain as they honor God in daily life and use Christ's Name and Blood against evil. In *God Wins* you will read many words of wisdom from Dr. Wagner, and also his report of eleven situations of severe demonic strongholds broken in various countries, in Jesus' Name. In other places in *God Wins* you will read Dr. Wagner's deep teachings about effective prayer. Dr. Wagner is the author of many inspiring, informative, and very useful books about spiritual warfare worldwide. *We thank Dr. C. Peter Wagner and highly recommend his books.*

Dr. Timothy M. Warner's book *Spiritual Warfare* was an invaluable resource in writing *God Wins*. Dr. Warner gives specific, biblically sound information about many aspects of the Christian's spiritual authority in Christ, strategies of satan and demonic beings, and aspects of spiritual war as they affect people in various circumstances. He illustrates his teachings with many compelling true stories of overcoming evil in Jesus' Name. *Spiritual Warfare* is a treasure; profound yet readable, interesting, excellent and applicable. *Roy and I thank Dr. Timothy M. Warner for writing this immensely instructive book, and we highly recommend it.*

We also thank Dr. Gregory A. Boyd for his profound teachings in *God at War—the Bible and Spiritual Conflict*, and *Satan and the Problem of Evil*. Chapter Ten of *God Wins* expresses a major thesis of Boyd, that God has chosen to allow personal freedom of thought and action to humans and angels, and situations on earth reflect the degree of their cooperation with Him. *Dr. Gregory A. Boyd has written important theological works and we recommend them for deep study.*

Roy and I also give special, *heartfelt thanks to our daughter, Robin Rosedale Kimmelshue, who was an invaluable help in many aspects of this book.*

PREFACE

ROY AND ELEANOR Rosedale have been in the international ministry of Campus Crusade for Christ more than 45 years. Roy loves people the world over and most of his adult life has been spent helping people overseas. At age 22, newly graduated from the University of California at Davis with a Bachelor of Science degree in Agronomy, Roy went to India to be the agriculturist on the Barpali village assistance project sponsored by U.S.AID and the American Friends Service Committee. He worked there for almost three years, developing and upgrading everything possible to help the people. At the time, Roy was religious but not yet "born again." His spiritual transformation came in 1957 after reading *Rees Howells, Intercessor*, about a man of prayer whose very effective wartime prayer ministry is reported in Chapter Eleven of *God Wins*.

When Campus Crusade began the International School of Theology, Roy taught Missions and helped start branch seminaries in Asia and Africa. He presently works with the International Leadership Consortium that includes graduate schools in Jordan, Singapore, Manila, Nairobi, Nigeria, Congo, Zimbabwe, and Burundi. While teaching, Roy completed a doctoral program at Fuller School of World Mission, training that helped him greatly in his international ministry and spiritual warfare counseling. Finding that most pastors and missionaries had received no spiritual warfare training, Roy developed a course on this subject and many people subsequently came to him and to Eleanor for counseling and help against demonic problems. Their desire in writing *God Wins* is to help Christians realize and experience that Jesus' presence within them is the power that can banish demonic harassments. It is Roy and Eleanor's earnest prayer that the true stories in this book will help people gain confidence in that area of their Christian life and ministry. Jesus overcame evil and promised His followers that they also would overcome it. He gave the command, "In My Name cast out devils" (Mark 16:17, NASV).

Out of their experiences with Christ in this realm, Eleanor has written *God Wins*. Eleanor holds a Bachelor of Arts in Education from California State University Long Beach, assists Roy, and travels with him when possible. They have three grown children and six grandchildren, a continual joy. The Rosedale family has experienced many wonderful answers to prayer for themselves and others. Eleanor first wrote a shorter version of this book for her grandchildren, to help them learn how to protect their lives and triumph in Christ. This expanded version is for their broader Christian family, to help each reader understand how to defend his or her life and *triumph* in Christ.

INTRODUCTION

I T IS WONDERFUL to know that if Jesus is in your life you have forgiveness of sin, life forever, fellowship with God, and His presence
with you in your daily life. Those are marvelous blessings. Yet virtually every person on earth has been aware of some degree of spiritual oppression as he or she has experienced puzzling troubles and
disappointments. People might not have words to express it, but they
feel it. Many of those problems come from the malicious activity of
satan, the evil spirit power on earth. He and his army of demons are
not make-believe, as many people in the Western world are deceived
into thinking; most of the rest of the world is aware of the reality of
spirit enemies. The purpose of *God Wins* is to help Christians understand how to be victorious over evil in Jesus' Name, so they can help
themselves and others.

As theologian Dr. Timothy M. Warner expresses it, "To ignore an
unscrupulous enemy who always seeks to take advantage of a difficult
situation by making it worse, and to fail to appropriate the victory of
Christ is folly" (*Spiritual Warfare*) pp. 91, 92, 109. It was because *God*
had pity on humanity that He sent Jesus into the world to indwell
those who ask His forgiveness, give them power against evil, and
eternal life.

Jesus said, "I came into the world *for this purpose, to destroy the
works of the devil.*" Devils were afraid of Him then and they are afraid
of Him today. In this book, Roy and I relate many kinds of situations
of Jesus' victory over evil, both in the U.S. and overseas. *God Wins*
will tell you exactly how to cooperate with *God* to do it. *All the stories
are true, and each will teach you how to win.* The Lord Jesus Christ,
His angels, and His people *work together,* forming a *triune* force for

good on this earth. All Christians can pray in the ways we teach. It is *not a "special spiritual gift."* It is just part of having Christ's presence within you and honoring Him.

But preliminary to applying what you read in this book, it is essential that you have Jesus' forgiveness and indwelling presence. That is far more important to your eternal welfare than being able to overthrow evil. However, if you do have Jesus in your life and know how to defeat satan in His Name, you have a *huge advantage.* God will use you to help yourself and others.

(*Please note:* I have an aversion to capitalizing the "s" in the name of mankind's enemy. Unless I am quoting someone else, in *God Wins* you will see satan spelled with a lower case "s.")

WISDOM FROM THE APOSTLE PAUL

A S YOU READ these accounts of victory in Christ, remember the counsel of the Apostle Paul: "Be strong in the Lord and the power of His might. Put on the whole armor of God so you will be able to stand safe against the devil's schemes. *For our struggle is not against people made of flesh and blood, but against principalities and powers, against the rulers of the darkness of this world, against the spiritual forces of evil in the heavenly realms* ["the air around earth"]. Therefore put on the full armor of God, that you may be able to stand your ground against the wiles of the devil...Use every piece of armor to resist the enemy whenever he attacks; *and when it is all over, you will still be standing up*" Ephesians 6:10–20. Verses 14–17 list the armor. (*Combination reference from several Bibles: King James, New American Standard, New International Version.*)

SECTION ONE:

TRUE STORIES OF VICTORY OVER EVIL

*The Son of God appeared for this purpose: to
destroy the works of the devil.*
(1 John 3:8)

SOME VERSES ABOUT CHRIST'S POWER OVER EVIL

REFERENCES ARE CITED from the King James Version Bible (KJV), the New American Standard Bible (NAS), and the New International Version Bible (NIV).

1 John 3:8   "The Son of God appeared for this purpose, to destroy the works of the devil" (NAS).

Mark 1:34   "And He [Jesus] healed many.... and cast out many devils" (KJV).

Mark 16:17   Jesus said, "These signs will accompany those who believe [in Him] In My name they will cast out devils" (KJV).

Mark 6:13   Empowered by Jesus, the disciples "cast out many devils" (KJV).

Luke 10:17   "Lord, even the demons are subject to us in your name" (KJV).

Luke 10:18   "Jesus said, 'I saw satan fall from the sky like lightning' [knocked out of power by the 70 disciples ministering without Him but in His Name], healing people and setting them free from demons" (KJV).

Luke 10:19   Jesus said, "Behold, I give you power to tread on serpents and scorpions [metaphors of demons], and over all power of the enemy: and nothing shall by any means hurt you" (KJV, note added).

Luke 4:34	A demon cried out, "Have come to destroy us? I know who you are—the Holy One of God" (NAS).
Acts 8:7, 8	"For in the case of many who had unclean spirits [demons], they were coming out of them, shouting with a loud voice, and many who had been paralyzed and lame were healed. So there was great joy in that city" (KJV).
Matthew 10:1	"Jesus gave His followers authority over all demons—to cast them out, and to heal every kind of sickness and disease" (NIV).
Acts 10:38	"How God anointed Him with the Holy Spirit and with power, and He went about doing good and healed all who were oppressed by the devil; for GOD was with Him" (KJV).
Acts 26:18	After His resurrection, Jesus' words to Saul, who became the Apostle Paul were: "I am Jesus,...who you persecuted...I am sending you to open their eyes [Jews and Gentiles] and turn them from darkness to light, and from the power of satan to God, so that they may receive forgiveness of sins and a place among those who are sanctified [set apart, made clean] by faith in me" (NIV).

CHAPTER ONE

OVERCOMING WITCHCRAFT AND OTHER EVIL

Example #1
Victory! Defeating a Black Witch
and "Dog Spirit" in Mexico!

"The weapons of our warfare are not of the flesh, but mighty through God to the pulling down of strongholds of evil."
(2 Corinthians 10:4, 5)

W
E WANT YOU to see Christ's victory over severe evil in Mexico. It is not uncommon to find witches in villages, not only in Mexico but in other countries, and in cities as well as villages. Many years ago, Roy and I were called upon to help in a strange and terrible situation of black witchcraft in a village not far from Cuernavaca, in the hills above Mexico City. "Black witchcraft" is the most evil kind, called that because the witch's motives are morally "black," and she sets her worst curses by the "black of night," paying homage to demons so they will attack people she hates or has been hired to harm or kill. Sometimes she attacks even those people's children and/or their animals, crops or livelihood. There are many kinds of witches, but all over the world the "black witch" is known as the most evil.

In the situation in Mexico, a lovely young couple had received Christ into their lives and helped start an evangelical church. But the "black witch" of the village was angry and jealous. She considered herself *the* spirit force in the village and wanted the Christian church kept out. So right in broad daylight, in the middle of the main street of the village, with people all around, she cursed the six-year-old daughter of the couple who were new Christians. She sent a "dog spirit" into the girl (a demon mimicking a dog). Immediately the girl became disoriented and howled like a dog. The villagers were horrified. Roy and I had never heard of such a thing. It was like from a fairy tale about black witches. The parents wept and prayed, fasted and prayed, lay on their faces on the floor of the village church and prayed all night long, begging God to help their little girl, take the evil thing away from her. The demon would leave for a little while but then come back. When it was "out," the girl was normal; dazed but normal. But when it was "in," she howled like a dog and didn't recognize even her parents. (Recently a missionary told me she saw the same demonic oppression in Istanbul, Turkey, as a disoriented man was sitting in the street, barking like a dog.)

Roy's cousin, Dr. Jerold Reed, Director of the Covenant Mission work in Mexico, and his wife Nancy had recently met this new Christian couple and were trying to encourage them. They knew we had some experience in overcoming evil in Indonesia, so they asked if we could come and help. God had taught us how to overcome a few difficult things there, including a death curse, but we had never encountered a problem like this before. It gave me the creeps just to think of it, that an evil person could send an "animal spirit" demon to oppress a little child. We did the only thing we knew to do; we prayed with the parents and told them the next time the howling started to *tell* the thing to "get out and stay out, in Jesus' Name." And we quietly prayed over the little girl. The next time the howling started, the couple did that. They *told* the demon to get out, and stay out, in Jesus' Name. *The howling stopped immediately* and the girl recognized her parents again. However, later it came back. Again they told it to "Get out, in Jesus' Name" and again it stopped immediately. But later it returned. *Back and forth, back and forth.* The demon had to obey the command given in Jesus' Name, but it returned of its own volition, usually a few hours later.

Was the demon so strong that the parents couldn't win? *No! Nothing is stronger than the name of Jesus!* It was not too strong, but *it was clever.* It knew it had to obey a command given in Jesus' Name, but it could avoid the intent of the command because it hadn't been forbidden to *ever* come back! So the dog demon came back whenever *it* felt like it. Roy and I knew some things about what is called "spiritual warfare" but we certainly didn't know everything. We just knew that in Mark 16:7 Jesus said, "In My Name cast out demons." The parents did that. Now, how to keep the dog demon out?

Then God helped all of us realize the missing thing. In Jesus' Name they needed to command that dog demon to *never* return! It didn't matter that they were new in Christ; He was *in* them. When they did that, the war was over. In Mark 9:25 Jesus rebuked a demon saying, "I command you to come out of him and *never enter him again.*" It was a good lesson for the new Christians. They learned what to do and how to do it. And they learned that when a Christian knows what needs to be done, he must *tell* it to happen, *in Jesus' Name,* not merely ask God to do it. The Bible, in Mark 6:7 and Luke 9:1 makes it clear that Jesus gave His disciples power and authority over demons. A Christian, even a very new Christian, has authority in Christ to give orders in Jesus' Name and the evil side *has to obey.* That was true for Christians in every era, and will be true until Jesus returns and banishes satan and all demons.

With their new knowledge, the parents were able to make the demon leave. Knowing specifically how to overcome evil in Jesus' name, they could withstand the evil woman and help other people in the village withstand her. A Mexican Christian friend who was born and raised in that country recently told us that now almost every little village in Mexico has an evangelical Christian church. Roy and I were glad to hear that! *Anywhere in the world that witches and other evil caused by demons are defeated, the Church grows.*

God is merciful and *loves to help us.* As you read these true stories in *God Wins,* please realize that these wonderful answers to prayer did not come about because Roy and I are missionaries. They came about because Jesus is *in us* and *in* the other people whose stories we relate. If you ever sincerely asked Him to forgive you and come into your life, He is in you, too. Thank Him. And if you have never asked Him for that, *do it.* Then you will have life forever, and on earth you will have fellowship with God, answers to prayer, and power against evil.

You might wonder why people have to pray at all. God has

power—why doesn't God just take care of whatever needs His help? It is because God has ordained that humans *participate and cooperate* in what takes place on earth. They will experience the blessing of that—or a lack of blessing if they neglect to cooperate with God. When you "pray in Jesus' Name," angels respond. Think of it like medieval times when a knight would say, "*By the order of the King*, I command you to (do thus and so)." An earthly king is only a single king and not even able to answer every need. The Lord Jesus Christ is *the King* over everything. If you have received Him into your life as your Lord and Savior, He is *in* you. If you are endeavoring to please Him, *you have His authority to call for evil to be vanquished*. Angels carry out the order. You become part of a triune team to bring God's blessings to earth: Jesus, His angels, and you!

Witches Send Objects That Carry Evil

Satan can legally attack us if serious sin has "opened the door" of our life, and he also acts upon the "offerings" of witches who give him worship. We have learned that witches have a common pattern in the way they work. It sounds very strange, but it is known world-wide that evil people often send curses *via objects* that they have "invested" with evil spirits to carry harm to the person who gets the object. Evil has always existed, in every country, but until fairly recently it was fairly hidden in America, where widespread Christianity brought God's angelic protection over this country. But now there has been a rise in evil as media and other public influences have aggressively promoted witchcraft and opposed Christianity. "Evil" means it is demonically driven and will harm individuals and society. Christians need to do everything we can help young people avoid that cruel trap.

Example #2
Victory! Night Terrors Defeated!

"The angel of the Lord camps around them who
reverence Him and delivers them."
(Psalm 34:7)

Years ago, the seven-year-old son of Christian friends began screaming in his sleep at night and his parents were unable to wake him or comfort him. It was as though the boy was in the middle of a nightmare he couldn't wake up from. In the morning he was dazed and uncooperative. It seemed much like what are called "night terrors," in which a sleeping child is badly frightened and screams and cries and sometimes even walks around in his sleep but can't be wakened. In the morning he might not remember anything about it, yet in his sleep he had been badly frightened. When a child has *not* watched violent TV or violent video games or been traumatized by an ugly life experience, yet has "night terrors," the cause is probably demonic because mental images come from somewhere. When those images are ugly, terrifying, it is reasonable to suspect that something evil has attacked the child's mind. Demons have access to minds, attacking people in their sleep when they cannot defend themselves. It is a mean thing, but "mean" is what demons are.

The boy had not suffered ugly visual input within his home, yet his troubled sleep pattern continued for an entire week. The desperate parents called Roy for help. He questioned them about anything unusual that might be in their home. They realized that the screaming nightmares *began after their boy had received a "gift" from the young son of an evil woman.* (That son probably was innocent.) Roy prayed over our friends' son in this sort of way: "Satan, if you are causing this problem, I rebuke you and forbid you to harass him any longer, in any way. In Jesus' Name leave him alone and never return!" Roy told the parents to burn the gift. *As soon as they burned the gift, the boy's nightmares stopped.*

The woman who had given the "gift" claimed to be a Christian, yet said hateful, cruel things about others and privately boasted that she had "special powers" that her evil father had called into her (with her permission) when she was twelve years old. She came from a classic case of "heritage of evil," a bloodline held by demons. Tragic. And dangerous. The woman had troubled others also, and evil literally surrounded her like oppressive electricity. Our adult son Michael was sitting in the middle of church, facing forward when suddenly his hair stood on end. He felt a presence of evil enter the church. He turned and saw the woman walk in. Others reported the same. If she ever actually wants Christ's forgiveness she will have to sincerely renounce the demonic bondage of her heritage. *Do not make friends with evil people.* If they truly repent, it will be obvious. (Our son Michael is a very clear thinking lawyer. I mention that to dispel any notion that he was frivolous in what he reported.)

Not only should you avoid accepting gifts from evil people, but you should avoid bringing questionable art objects home from foreign countries. Even if the object is beautiful, well-crafted, *if anything about it makes you feel uncomfortable,* don't buy it or accept it. Many such objects carry demonic presence, particularly if they were used in a ritual, or if the artist called upon a demonic spirit to help him create the object, or if the person giving you the gift is someone you don't trust. When mission expert Dr. C. Peter Wagner and his wife experienced strange difficulties in their home after ministering in Bolivia, they traced the problems to a carved wooden animal and some decorative animistic ceremonial masks that they had brought home from Bolivia. Dr. Wagner reported that when they destroyed the carving and the masks, the trouble stopped. Please remember that when an object has carried evil into a place, or against a person, that object *must be burned. Burning the object denies the demon a "home." Then it has to leave.* That, too, must sound strange to a reader, but it is true. Demons like to have a physical place to live and cause trouble.

Example #3
Victory! Witchcraft Attacks Defeated!

"The Lord is my rock and my fortress and my deliverer; my God, my strength; in Him will I trust. The righteous run to Him and are safe."
(Psalm 18:2)

Several other situations of black witchcraft harassment occurred as a result of our friends' contact with a couple they had reason to consider evil but were trying to help spiritually. (Fortunately that couple later moved away.) In one of the situations, our friends kept the offending couple's children while they went on vacation. Upon their return, that couple gave our friends the gift of an olivewood nativity scene. It wasn't yet Christmas, so our friends stored the crèche in their attic and forgot about it. However, later they began to smell a "strange unpleasant odor." They searched everywhere for the source of it. They found the trouble in their attic. A heavy mattress, formerly leaning sharply against one side of the ceiling, had somehow flipped completely the other direction and was smoldering against a burning light bulb close to the nativity scene. That is what smelled bad. There had been no earthquake and no non-family member had access to their house. If our friends had not located the problem, there might have been a fire. In case you wonder, the phenomenon was not their imagination. These friends are stable, highly intelligent people.

Other odd situations involving the woman illustrate the difficulty of trying to help people who don't want to be helped. During the time our friends were trying to help the disturbed woman spiritually, two *apparitions* appeared in their home, one of them a monkey-like animal at the foot of their bed. My friend woke her husband and said, "Look at that!" and they both watched it until it (the demon) scampered off the bed, down the hall and disappeared. (A demon can come in with an evil person or be sent in by that person, and if the evil is strong enough it can take visible form.) Then, directly after they reported to the woman's Christian employer the trouble they were having with her and she was dismissed, a death curse spirit appeared beside our friend's bed; a tall, black-robed demon with a death mask face. Our friend cried out, "Jesus!" and it vanished. Since the evil woman moved away there has been no more trouble, however it is well to know that distance is not an issue in the spiritual realm.

Note that when our friend cried out, "Jesus!" the evil thing vanished. The intent in sending a "death spirit" was to cause our friend to have a fear-induced heart attack. But the Holy Spirit within her defended her. He caused her to automatically call on Jesus, her savior and King. *Jesus is the power all evil beings are afraid of.* They know that He will be King forever while they, the demons, will be in hell. That's why demons cried out fearfully to Jesus when He was on earth,

"Have you come to destroy us?" (Mark 1:24) They know that time is coming.

The evil sent against my friend *could not have occurred accidentally.* That kind of witch makes contact with demons in order to cause harm, and the harm can be of many kinds, including injury or illness or even financial disaster. People need to learn to forbid any such thing, in Jesus' Name.

God's Punishment for Witchcraft

This friend asked me to caution you: Even though you are a kind Christian, do not try to help a "black witch." She doesn't want help and you would be harmed. Stay away from people like her, and in Jesus' Name forbid satan to *ever* do such things to you or to any member of your family as were done to her family. And *do not accept any kind of gift from an evil person. Sending evil via "gifts" is a common way witches operate.* Pray the Blood of Christ's protection over yourself and your family and ask God's angels to surround you and warn you if there is someone you need to stay away from.

A corner of my heart still pities the evil woman because she was born into a heritage of evil. I would like to see her set free. But until she is free of the demons her father called into her, she is dangerous. And it is probable that she likes being dangerous. She will have to repent and renounce all contact with evil if she ever wants to be free. And she will need strong prayer help to expel her demons and keep them out. Otherwise there is no hope for her. She will suffer God's punishment for witchcraft.

In the Bible, in Isaiah 47:12–15 God warns all people involved in witchcraft: "Stand fast now in your spells and in your many sorceries with which you have labored from your youth; perhaps you will be able to profit. Perhaps you may cause trembling...Let now the astrologers, those who prophesy by the stars, those who predict by the new moons, stand up and save you from what will come upon you. Behold, they have become like stubble, fire burns them up; they cannot deliver themselves from the power of the flame—there is none to save you." That is a sad end for those people. God says He "has no pleasure in the death of the wicked" (Ezekiel 33:11) He urges all people involved in evil to turn away from it. In the meantime, stay away from such people. Pray for them, but stay away from them. If they repent, it will be evident.

Example #4
Victory! Demons Flee Hunting Lodge!

"Be strong in the Lord and the power of His might. In nothing be frightened by your enemies."
(Ephesians 6:10 and 1 Kings 2:2)

The wife of one of Roy's seminary students led a friend to Christ, and then that woman phoned a friend in Wisconsin and led her to Christ over the telephone. The Wisconsin woman was the fairly new owner of a hunting lodge, and everything had been going fine *until* she became a Christian. Then weird things began to happen. She would make beds and ten minutes later find the bedding ripped off. The woman phoned her Christian friend in California for help. That friend contacted Roy and he told her to advise the lodge owner to go through all the rooms and *tell* the invisible evil spirits to leave. But that didn't help. The sheets kept getting ripped off. They phoned Roy again. "Tell her to go through the lodge," he advised, "to see if she notices anything evil looking. Did she check the basement?" No, she hadn't. The lodge was big and fairly new to her. She'd been too busy to even go down there. The basement turned out to be the problem. In it she found a chest full of witchcraft paraphernalia: books on black witchcraft, a human skull, a cape, tarot cards, and a dagger. Evil rituals had taken place in that lodge. That was where the evil spirits resided. Those witchcraft objects gave demons "legal right" spiritually to be in the lodge and cause trouble. (The "sin right," because previous people in the lodge had made deliberate contact with demonic spirits, which is a grievous sin.) The new owner needed to destroy *all* of it; burn what she could and throw any bits of residue into the trash. But first, burning it is was the important thing. *When she burned the witchcraft objects, the trouble stopped immediately.* No more ripped up beds. The demons were so furious that the woman had become a Christian that they had tried to scare her away. And they almost succeeded. The demons feared that a Christian would be a threat to them. And she was! She had Jesus! She burned up the demons' house (the chest of evil things) and the demons had to leave!

Note again: The woman at the lodge had no trouble *until* she became a Christian. *That made her a feared enemy of the evil side.* Demons know that Christ is *in* each Christian, and that Jesus' power is greater than theirs. For that reason, they fear Christians.

At the beginning of this situation, Roy asked his student's wife to find out if the lodge keeper had asked her pastor for help. She had, but was told that he "doesn't deal with it." Because so many people in various churches have reported the same thing, that their pastor "doesn't deal with it," Roy was determined that his students would not leave his seminary classes without knowing the issues and techniques of spiritual warfare. Wherever he teaches, and whatever type of mission class it is, he includes a practical segment on "spiritual warfare," because *that is the war we are in.* As a result, many of his students who became pastors and missionaries say this information has helped them greatly.

Example #5
Victory! New Age Painting Destroyed

"Above all, taking the shield of faith, with which you shall
be able to quench all the fiery darts of the evil one."
(Ephesians 6:16)

When our son Michael and his wife Kristen lived on the mountain years ago, they were friends with a couple who continually suffered hard times financially. Mike wondered if perhaps something evil in their home was causing it. He asked Roy and me to go to the home with them to see if we could sense anything. Roy and I never know whether we'll recognize something that is wrong, but we always pray that God will "show our eyes and our spirit" if something is there that harbors evil.

In their friends' home we looked around. Nothing seemed to be amiss, except that I felt uncomfortable about a strange "New Age" type painting that hung at the top of their stairs. It had a unicorn on it and other occult symbols. The woman told me her brother had painted it. I asked her to tell me about her brother. She said he was not a Christian, and was involved in New Age, a form of witchcraft (although many New Age followers possibly don't realize that at the beginning). The woman said she didn't like the painting either, but kept it because it was a gift from her brother. It was the only thing in their house that "felt strange," so Roy and I suggested they burn it. They did. Suddenly everything in their lives turned for the better, financially and in other ways. We don't know whether the woman's brother meant his painting as a deliberate curse, hopefully not, but *because he was involved in witchcraft, demons were involved with him and everything he did,* including his painting.

Remember, demons hate Christians and want to harm them, so again, *do not accept a gift from anyone who seems to be involved in evil.* Don't even buy items from places that give you reason to think the proprietor is involved in evil. When my daughter Karen and I attended a Campus Crusade for Christ staff conference in Fort Collins, Colorado, we enjoyed walking through the shops in the charming town. In one of them, Karen saw a dress she really liked and it looked lovely on her. But then we noticed that there were New Age and other witchcraft symbols on the dressing room walls. We left. Karen liked the dress, but she didn't want *anything* from a place involved in evil. The store felt contaminated. We were glad to get out into the fresh air.

Roy wants me to comment here that it is best to work as a team if you are asked to help someone because people have various gifts from God's Spirit. Roy thinks I can sense evil presence more easily than he can, and I think he has great wisdom in what he says to people, and what he prays. Ask God for discernment before you go. If one person misses a clue, the other might catch it.

CHAPTER TWO

OVERCOMING OPPRESSIONS OF INFANTS AND CHILDREN

Example #6
Victory! Apparitions Gone!

"Now thanks be to God, who always causes us to triumph in Christ."
(2 Corinthians 2:14)

YEARS AGO ROY and I were asked to help a young family in a community near ours. The couple's three-year-old daughter was frightened by apparitions (visible spirits). She could see them in her bedroom at night and pointed at them, crying and begging to get out of the crib, but her parents couldn't see what she was afraid of. Evil spirits are mean; they love to pick on little people because young children either cannot express their fears or they are not believed. And a very young child has no way to express the problem or escape it. The parents were Christians, but they didn't know what to do. So they phoned Roy. Before we go anywhere to try to help people, we pray that God will give us wisdom. At the home we were puzzled. We didn't sense anything odd in the girl's room. But clearly something was there or she wouldn't have been so frightened, and she even pointed at what she saw.

What had permitted evil spirits to be in the house? Roy asked if anyone in the family was involved in witchcraft. "Well, yes," the woman's mother, but the mother didn't live with them. Had the mother given them any kind of gift? "Yes, the dining room table." As strange and extreme as it sounded, Roy suggested they get rid of the table because it was a physical thing that had been handled by someone who practiced witchcraft. He thought it possible that evil spirits had attached to their home by way of the table, just by physical contact with the woman's mother. She probably had used the table to consult tarot cards or do other things designed to attract evil. Sure enough, *when they got rid of the table, the apparitions stopped.* The little girl wasn't bothered any more. It is so odd to think that evil spirits can be present in a "thing," but they can be. Good spirits, which are angels, and bad spirits, which are demons, are not limited to one form, or one body, or one location, as humans are. A demonic spirit was "with" or "in" the table that was used for evil. And at night those spirits cruelly frightened someone who was too little to explain what she saw or be able to get rid of it. Demons are *nasty, malevolent* creatures.

Please note: Never dismiss a child's fears because you can't see what the child is afraid of. If he has seen something frightening, or even just thinks he has, and you disbelieve him and try to talk him out of it, *then the child has two things that frighten him:* what he saw or thinks he saw, and the fact that the big people in his life won't protect him. At the very least, hold the child and speak words of comfort, even to an older child. And it is a very simple thing for a Christian to whisper, "satan, if you are doing this, in Jesus' Name I forbid it!" *If it is there, without sit having allowed it in, it will stop.* And pray the Blood of Christ's protection over yourself and your family and your home, and in Jesus' Name forbid the trouble to ever come back. *All* Christians can "speak against" demonic spirits. It is not a "special" gift; it is just part of being a Christian. The one exception would be if the Christian is deliberately involved in sin, behaviors God forbids (i.e. cooperating with demons). Then God doesn't promise to protect him from the bad effects. He won't be protected by God until he at least tries to turn away from the sin.

(Possible problem: Where is that table now? We hope it was broken up and burned, as it needed to be, because evil spirits won't leave their *physical* home voluntarily. If the young couple gave the table away instead of destroying it, people who have it now might be suffering baffling problems.)

Example #7
Victory! "Little Men" Gone!

"The Lord will not fail you or forsake you."
(Deuteronomy 31:6)

When Roy and I attended a Campus Crusade for Christ Directors' Conference on the island of Cyprus in the Mediterranean, we met a Turkish man who directed the CCC work in his country. The young man and his little Russian wife asked to meet us, saying an article we wrote had helped them. It was titled, "How We Learned to Overcome the Enemy in Jesus' Name," published at the Fuller Seminary School of World Mission when Roy was working on his doctorate. The article had been given to them by another Campus Crusade worker in Istanbul. This is the story they shared with us… The Russian wife told us that every night from earliest childhood she "saw little men" moving around on her bed. She could see them; but her mother could not. It frightened her so badly that she slept in her mother's bed until she was twenty years old! She became a Christian and got married, but still she saw the "little men." She and her husband had no idea how they could stop the problem until they read Roy's article. Then they were sure it was demonic and did what we said to do: In Jesus' Name they told it to stop and never come again. And they prayed the Blood of Christ's protection over her. *That was the end of the "little men."* The woman told us *she never saw them again.* They were very relieved and thankful.

Note again that satan loves to oppress little children. He is a bully, and children are helpless to combat him. If the "little men" had been the harmless, friendly elves of fairy tales, the little Russian girl would have been delighted, not frightened. People in many countries have seen demonic "little men" and "elves" and could cope with the fear only by pretending they were harmless little fairy tale creatures. The Norwegians are realists; they don't even pretend their troublesome "trolls" are pleasant.

What had permitted that evil spirit oppression of the little Russian girl? It isn't known, except that *sin of some kind brought it in.* Any kind of trouble with demons is brought about by sin. But it is not necessarily the suffering person's own sin that brought the trouble. Evil can *come in* with an object (like the table in example #6) or it could have *been in* the house before the Russian girl's family lived there. Or it could have been attached to something evil that a parent had done or was doing. Or it could have been sent in by a witch. Or it could have been what is called a *"generational curse,"* a curse set against the family line long ago by someone who made a pact with the devil to oppress all future generations of that family. Through the generations, members of the family "feel it," suffer emotionally or by illness or severe disappointment. They feel a lack of freedom to live normal lives such as people around them seem to have. It disappoints and puzzles them. They don't know why their own lives are different, restricted. *Such curses can be broken, in Jesus' Name.*

Example #**8**
Victory! Little Gray Spirits Flee!

Jesus gave the 12 disciples (and all Christians) authority over all demons—power to cast them out. (paraphrase of Luke 9:1)

From a home in a distant community, we got a phone call from a young couple who said they felt something evil was in their house. They said it was located just beyond their kitchen, by the door to their garage, and they saw it only there. Out of the corner of their eye they each saw little gray creatures darting from the freezer into the garage and back again. But when they turned to look, they couldn't see anything. This had gone on for many weeks and the couple was unnerved, so they phoned us for help. Roy told them to look through their house for anything occult (evil). They did, but found nothing. So we went to their home. We didn't sense anything bad either, but we "spoke against the enemy" just in case. We told satan if he was there, to "get out and stay out, in Jesus' Name."

Two weeks later the couple phoned again, saying they still had the trouble. What could be wrong? We prayed for wisdom. Then Roy asked if they had checked the garage for anything occult. They hadn't. When they did, they found a trunk the woman's mother had left in the garage a few months earlier. It was filled with books on witchcraft. Because evil spirits inhabit items that glorify evil, the demons had the "legal right," the "sin right," to be in that garage and the area close by. (Just as at the hunting lodge of Example #4.) Roy told the couple to *burn* the books or return them to the mother, but *get them out of their garage, away from their home.* As soon as they did that, there was no more trouble.

Example #9
Victory! "SIDS" Baby Back to Life!

"The weapons of our warfare are not of the flesh, but mighty through God to the pulling down of strongholds of evil."
(2 Corinthians 10:4, 5)

A few weeks before the following crisis occurred, our daughter Robin had brought a book about word origins home from college. *The Etymology of Words.* In it I saw that the origin of the word "nightmare" is "nacht mare," "the female demonic spirit that sits on people's chests, (usually when sleeping), to crush their breath away." Several years ago, *Reader's Digest* reported that more than 40% of adults have experienced that alarming weight on their chest at night. An adult can throw it off, but an infant or small child cannot, and dies. The result is called a "SIDS" death, "sudden infant death syndrome." It is still a mystery to medical people looking for consistent physical reasons for the deaths. They know it is a suffocation death but evidence of cause is not always there.

The ancient name of the "nacht mare" is "Lilith," the demonic female leader of a legion of child and baby-killing demons associated with the "sudden infant death syndrome" known as SIDS. (Google: "Lilith." You would be shocked. Some of it had to be blacked out.) Interestingly, a women's lib group that promotes abortion goes by that unusual name. I experienced that at least one sleeping baby was killed by that type of demonic spirit. My proof is that when I whispered, "satan, get *off* that baby's chest! In Jesus Name, get *off* her chest!" the baby began to breathe. The father's grief turned to joy.

It was Sunday on a Memorial Day weekend and Roy was away, speaking at a church in Ventura. I was at home, and suddenly heard screaming from the house next door. It had been rented for the holiday weekend. "Help me, help me, help me," a woman's voice cried, on and on. I ran across the ravine and up to the house to find out what was wrong, and if I could help. A young red-headed woman was running back and forth on the deck, crying, "Help me, help me, help me!" "What's wrong?" I asked, as I ran up on the deck. "Help me, help me, my baby's dead!" Tears streamed down her face. I ran to the open sliding glass door and went quietly in. Such a sad sight, the father on his knees on the floor, tears streaming down his face, trying to jiggle life into his little girl. I'd never seen a dead person before (except at funerals) but this child was clearly gone. Her skin was gray and she was as floppy as a rag doll, her eyes rolled back. They'd found her in her crib that way. So tragic.

The father glanced up at me with grief-stricken face. Suddenly, because I had just read about the "nacht mare" that suffocates people, I whispered, "satan, *Get off that baby's chest!* In Jesus' Name get *off* her chest!" *The baby began to breathe!* The father exclaimed, "She's alive, I think she's alive!" We watched gratefully and with wonder as color began to rise on her little gray face. Then her eyelids fluttered, and she drew a breath and cried. What a beautiful sound! In my heart I was praising God that this suffocated child could draw a breath and cry! She was alive again! The father was ecstatic! His tears of grief had become tears of joy. I went out on the deck to tell the young mother that her baby was alive, but she couldn't believe it. "No, no, my baby's dead..." She was inconsolable. "Help me, help me, help me!" She continued to cry to people walking by on the road below.

Someone had called the paramedics and I left as I saw their truck arriving. Back home in my kitchen I danced for joy! "Oh, Jesus, thank you! Thank you, thank you, thank you!" But not long after the paramedic truck drove away with the mother and baby, He said to me,

"You didn't forbid it to return." "Oh, that's right, I didn't!" "Satan, in Jesus' Name I forbid you to kill that little girl! I tell you to leave her alone and *never attack her again!*" And I prayed the Blood of Christ's protection over her.

The next morning Roy and I had guests for breakfast out on our deck; a young man Roy had led to Christ, and his girlfriend, a volunteer paramedic. Looking over at the house across the ravine, we talked about the emergency. She told us there had been a "code blue" in the paramedic truck on the way to the hospital. "Code blue" means a life-threatening medical emergency. The baby had stopped breathing. Then, inexplicably, she began breathing again and had no more trouble. Praise God! That was why in my kitchen God warned me to forbid the suffocation spirit to *ever* kill that girl! Why didn't God just take care of it in the ambulance and not allow a suffocation demon to attack the girl again? Because God has ordained that His people participate with Him in the spiritual war. Christians speak orders in Jesus' Name, and God's angels enforce the order.

Why had the emergency happened? Why had an evil spirit been sent against the tiny girl? We didn't know. Could a witch who hated the family have sent a death curse against the child? Possibly. That kind of thing has been known in virtually every country. Certainly it was a "death spirit," a "suffocation spirit," or God wouldn't have urged me to forbid that spirit to ever attack her again. My heart is filled with praise! God is our "shield," our "high tower," our "strong defense!" (Psalm 3:3, Psalm 91 and other Psalms). God was concerned about that little girl. *He knew in advance what was going to happen to her* and I have marveled that He brought the family right next door to me and had instructed me about the "nacht mare" through the book on word origins. A month earlier I would only have been able to weep with them. But because I saw that book, when the emergency happened, I was able to tell satan to get off the child, in Jesus' Name, and *His angels kicked that child-killing demon right off that helpless little girl. Victory!*

When Roy returned from Ventura, I told him about the crisis and he went next door to visit the father. The man's wife and baby were in the hospital for overnight, being monitored. Roy expressed how glad we were that his baby lived, and he told the father that it was Jesus who saved her. The man didn't respond much, except to tell Roy that he is an Israeli commando, in California on vacation. As a commando, he said he recognized death, knew that his little girl was dead, even though he tried desperately to get her to breathe. He told Roy that when he saw me enter the room and "whisper a prayer," his baby came alive again, that whatever I "prayed" had brought her back. (Well it did! But Roy didn't tell him what my "prayer" had been, for the man wouldn't have understood. It was a *war command*, so angels could kick that wretched death spirit off the little girl's chest! Picture it happening! How exciting is that!) I praise God!

Roy said the Israeli wanted to come over to thank me for praying. He did, and was beaming! We rejoiced together! I told him the truth: that "Jesus, (Yeshua in Hebrew) saved your baby!" The Israeli said he isn't a religious man; that he doesn't know much about "those things," meaning God. But he expressed gratitude to God for the miracle of his baby and said, "You people [meaning Christians] use one of our words." I smiled, "I know! Hallelujah!" And he beamed. "Hallelujah" is Hebrew for "Praise God" and is spoken the same way in every language. So appropriate! We were standing outside in the soft sunshine and joined our hands together and raised them to heaven, beaming, praising God! "Hallelujah! Hallelujah dear Lord, Hallelujah!" Tears of gratitude were on all our faces. Roy prayed aloud, thanking God for saving the little girl's life. And he asked God to *bless* her and her family, and protect them in every way. And privately we "prayed the Blood" over them. Our new Israeli friend wouldn't have understood that either, but *he knows that Jesus saved his baby.* We hope that knowledge continues to work in his mind and heart until he understands that Jesus is the Holy One of Israel, the Messiah, and receives Him as *his* Messiah.

Please Note: In the unseen realm, the thing that happened when I told satan to get off the baby's chest in Jesus' Name, is that *His angels* were then *authorized* to drive the suffocation demon away. They had been present the entire time, but they seem to have had to wait for an order given in the Name of their King, the Lord Jesus Christ. Why this is required at times, and at other times not, I don't know. But they are Jesus' warriors, His army. In this Church Age, Christians have the high privilege of *cooperating* with them to bring God's mercy to people.

It is true that in this world mankind has a cruel enemy, but we also have a *Great Friend*, our *Lord Jesus Christ*. I will thank Him forever for saving that little girl. He is so merciful. It ought to be our deep desire as Christians to learn how to cooperate with Him, more and more. It is His plan that we be a team together: Jesus, His warrior angels, and Christians. A triune team. Did you ever think you would be on the same team as Jesus and His army of angels, the three of you working together? What high privilege!

CHAPTER THREE

OVERCOMING NIGHTMARES AND APPARITIONS

Example #10
Victory! Nightmares Stop!

"I will say of the Lord, He is my refuge and my
fortress: My God, in Him will I trust."
(Psalm 91:2)

ROY AND I befriended Sopheary, a refugee from Cambodia whose family ran a donut shop. When I told her about Jesus and pointed to my heart, she beamed and pointed to her own heart. In broken English she said, "I Christian too." She had escaped Pol Pot's murderous regime in Cambodia and made her way across a jungle into a Thai refugee camp. There she saw the Jesus film and asked Jesus to come into her life. When I learned that she slept on a mat on the floor of the donut shop every night, I invited her to stay at our house. We have an extra room with a comfortable bed, and I knew she would love to walk among my flowers.

But the next morning when I asked Sopheary how she had slept, thinking she would exclaim, "Wonderful," instead she shook her head sadly. "Not good." She told me that *every night* she had a terrible dream, the *same dream every night since the terror of running through the jungle to escape Cambodia.* In the nightmare, she was running toward the refugee camp in Thailand, carrying her little brother, chased from behind by Cambodian soldiers and sought from the front by Thai soldiers who didn't want any more refugees in Thailand's overcrowded camps. Every night Sopheary was running and running through the jungle and soldiers almost caught up to her when suddenly she tripped on a tree root and fell. Then a gun was at her head.

Tears ran down Sopheary's face as she told me. She said that every night she woke up in a cold sweat. I comforted her and asked if she would let me pray that the dream would stop and never return. "Oh, yes, please." I quietly said, "satan, in Jesus' Name I forbid you to *ever* give Sopheary that nightmare again! And I pray the Blood of Christ's protection over her mind and over me also" (so satan couldn't do a strike-back at me; he's a bitter spirit, hates to lose). Sopheary has *never had the dream again*, praise God! It has been more than 20 years. She lives in Long Beach now but still phones me occasionally. On this earth we have a *friend*, Jesus. And we have an enemy, satan. We want to stop him whenever we can!

Example #11
Victory! War Victim Comforted

"As one whom his mother comforts, so will I comfort you."
(Isaiah 66:13)

As Roy and I were returning from a family Thanksgiving dinner at my brother's house, we stopped at a Jack in the Box to get a cup of coffee for the long drive home. Roy is very friendly and has been in many countries, so he felt comfortable beginning a conversation with the Cambodian manager. Roy showed the Cambodian one of the little evangelistic booklets he always carries and the man's eyes lit up. He was already a Christian! Like our friend Sopheary, he had received Christ in a refugee camp in Thailand as the Jesus film in Cambodian was shown to refugees. Roy asked if the man also suffered bad dreams about the war and his eyes filled with tears. He told us he had terrible nightmares; so many of his family members had been killed. (The murderous communist despot Pol Pot killed one third of the people of Cambodia, his own country.) We three joined hands there in the restaurant and bowed our heads and prayed together. In Jesus' Name, Roy quietly prayed aloud that the bad memories would no longer torture the man's mind and heart. In Jesus' Name Roy forbade satan to *ever* torment the man's mind again. Then we prayed the Blood of Christ's protection over him and his family and all that concerned him; that God would BLESS them. The man had tears of relief and gratitude. It was God's "divine appointment" to comfort him. He felt that and was comforted. We were glad we had stopped there.

Example #12
Victory! Teenagers Freed From Nightmares!

"For I am convinced that neither death, nor life, nor angels, nor principalities, nor things present, nor things to come, nor powers, nor height, nor depth, nor any other created thing will be able to separate us from the love of God, which is in Christ Jesus our Lord."
(Romans 8:38, 39)

The enemy is cruel, a sender of nightmares, attacking people's minds when they are sleeping and can't defend themselves. A teenage girl told me she had suffered terrible nightmares for several years until she did what I advised, and *told* satan to "Stop it! in Jesus' Name." She forbade him to *ever* give her another nightmare. And she "prayed the Blood" of Christ's protection over herself. That was several years ago, and *she has not had a bad dream since then.* She treasures being able to sleep peacefully, and she treasures having learned that in Jesus' Name she can get rid of any evil thing.

Not long afterward, a high school girl friend who is also a Christian (and who didn't know anything about the first girl's nightmares), confided in her that she didn't sleep well because she has nightmares. The first teenager was able to tell her exactly how to stop them. The next day the friend beamed that she had followed that advice, forbidden satan to bother her sleep, and had slept wonderfully all night. All those classic old hymns about "There is Power in the Name of Jesus" and "There is Power in the Blood of Jesus" are *true!* The first girl later went on a mission trip to Africa and when the other girls on the team reported that they were having terrible nightmares, this girl shared with them how to stop the bad dreams, in Jesus' Name. They did that and had no more nightmares.

Pray the Blood of Christ over your sleep and be careful what you take into your mind. Don't watch scary movies or read scary books, especially not at bedtime. Think only of good things at bedtime. *You have to guard your mind, which is your master computer.* The Bible says to guard *your heart (your mind) with all your strength, for out of it comes everything you are in life* (Proverbs 4:23). Philippians 4:8, 9 reminds us to dwell on whatever is true, noble, right, pure, lovely, admirable, and of good repute…and the God of *peace* will be with you.

Avoid anything that tears you down in your mind, because invariably it will tear down your life, also. Avoid books and games that have an occultic theme, such as the Harry Potter stories or a Ouija board or objects that carry occultic themes or words. Get rid of them. Don't throw away a family heirloom (unless it makes you feel creepy) but if anything is an obvious representation of evil, *get rid of it!* Take charge: *Tell* satan to "*leave!*" in Jesus' Name. Forcefully forbid him to ever give you another nightmare or trouble your sleep in any way. Or you can be specific and say, "spirit of nightmares" or "demon of nightmares." They know who they are, and each of them has a specific, cruel assignment against mankind. Out loud, if only in a whisper, tell any such thing to "*Get out* and *stay out,*" in Jesus' Name, and command it to never come back! Whisper "the Blood, Lord, the Blood" over yourself and your room and whatever concerns you, Ask your angel to guard over you, and wrap yourself in the consciousness of God's great love for you as you drift off to sleep. And when you wake up, make every effort to please God, in your thoughts and actions and friendships.

Example #13
Victory! Nightmare Apparitions End!

"The name of the Lord is a strong tower; the
righteous run into it and are safe."
(Proverbs 18:10)

I know a young Christian woman who did not read scary books or watch scary movies or scary TV, yet she had very frightening nightmares in which she saw gigantic demons. What made the nightmares doubly bad was that in her dreams she was "mute." She couldn't speak Jesus' Name to make the evil creatures leave! This had gone on for months, so she went to a healing service at her church to ask for prayer.

The prayer team prayed for her and gave her a cloth that had been blessed in the way the Apostle Paul prayed over bits of cloth that were sent out to suffering people and carried angelic healing to them. The young woman put the little cloth under her pillow, as they instructed, and the nightmares stopped for six months. But then she had another "mute" terror dream. Back at the church, after the service, she asked for prayer again. God led a woman on the prayer team to pray that in any future nightmare the young woman would "have a voice," and she spoke against the "spirit of muteness." Demons know that humans have to verbally *speak* against them, so being mute in her nightmares made it impossible for her to defend herself. When the praying person *spoke against* the demonic spirit of *muteness*, the young woman's nightmares *stopped!* She then would have had a "voice" in her dreams and been able to defend herself. That forced the "demonic spirit of muteness" away. The young woman never had that bad dream again! (Demons are such cowards; they don't want an equal fight.)

Example #14
Victory! Chest Pressure Stops!

"Above all, taking the shield of faith, with which you shall be able to quench all the fiery darts of the evil one."
(Ephesians 6:10)

A number of years ago Roy and I got a desperate phone call at 3 a.m. A pastor's wife begged, "Come over, please come over! We've just had a terrible experience! We were in bed, sound asleep, when suddenly we both felt heavy weight on our chests and a dark, evil presence was in the room! Come over, please come over!" I said we would, but asked what they did (knowing what she would say). "I cried Jesus!" (Exactly the right thing. God brings "Jesus" to the lips of a Christian in trouble; His Name brings angelic help, scares the evil side away.) "And the evil left, didn't it?" "Yes, but it was so terrible, please come over." So we did. The couple looked pale and shaken. And they were suffering from the misconception that they "must have sinned" or it couldn't have happened. Not true. They grieved, "How have we sinned that such a thing could happen to us?" "You didn't, you were a *target*." If they had sinned they wouldn't have had to wonder what the sin was; God would have put it uppermost on their minds so they could ask forgiveness and be restored. Probably some evil person sent that evil against the pastor. We forbade satan to *ever* do that to them again, or to any member of their family. And we prayed the Blood of Christ's protection over them. Then they were at peace. The denomination they served taught (innocently but falsely) that a Christian can't be attacked by evil. We assured this couple that Christians most certainly *can* be attacked, and *missionaries and pastors are probably the most attacked*. If the same weight the pastor and his wife had felt on their chests had been on an infant or toddler's chest, that child would have died. Roy taught them to pray the Blood of Christ's protection over their lives.

In his book, *Your Adversary the Devil*, p. 147, Professor Dwight Pentecost states, "Much that we suffer in the physical realm, the emotional realm and the mental realm we suffer because we are subject to Satan's attacks against us as an ambassador of Christ." A Bible translator in one of Papua, New Guinea's remote jungle villages was struck from behind by an ax, killed by his formerly faithful language helper. The other villagers were appalled. "Why did you do it?" "A voice told me to kill him," answered the man. A demonic voice. Roy and I were sad that the missionary seemingly hadn't known how to protect himself, how to "pray the Blood" of Christ's protection over his life. If he had known to quietly speak that blessing over himself each morning, and in Jesus' Name forbidden satan to harm him, I think the language helper would not have been able to hear the demonic voice. It was a tragedy and a great loss to God's work among the people of that village.

About two weeks later, Roy got a call from the same pastor that a Christian man in a nearby community had just had the frightening experience of "pressure on his chest and sense of evil in the room." Roy went with the pastor to the man's home to pray with him, and in Jesus' Name forbade the thing to *ever* return. They prayed the Blood of Christ's protection over him. The man then pointed out his window to the house below, which he said was used for satanic worship. He wondered if that group had anything to do with his frightening experience. Probably. If possible, avoid living close to evil people. If you can't avoid it, pray in groups against the evil influence and in Jesus' Name forbid the evil people to harm you. If you want to stay where you are but don't have people to pray with, then fast and pray that God will remove the evil people.

Example #15
Victory! Apparitions Gone!

"Resist the devil and he will flee from you."
(James 4:7)

A single mom who had attended a spiritual warfare class I taught at church phoned for help. She and her teenagers were having strange difficulties in a home they had recently moved into. The daughter was having nightmares, and both her daughter and son were seeing apparitions in their bedrooms at night. Equally alarming, the entire family heard unexplained footsteps in the hall and on the stairs at night. The mother wondered if something evil had "come with" the house. She asked if Roy and I would check around the yard and under the build-up (the dirt below the first floor of a mountain house), to see if we felt uneasy about anything. We prayed with her that together we would be able to discover the cause of the trouble. We checked under the build-up, as she requested, but the area felt peaceful. What could be wrong?

We asked the mother to take us into the bedrooms where her teenagers had seen the apparitions, in case we sensed that something evil was present. We did, in both bedrooms. In the girl's bedroom was a strange, black-edged fabric canopy hanging over her bed. It had recently been given to her as a gift from someone in Guatemala. I didn't know where the curse was set, or if the fabric had been used in an evil ritual, but I had a strong feeling that it was carrying demonic presence. In the teenage boy's room the only thing I felt uncomfortable about was a poster of a rock star with a mean, rebellious looking face. Roy and I suggested to the mother that they get rid of the canopy and the poster. *Burn them.* They did that and all the problems stopped immediately. There were no more stair-step sounds or apparitions. Certainly not every canopy fabric carries evil, but that one did. About the poster, avoid any kind of portrayals of violence or rebellion or other evil. Avoid violent video games and violent movies and insist that your family do the same.

Satan is called the "prince of darkness" because he is a coward, hates light, and his deeds are evil. He loves to disturb people in their sleep, when they can't defend themselves. Any Christian can forbid nightmares in Jesus' Name, *but it must be spoken, if only in a whisper.* And then remember to "pray the Blood" of Christ's protection over yourself when you give that command.

Negative Effects of Violent Media

Frequent viewing of violence conditions the mind to accept it and even be thrilled and excited by it, creating a demonic "blood lust" similar to what serial murderers say they feel. That is a growing problem in schools today, as even junior high kids viciously beat up on each other. Other youngsters film it on their cell phones instead of breaking it up. That causes insensitivity to human suffering, a social regression to barbarism. It is what results when Christianity is restricted and violence is accepted, fed into the minds of children, teaching them patterns of hatred and violence. In that way, our society has become increasingly "sick" (evil). God is angry at people who tear down young people's lives with violent, obscene, and occult books and movies and videos. Unless the greedy promoters of those evil things turn away from the evil they are doing, they will face God's severe judgment.

Why the Rise in Demonic Activity?

FATHER AMORTH'S CONCLUSIONS: In Italy, Father Amorth fought to ban the sale of Harry Potter books because, he said, "They teach sorcery to children." He argues that "The growth of evil in the world constitutes overwhelming proof that satan is working overtime. One need look no further than ritualistic murders, satanic cults that torture and rape victims, a spate of horrific child abuse cases, and so forth. A society bereft of values and moral codes has created a fertile field for evil. Who could deny it? *In fact, the devil's most clever trick is to make people doubt his existence"* *(The Vatican Exorcists)* p. 29.

Negative Input of Media

Dr. Nancy Carlsson-Paige, professor of early childhood education and conflict resolution at Lesley University in Cambridge, Massachusetts, wrote Taking Back Childhood, about raising "confident, creative, compassionate kids" in a negative world. We recommend it. Her work has been featured in *Time, The Wall Street Journal,* and *USA Today,* and on NPR, the Discovery Channel, and ABC. Dr. Carlsson-Paige presents data on the bad effects that violent media has on children's minds and security. In the 1970's, violence on TV was minimal. Now, despite complaints to media producers, their programming for 5-10-year-olds averages 7.86 violent incidents per hour. Even omitting "cartoon violence," there were 6.30 violent incidents per hour. Adult programs have less violence, averaging 4.71 violent incidents per hour. Many problems are associated with that violently negative mental input. *Young children often can't distinguish between what is "real" and what is not,* as situations are depicted on TV. Many parents interviewed described specific instances of media violence that frightened their children. In the 1970's most mothers stayed home full-time [providing guidance and security for their children], but by 2000, two-thirds of the children of America had working mothers. That left most children alone after school to watch TV, and many watch 5 to 6 hours of it. Not everything on TV is bad, but a lot of it is, and plants ugly images into children's minds. *Everything teaches,* not just what children learn in school.

The author documented the increase in violence in children's behavior since federal deregulation of children's television. Many programs now glorify relationships built on coercion and force, rather than on empathy and love. Via TV and video games, kids "learn" that violence is the way to solve problems. On average, on *Power Rangers,* a popular kids program, there are more than 200 violent acts *per hour.* "Children are active learners; they take in what they see and then try it for themselves." *So at school there is escalating aggression. Out of 3,500 research studies* examining the relationship between violence in the media and violent behavior, almost all of them; 3,482, *showed a strong correlation.* Only 18 did not. Against those overwhelming findings one wonders if the remaining 18 were conducted by groups with a vested interest in negative media.

The American Medical Association and the American Psychological Association have warned that viewing *entertainment violence increases aggression and antisocial behavior and desensitizes children to violence, hardening them to the pain inflicted on others.* Yet the media culture continues to barrage children with images and models of violence on a daily basis. That violence deeply affects children's minds and ability to relate positively to others (*Taking Back Childhood*) p. 20. And video games engage children in participating in killing people, in shockingly violent ways. (*Taking Back Childhood*) p. 21–22. *Those horrible images remain in kids' minds*, like being brain-trained criminally. People who produce that type of media seem without conscience, undermining society's responsibility to raise children who can relate peacefully to the community. The world has suffered enough grief without violence being taught by greedy film makers as "entertainment," without regard for peace in society.

Withholding wholesome words of scripture in schools, while permitting violent, evil words to be spoken is producing a rising tide of mindless violence among impressionable young people. Parents need to bring their children under firm but kind control, with responsibilities and the expectation of obedience and good attitudes. Attending a church where the child can have positive friendships and good Bible teaching is a big help. *The brain can be trained toward a positive life or a negative one.*

Note: Keep in mind "what kind of person you want to see when your child is 23."

CHAPTER FOUR

OVERCOMING EVIL AND ILLNESS

Example #16
Victory! Keeping Evil People Away From Medical Office!

"Fear not, for I am with you."
(Genesis 26:24)

SEVERAL YEARS AGO I was told that some disreputable looking men were hanging out across the street from a medical office, and ugly graffiti was being scrawled on the side of the building every night. I had noticed the men as I drove in; scruffy looking guys dressed in black, with satanic jewelry, "death" T-shirts, and skull and bones tattoos; guys who looked like they were involved in things that weren't good. A friend in the medical office knew Roy and I had some experience in praying against demonic problems. I was asked if I could pray that the guys would leave. I answered that I could, but that they didn't need me. Any Christians can easily do it themselves and I would tell them how. However, they didn't feel they wanted to try.

So as I stepped outside the office I whispered, "satan, in Jesus' Name I tell you to get your guys away from this building and I forbid them to *ever* return." *They have never been seen there since.* My friends were grateful and relieved. After I "spoke against the enemy" (satan) I prayed the Blood of Christ's protection over myself, the medical staff, and their office, so there couldn't be any kind of strike-back from the evil side. It is wonderful to be able to cooperate; "co-operate" with Jesus to put down evil. Participating in that battle makes you part of God's triune force for good: *Jesus, His angels,* and *you.*

Note: This pattern of prayer cannot be separated from genuine heart worship of God, reverence for His words in the Bible, especially the New Testament, and an earnest desire and effort to obey Him. Then

He can speak to you and you will hear Him. God will impress upon you when something is wrong, and you will know to pray.

Example #17
Victory! Late Night "Boom Boxes" Gone!

"I will deliver him and honor him."
(Psalm 91:15)

I'll tell you about someone else's experience so you'll know it isn't just Roy and me who can do this; it's *any* earnest Christian! A woman who attended a Bible study I taught in our church on the topic of spiritual warfare has a daughter whose lovely neighborhood was being harassed by cars and trucks roaring up and down the streets at 11 p.m., their loud "boom boxes" blaring ugly music. Her daughter was alone with a baby and frightened; her husband worked nights. Residents complained but the police did nothing. And after the young mother reported the trouble to the police, her house was pelted with raw eggs, indicating that the youths were made aware of her complaint.

My friend was desperate to help her daughter. She told me she had prayed and prayed for weeks, but there had been no change; the guys were still frightening residents. I told her that in Jesus' Name she had authority to just *tell* those guys to get out of her daughter's neighborhood, and forbid them to return, and the evil side would have to obey. I told her she didn't even need to be there to do that. Later she told me that the next day as she drove toward her daughter's distant neighborhood, from inside the car she yelled, "satan, in Jesus' Name I tell you to *get those guys out* of my daughter's neighborhood! *Get out! Now!"* And she forbade them to return! (I had told my class that commands against satan need to be spoken, but they can be whispered and he has to obey. But she was angry, so she yelled.) I had to smile as I thought of her bouncing up and down in the driver's seat, yelling at satan. But guess what! Those fellows with their offensive boom boxes were *never seen in the neighborhood again!*

Example #18
Victory! Boy Freed From "Spirit of Murder"!

"Depart from evil and do good; So will you abide forever."
(Psalm 37:27)

Years ago I substituted for one day in a third grade class of a church school. In the class there was a boy the other eight-year-old children avoided. They refused to sit by him or play with him during recess, and when I asked why, they said he was always talking about killing them, and even drew gory pictures of doing it. So I asked him to stay inside and visit with me while the other children were at recess. I asked him if he ever had thoughts about killing people, and he very openly admitted that he did, and that every night he dreamed about doing it. I asked if he had ever asked Jesus to forgive him and come into his life, the way we all have to do. He said he had. I asked if he thought killing people was the right thing to do; if he thought Jesus would want him to hurt people. "No." But he said it didn't matter, he dreamed about killing them anyway. "And I'm gonna do it."

Then I knew that the boy wasn't just having nightmares, he was afflicted by a "spirit of murder" (demon of murder). It was oppressing him and using him to oppress the other children. "Would you like those violent dreams to stop?" He hesitated a moment, pondering that. Then he answered a very meek, "yes." So I asked him to take my hand and we would pray. I told him he would need to ask God to forgive him for those cruel thoughts, and I said he would have to mean it or nothing would change. In an audible whisper he asked forgiveness. Then, quietly but out loud, I said, "Spirit of violence, of murder, in Jesus' Name I tell you to leave this boy's mind alone, and never return, never give him thoughts or nightmares of violence again. I pray the Blood of Christ's protection over both of us and ask you, dear God, to surround him with a sense of *your love* for him, and give him love for others."

That was my only day in the boy's class. I wondered what changes there would be in him. A couple of months later I saw his regular teacher and asked about him. She reported that the boy had become happy and cooperative and no longer threatened the other children. So other children accepted him and played with him and all was well. She beamed, "God must have done something in his heart!" He did! In the Name of Jesus, in that boy's life, the demon of murder had been knocked out of power. *Any Christian (who knows Jesus lives within him) can do that,* just as Jesus' disciples were able to do when He sent them out to minister in the community. I could imagine Jesus smiling that this young boy was now free from that terrible oppression.

And then other people were safe also, people who might have been harmed by him later in his life if the demon of murder had not been banished from him. I don't know where it came from; whether a demon of violence came down his family line, or someone was violent toward him, or if he saw repeated violence on TV and it fastened into his mind. But Jesus rescued his mind, and because of that his *life,* and perhaps the lives of other people were rescued as well.

I didn't tell the boy's teacher about praying with him because at that time the denomination didn't believe satan could bother a Christian, certainly not a child. Not true. He can and he does, especially if there is deliberate sin or "hereditary evil" in the family background. Satan is predatory. Severe sin of some kind gave evil the legal right to attack the family, even a very young member of the family, as that boy was. In the early days of Christianity, when most Gentile converts came from pagan backgrounds, it was customary that Christians who were older in the faith prayed with the new Christians to get rid of those demonic hangings on. Then the new believers could grow in their Christian lives without the kind of mental harassment that oppressed the third grader and other children through him. Satan is always your enemy. And if you are a Christian, or even have reverence for God, Jesus is always your friend!

Example #**19**
Victory! Man Freed From "Spirit of Child Molestation"!

"In the name of Jesus and His wounds there is victory! Jesus Christ has tread upon the head of the serpent [satan] and also conquered its power over me. The victory has been won. Hallelujah!"
(African Song of Victory)

This account was reported a number of years ago by a church on the west coast of California and relates to the safety of children. The pastor has the spiritual gift of a "word of knowledge" from God's Holy Spirit, knowing things he would not know unless God told him. And like Roy and me, he knows Christians can be oppressed by evil, especially if the evil took root when the person was very young. Perhaps evil was done to him, such as molestation or other abuse. In this situation, a Christian man was afflicted by a "spirit of child molestation." He *hated* himself for it. He drove all the way from the east coast to the west coast trying to "get away from himself." That he loathed himself was a good thing; it meant he could still hear God talking to him. He hadn't hardened his heart. He had repeatedly begged God to forgive him and change him, but the problem was too strong for him. In any kind of moral difficulty, "too strong" indicates a degree of demonic control. The person needs prayer help.

In California the man sought employment in the children's program of the church. Although most people who work with children would never harm them, unfortunately child molesters tend to seek jobs around children. As the pastor conducted the interview, God revealed to him that the man was a molester. The pastor confronted him: "You're a child molester, aren't you?" The man broke down and cried. He told how he hated himself. "Would you like to be free of it?" "Oh, *yes!*" So the pastor did what I did for the school boy. He *told* the demonic "spirit of child molestation" to *get out* of the man and *stay out*, in *Jesus' Name*. The man immediately felt free of his wrong interest in children, as though that sexual aberration had never existed in his life. God had mercifully led him to where he could get help. God has pity on anyone who wants to do right and will arrange circumstances to help that person.

The man then no longer had any desire to work around children. Being set free saved a lot of grief for everyone; the man, society, children, law enforcement, the courts, and the prison system. Counseling does not help molesters, as the vast majority of psychiatric agencies know. *Molesters remain a threat their entire lives unless someone like that pastor recognizes the cause of their problem and sets them free.*

To most predators, their desires seem normal and their concern is only for themselves. I doubt that many of them realize that their aberration is demonically driven. Or maybe some of them do, but don't care. In Thailand, little children, boys as well as girls, are "bought" for sexual use and abuse by child molesters from around the world. Several years ago Reader's Digest reported that most of those children die within three and a half years, from abuse, disease, fear, loneliness and despair. From the time they left their childhood home, they had no "life" at all, nothing beyond abuse and death. What satan does is always destructive; he can be counted on for that. The Bible calls him "a liar and the father of lies" (John 8:44). "The destroyer," "the murderer," "the deceiver," "the thief." He is also "Beelzebub, the ruler of demons" (Matthew 9:34, Mark 3:22). The "god of this world" (2 Corinthians 4:4). The "serpent of old" and the "deceiver of the world" (Revelation 12:9).

Any perpetrators who can think at all must realize that their desires *are not normal, and that they are doing an evil thing.* Condemning it is not an issue of discrimination; it is an issue of protecting helpless children. That is the number one responsibility of any decent society.

Example #20
Victory! Mean Prison Guard Gone!

"God is our refuge and our strength, a very present help in trouble."
(Psalm 46:1)

A friend who ministered in a women's prison had a very difficult time with a huge and very mean guard, who was harsh to the women prisoners and hostile to Christianity. In fact the man was mean to the point that his behavior seemed illegal. He did everything he could to demoralize the women, and on their infrequent ministry weekends, when California law permitted my friend to meet with the women for Bible study and singing and prayer together, the guard deliberately kept the women in their cells overtime so they would be late to that meeting. Now a ministry weekend was coming up and my friend asked a group of us to pray that God would change the man, help him not to be so mean. She had been asking that for several months, but there had been no change in him. Her eyes filled with tears as she told me privately that "the guard was worse than ever." *"Then it's time to make a direct strike,"* I told her. *"Let's pray."* What I was going to do was not really a "prayer," but you'll know what I mean. It was what theologians call a "power encounter," contending with evil.

I said, *"Satan, if that guard is your man, in Jesus' Name I tell you to get him out of that prison, away from those women, and I forbid him to come back."* When my friend went to the women's prison a few days later, *Victory!* The guard was gone. (He had been caught with explosives in the trunk of his car.) With that hostile man gone, the women prisoners had a wonderful, happy, relaxed time together, studying the Bible, singing, rejoicing, and praying together about their needs and the needs of their families.

Note: If any state wants to cut down on crime and the high cost of continually building and maintaining "yet more jails," *send in Bible teachers.* Give inmates a chance at a new life. Roughly *70% of those who have attended Bible studies stay out of prison when they are released.* In contrast, at least 50 to 70% of released inmates who did *not* receive life-changing spiritual help commit new crimes and are sent back to prison. That is *very expensive in terms of tax dollars, heartache, and wasted lives.* If young people lack a moral compass, how can we expect anything else but that many of them will crash on the rocks of bad behaviors that will affect their entire lives, harming themselves and others.

Example #**21**
Victory! "You Can't Let Her Die!"

"Now thanks be to God, who always causes us to triumph in Christ."
(2 Corinthians 2:14)

I wish I knew more about how to pray for sick people to be healed. I'm asking God to teach me. But I did have one very wonderful answer. A woman very dear to our family was in the hospital with advanced uterine cancer and not expected to live. She was well known, and hundreds of people had been praying for her. There was a new medicine the doctors hoped would stop the cancer, but it didn't seem to be working. If it would be effective, canker sores would have developed in her mouth within 24 hours. But 48 hours had passed and she still had no canker sores. One of her relatives phoned me, saying the woman was close to death, and if I wanted to see her alive I would have to go to the hospital immediately. After we hung up I began to cry, and (sorry to say, but God understands), I yelled at God. "You can't let her die! She's a pastor's wife and has two little boys! You can't let her die!" God spoke a command loudly to my mind: *"Go to the hospital and tell satan to stop interfering with the medicine."*

I jumped in my car and zoomed to the hospital. The precious woman was skin and bones but still radiant, and smiled at me. I asked her if I could pray, and she nodded. I felt awkward because I didn't know if she understood about giving a command against satan. I didn't want to frighten her, so I went to the foot of her bed and turned away a bit, so she couldn't hear what I was saying. (Remember, giving a command against satan isn't a prayer. A prayer is only to God.) This was a "battle command" against a demonic enemy just as God had commanded me to do. I whispered, *"satan, in Jesus' Name I tell you to STOP interfering with the medicine. Get away from her and get out of this room! And in Jesus' Name I forbid you to come back!"* And I asked for God's angels to fill the room.

I quietly prayed the Blood of Christ's protection over her, and myself, and then prayed for her body to recover. I turned back to her and we said a few words and smiled at each other and said a gentle "good-bye." Maybe some other people who loved her were saying, "Good-bye," as in "I'll see you in Heaven," but I didn't. I knew she was going to live because God had told me what to do and His angels would make it happen. They would drive away the enemy so the medicine could work. Back at home, just a few hours later, I got the victory call. "She has canker sores!" The sign the medicine was working! The relative who phoned me was so happy, she was crying. I danced with joy in my living room! "Oh God, thank You, thank You!" The sick woman recovered and even had another baby! All these years she has been a *blessing* to everyone, her beaming face radiant with God's love. *She is precious to God* and Jesus *saved her life.*

Hindrances to Healing?

Why are some people healed and others not? How important is a "gift of healing?" What about evil spirits that "own" cities and territories? A pastor in Evanston, Illinois hadn't seen much progress in his church until he seriously fasted and prayed. Then a ruling demon appeared to him, complaining, "Why are you bothering me?" The spirit identified itself as a demon of witchcraft that had supervision of that area. In Jesus' Name the pastor *demanded* that the demon give up the territory, and named the streets he wanted. *Immediately* the sick began to get well and many people came to church. *Fasting and prayer brought God's angels in great numbers to contend with the evil spirits.*

Several years ago our family lost a much loved niece to cancer despite the prayers of hundreds of people. And a beloved child in the church died also, despite hundreds of people praying for her, also. Was there a different way we needed to pray? Did we need to fast more? Might there have been a territorial spirit even in that lovely, well-churched community. It is a painful mystery.

Let's ask God to teach us *how* to be of help, how to cooperate with Jesus and His angels to gain answers to prayer. Was it "God's will" for my dear niece and the precious young girl to suffer and die? I don't think so. God is our comforter and healer, not the oppressor of His children. *He is the one we want to run to, not the one who harms us.*

When people have lived a lifetime that's different, because our bodies are "perishing," as God says, preliminary to going to Heaven. But that should not be the case with a young person. *I pray that all of us will learn how to cooperate with God better and better,* so His mercies can be accomplished.

CHAPTER FIVE

OVERCOMING SPIRITISM

Example #22
Victory! Postcard Carrying a Curse Is Destroyed!

"Put on the whole armor of God that you may be
able to stand against the schemes of the devil."
(Ephesians 6:11)

THIS WILL BE the strangest story you ever heard. But the story is true. This crisis occurred when Roy was teaching Missions at Campus Crusade's International School of Theology in California. *In this situation, an evil spirit had been attached to a physical object.* That method of sending evil is well-known in Asia and South America and the Middle East, but not so much in the West, where Christianity has been a restraining influence on evil. This is what happened...

One of the students in Roy's Spiritual Warfare class led a young Chinese man to Christ around Christmastime. Soon after Christmas, the Chinese man asked the student for prayer. He said everything had been going well for him *until* he became a Christian. Then his wife had gotten sick and he lost his part-time job and his car broke down. The young man was very discouraged. Roy's student brought him to Roy's office at the School of Theology to talk to Roy and pray. Roy asked him about his situation and thought it odd that all those troubles had happened at once. (A sudden cluster of troubles is always something that should raise a question.) Roy asked if anything unusual had happened in his home, or if there was anything in his home that made him feel uncomfortable. Rather reluctantly the young man said there was, but he felt embarrassed to mention it. Roy encouraged him, "Mention it anyway." The young man told him a Christmas postcard had come from an uncle in China, and for some reason the postcard made him feel creepy. He didn't want to touch it. Roy thought, "Bingo!" and said, *"Burn it!"*

After the weekend, the Chinese man came back to Roy's office and reported that the most extraordinary thing had happened. He had put the postcard into the fireplace but had an extremely difficult time getting it to catch on fire. When it finally did, and it went up in smoke, *all the dogs in the neighborhood howled.* It was as though they could see or sense something bad. And then the man's troubles were over. He got his job back, found a way to fix his car, and his wife was better. (Sounds like country western lyrics, but true.) The uncle in China was either involved in witchcraft himself or had gone to a witch to have demons attached to the postcard. Perhaps he was angry that his nephew had become a Christian. Note again that an evil spirit or spirits had been attached to a physical object to carry harm to someone, and *burning got rid of it.*

ALL EVIL SPIRITS IN OBJECTS CAN BE MADE TO LEAVE. IT REQUIRES BURNING THE OBJECT, THE "HOUSE" THE DEMONIC SPIRIT OR SPIRITS ARE LIVING IN.

Note: A new Christian from a non-Christian background often faces strange, discouraging troubles. Satan has owned the family line and doesn't want to let go. That's why the Chinese man was attacked. Unless someone has prayed protection over them, it is common that new Christians from unsaved families *at first feel their lives are worse* than they were before they received Christ. Be very patient and helpful and prayerful with them. In Jesus' Name forbid harm, pray the Blood of Christ's protection over them, and yourself. Teach them to protect themselves the same way.

Example #23
Victory! The Indonesian "Kris"!

"At such time as I am afraid I will trust in thee."
(Psalm 56:3)

This story will also seem very strange to Westerners, but it is true. When we were missionaries in Indonesia, a young missionary couple with a baby who were new in Jakarta, stayed in the home of Roy's good friend, an American Christian who owns a print shop in that city. *The printer warned his young guests not to buy any "interesting souvenirs,"* but perhaps he didn't explain why. In the Hotel Indonesia (where our family went occasionally for the luxury of an icy Coca Cola) the young man saw a beautiful, wavy-bladed dagger called a "kris." He bought it. What he didn't know was that every elaborate kris is specially made for a wealthy, important man, and one or more "spirits" are called into the kris to guard that man. I don't know whether the spirits are "in it" or just "with it," but it is the spirit's "job" to protect the owner of the kris. It will attack anyone else who gets hold of it. We know that sounds strange, but it is true. There are many strange things in this world that most Westerners don't know about.

The inexperienced young missionary took the kris home to the print shop, and without the printer's knowledge he hung it over his baby's bed in the guest bedroom. (Bad move.) The first evening, during dinner, the baby screamed as though in fear or pain. The missionary jumped up and checked the baby, but couldn't find anything wrong. The second evening the baby screamed again. As the missionary ran into the bedroom he saw an amorphous (transparent) man bending over his screaming baby. He yelled, "Get out! In Jesus' Name, get out!" The spirit turned, looked at him, and disappeared. Back in the dining room the shaken father told our friend what he had seen. "How was he dressed? What did his cap look like?" (Dress varies according to island.) The shaken man described the spirit's clothing. The printer declared, "He's Balinese!" (from the Indonesian island of Bali). *"I told you not to buy any interesting souvenirs!"*

The printer said they would have to smash and burn the kris in order to get rid of the trouble. ("Burn the spirit's house," just as the young Chinese man burned the postcard that carried an evil spirit.) The dagger was so beautiful that the young missionary couldn't bring himself to destroy it. And like most American seminary graduates, he hadn't been instructed about such things. So he offered the beautiful and very expensive kris to the printer's Indonesian helpers. *None of them would touch it, even though they were poor.* They knew what was in the kris, and that anyone who accepted it would be harmed. Finally, the two American men smashed the beautiful kris with a sledge hammer and burned the fragments, melting them down, to deny the spirit a "home." That ended the trouble. It was a costly lesson. *It is false to think a Christian can't be attacked.* As we have said, most of Roy's work has been in helping harassed Christians.

Example #24
Victory! Set Free From Evil Spirits!

"No one can enter the strong man's house [satan's]
and steal his property unless he first binds the
strong man. Then he will plunder his house."
(Mark 3:27)

(What we want to do in Jesus' Name is "bind" satan, tie him
up spiritually, so we can reclaim people he currently owns.)

In Bonggaw village, northeast Thailand, a spiritist had been able to cast out spirits for people in the village. To do that, he used a more powerful spirit to cast out weaker spirits. Then, to protect *himself*, the spiritist collected idols inhabited by spirits *yet more powerful* than the ones he was using. (There is no love in the demonic realm, only degrees of size and power; satan at the top and lesser spirits at the bottom. They all hate each other, but seem locked into a system of having to obey whichever evil spirit is larger, more powerful.)

Five years before the *Jesus* film team came to his area, the man had stopped casting out evil spirits in the village. But *then the powerful spirits living in his own idols attacked him.* They caused his mouth and eye to be so severely twisted that he could not speak or see, and crippled both his hands and feet so that he could not walk. He remained in this condition for five years. When the Jesus film team came near his home, 26 villagers received Christ, including his wife. She asked the film team to come to her home and pray for her husband. At the house the film team asked the man if he wanted to receive Christ, but the man could not answer because of his twisted mouth. His wife again urged the Jesus Film team to pray for him. They prayed, and the man's mouth and eye straightened out and he could see and speak. Now he can walk and move his arms. He tells everyone that it is *God* who helped him (CCC New Life Training Center Report, quoted in Roy's dissertation) p. 309.

Example #25
Victory! Demon-Possessed Chinese Woman Set Free!

Fearful evil spirits confess Christ's divinity: "What have
we to do with thee, Jesus, thou son of God. Are you
come to torment us before the time [of judgment]?"
(Matthew 8:29)

In his book *Spiritual Warfare* (pp. 69–71), Dr. Timothy Warner tells about an experience Dick Hillis had with a demon-possessed Chinese woman. Hillis, longtime Director of Overseas Crusades, a well-known mission organization, was a relatively new missionary in China. A young Chinese soldier came to his door and asked for help. "Is your Jesus all-powerful?" "Of course He is," responded Hillis with no hesitation. "Good," replied the soldier. "My wife is in the courtyard, and she is demon-possessed. Twice the demon has ordered her to kill herself, once by hanging and once by jumping into the moat. Both times she obeyed him, but I was able to rescue her. However, I don't know what to do now, as I must go back. So I have brought her to you." (That was a shocker for a Western-trained missionary. Most Christian missionaries would quickly tell nationals that Jesus can solve their problems, but the reality is that most seminaries in the U.S. don't teach their students how to contend with demons. Probably the professors themselves had no instruction or experience in that area of ministry.)

Even though Hillis' theological education had not equipped him to deal with demons, he knew he had to do something. He and his wife and a Chinese Christian woman took the young soldier's wife to the women's compound and began praying for her. Hillis says, "I confess that I prayed in doubt, wondering if I would need some special gift of healing." To make matters worse, Hillis says, "the demon-possessed woman would take words from our prayers and make ridiculous poems out of them…She would scream and yell and make fun of what we were doing." They struggled in prayer for three days with no results. The soldier showed up to get his wife, but Hillis asked for more time. *The Lord also led him to ask if they had any idols in their home.* When the soldier answered that they did, he was told to *go and destroy them.*

The result was that the next morning the demons were complaining that their home had been destroyed (speaking through the woman in a different voice). So Hillis knew the soldier had indeed gotten rid of the idols. But the demons remained in the woman. Hillis then reported that in their reading of the scriptures, Ephesians 1 and 2, God suddenly revealed that (as Christians) they were not only identified with Christ in His death and His resurrection, but were "seated with Christ in heavenly places far above principalities and powers." That meant they had Christ's authority to set the woman free. He and his wife and a Chinese Christian began singing "There's Power in the Blood," and then after singing, they commanded the demon to come out of the woman in the name of Jesus. *She was instantly delivered!*

The young missionary Dick Hillis had learned two important lessons. The first was the necessity of clearly understanding the believer's position in Christ—seated with Him in the heavenly realms—and the implications of that for our encounter with the enemy. The second was that, "It is not enough to pray or to sing, though I believe that satan hates both prayer and song. *We must resist the devil and command that he depart.*"

CHAPTER SIX

OVERCOMING SPIRITISM, continued

There are two things evil spirits always do:

1. Attempt to force people to worship them.

2. Make people afraid.

IN EVERY WAY they work in the world, whether in private lives, religious systems, or social systems, those are major things demons do. One of the great luxuries we have in Christ is that we don't have to be afraid of evil spirits or death. We have the great God of Heaven who loves us and created us with a free will to choose Him. His relationship with us is based on love; He *wants* to help us. His desire is for good to happen in our lives. *As Christians, in Jesus' Name we have authority to give the order for good to overcome evil.* So we can stop whatever harm evil spirits are doing or intending to do. Think about that, how blessed you are if you are a Christian! Jesus came to help mankind defend themselves against that really nasty demonic enemy! And He did that because He loves us. *If you have ever asked Jesus to forgive your sin and come into your life, you have a very powerful Friend who will help you!*

Example #**26**
Victory! Evil Spirit Banished From Weang Pong!

"O sing to the Lord; His right hand and His holy arm have gained victory. The Lord has made known His salvation."
(Psalms 98:1–3, abbreviated)

When Roy was in northeast Thailand, close to Cambodia, he visited a fishing village called Weang Pong, next to a large lake, and learned of a strange situation that had occurred there. A formerly "sacred" tree stands on the main path going to where men would launch their boats, and in years past it was well known throughout the area that a very strong "spirit" lived in the tree. Whenever anyone went by the tree he had to bow in reverence to the spirit, and if he did not, a catastrophe was sure to happen. Fishermen had drowned in the lake when they refused or neglected to bow to the spirit. The farmer who owned the land next to the tree could not plant his rice any closer to it than 20 meters, or one of his family members would become sick or a water buffalo would die. So he kept his cultivation a respectful 20 meters away, even though he needed the land for food crops. For as long as anyone could remember, they had been afraid of the "spirit in the tree."

One day a Thai Campus Crusade for Christ "Jesus film" team came to Weang Pong, and after hearing the story of the tree spirit, they decided to do something about it. First they dug away the dirt that was piled up against the trunk of the tree. In this dirt they found a wooden head made of teak wood and carved like a king's head. They felt it was the source of the problem, that at some time in the past, demonic power had been "invested into" (put into) the wooden head as a place for the demon to live. A "residence," like the Balinese spirit was put into the kris. The villagers were alarmed, but not surprised, at what the Christians found, and they were sure the Christians would be killed by the strong spirit. However, *the Christian team commanded the spirit to leave, in the Name of the Lord Jesus Christ, and then they burned the wooden head.* When the villagers saw that no harm came to the men, they knew that the film team's God was *greater than the evil spirit, and many became Christians.*

There were about fifty Christians in the village when Roy was there many years ago, and there would be hundreds now. The people built a village church, and *no one was ever bothered by the "tree spirit" again.* The farmer could plant right up to the edge of the tree without anything bad happening, and the fishermen didn't have to bow to the tree on their way to the lake any longer, or risk drowning. They were so glad to be rid of the demon! *And they are so glad to have Jesus, who is vastly more powerful than the malicious demon.*

Example #27
Victory! Malicious Spirits Leave Phu Khiaw!

*"And the devils also came out of many, crying out and
saying, 'Thou art the Christ, the Son of God.'"*
(Luke 4:4)

The following situation is an example of what Dr. C. Peter Wagner terms "Strategic Level Warfare," confrontation with "territorial spirits." Those spirits hold large numbers of humans in spiritual bondage in a physical "territory" of a village or city or nation.

While Roy was visiting the Thai Ezra Bible School in Phu Khiaw, northeast Thailand, the Thai Director of Campus Crusade for Christ in that country told him about a severe problem they were having. People of surrounding villages complained that they were being harassed on the main road that runs from their villages to the market town of Phu Khiaw. They reported that *as they rode their bicycles or carried produce baskets on that road, right where the road runs beside Bible School property they were being pushed off their bicycles, or knocked over, or thrown down.* Yet when they got up to see who had attacked them, *no one was there.* From experience in their pagan country they recognized it to be the work of evil spirits. And the fact that it happened right beside the Bible School property made Christianity look bad. Roy said, "It's not right that a road going by a Bible school should have this problem. Let's try something."

So Roy and the Thai Director walked to each of the four sides of the property and stretched their arms out wide along the fence. Together they rebuked the spirits, commanding them to *leave, in Jesus' Name.* (Roy and the Director had never given a "distance" command before, so their big question then was, "How *far* should we tell them to go?") They pointed to the distance and commanded the spirits to get away from the school "as far as the eye could see" and never return. *That evil was broken and never returned.* No more people have been knocked down by invisible beings and Christians were finally able to plant churches in the surrounding communities.

Before then, the people were resistant to Christianity. For ten years after that, Roy checked with the Director, to make sure the spirits were gone for good. They were.

The strong territorial spirits not only harassed people along the side of the church property, but must have held minds captive, because when those spirits were banished, the people could "hear and understand" the Gospel. In that area of Thailand, after Christians proved to be more powerful than evil spirits, *a great turning to Christ took place.* The same principle holds true everywhere in the world, because the "god of this world [satan] has blinded the minds of the people who don't believe in Christ, lest the light of the glorious gospel of Christ, who is the image of God, shine in unto them and they be converted" (2 Corinthians 4:4).

Example #28
Victory! Demonic Bull Banished!

"Stand firm in one spirit, in no way alarmed by your opponents,
which is a sign of destruction for them, but of salvation for you."
(Philippians 1:27b, 28).

In northeast Thailand, a Jesus film team that showed the film to villagers needed a place to sleep for the night. Some unscrupulous village leaders planned to steal the film team's equipment, just as they had stolen from other visitors they had lodged in the Buddhist temple. How would they accomplish that? The Buddhist temple had *a resident evil spirit that appeared as a large black bull.* Other visitors that the Thai village leaders had housed in the temple had run in fear, leaving their belongings to be stolen and sold. The film projector was expensive; the village leaders figured they'd make a lot of money selling it, and it was going to be so easy to get.

When the men of the Campus Crusade for Christ film team were in the temple, sure enough, the big black bull demon appeared. But because they'd heard about the problem, our film team just told it to "Get out and stay out, in Jesus' Name." The bull vanished and the men of the film team went to sleep. The next morning their hosts were surprised to see them still in the temple. "Didn't you see anything?" "Yes, and we told it to leave and not come back, in Jesus' Name." The Thais were astonished. Their "bull" was known far and wide as being the most frightening demon. "This Jesus must have greater power" Eshleman (*I Just Saw Jesus*), which reports wonderful accounts of how God has used the Jesus film overseas.

Personal note: When Roy and I were in Thailand we saw a sparkling Buddhist temple in the distance, glinting lovely colors after a rain. I wanted to see what made the white and pastel colors "sparkle." So we walked to it. The exterior was tiled with colorful pieces of shiny broken china, which looked beautiful and reflected light. But the interior of the temple was filthy. The term "whited sepulcher" came to mind. (Sepulcher means tomb for the dead.)

Example #29
Victory! Opening Minds by Binding satan!

"They tell how you turned to God from idols, to
serve the living and true God."
(1 Thessalonians 1:9b)

Thais generally call themselves Buddhists, but for many it is just the "national religion," like many people in America call themselves Christians but don't understand what it really means to be a Christian. However, Thais who have studied Buddhism tend to be proud of being Buddhist.

On one of Roy's trips in Thailand he was in a village with a group of our Thai Campus Crusade for Christ staff in a home where a "New Life Fellowship" meets. That is a Bible study group that builds new Christians in their faith in Christ. While they were there, two men stopped by to visit with the owner of the house. One of them was a prominent Buddhist businessman who boasted that his son was an important Buddhist monk in the big Buddhist temple in town. The other was the head layman responsible for building and maintaining that temple. The New Life Training Center Director translated the men's boasting so Roy could understand what they were saying.

Roy then asked the Thai National Director to have someone share the Campus Crusade Four Spiritual Laws evangelistic booklet with the two older men. While the local CCC staff man did that, Roy and the rest of the Campus Crusade staff prayed that the Buddhists' eyes would be opened to the Gospel. At the same time, they bound satan and the spirits from "blinding the eyes of the men's understanding." In a short time, both Buddhist village leaders prayed to receive Christ. A trainer from the New Life Training Center immediately began following them up with materials of two follow-up appointments, to build them in their new faith in Christ. Then those two converts committed themselves to come to the New Life Fellowship, which met at that home. When satan was bound, God's light came into the men's minds and hearts.

Example #30
Victory! Problem Pig in New Guinea!

"We were the first to come even as far as you, in the gospel of Christ."
(2 Corinthians 14b)

Dr. Warner relates this missionary report: "Otto Koning, a missionary to New Guinea, tells of going to a village for the first time to hold services there. The people had built a special shelter for the meeting, and it was packed to the palm-frond walls with curious people. But conducting a service was another matter. The babies cried, the dogs outside barked, and to top it off, a very large pig came crashing through the wall of the shelter, causing pandemonium among the people. Koning finally gave up in defeat and headed for home. He was understandably not too eager to return to the village, but he had promised he would. Fortunately he had also been learning about spiritual warfare and the reality of demonic interference toward attempts to bring the gospel to a new village. So he began to wonder if demons might have been behind the disturbance in the village and if they could be bound before he went there. It was worth a try; so [in Jesus' Name] he commanded the demons not to use the animals to disturb the service. This time even the babies didn't seem to cry as much, and the animals stayed at the other end of the village. The result was that the gospel was heard and people came to Christ."

Dr. Warner comments: "Satan will use any avenue he can to prevent missionaries, or any Christian workers, from carrying on their ministries. And when the local people see that the missionaries do not know how to handle an encounter which they [the villagers] clearly perceive to be demonic, the cause of the Gospel is hindered, to say the least. In the minds of the people, when the missionary fails to win a power encounter, the power of the demon is assumed to be greater than the power of the Christ the missionary serves. A successful meeting of such a challenge, however, is powerful witness to the gospel. The typical Western mind will attribute this to coincidence, but anyone who has been in the battle has no difficulty understanding the reality of the power of demons to use animals or other objects in the physical world to hinder the work of God and of God's servants. Understanding this is the first step in claiming victory over it" Warner (*Spiritual Warfare*) pp. 95, 96.

Example #31
Victory! Cleansing "The Devil's Hill" Mission House!

"We don't wrestle against flesh and blood, but against the rulers, against the authorities, against the powers of this dark world, and against spiritual forces of evil."
(Ephesians 6:12)

From his own experience Dr. Warner gives another example… "In a village in Sierra Leone, West Africa, early missionaries were given 'the devil's hill' on which to build the mission house. No one took the danger of this seriously because [they thought] 'demons couldn't do anything to Christians.' When I was on the field I had a nonfunctional theology about such things, but I vividly remember watching the family living in the house go through attacks of physical disease which eventually took them off the field. A recent occupant of that house told me that until two years ago, people who came to visit would become ill when they arrived but would lose the symptoms as they left the village. Why the change? *Two years ago they finally cleansed the hill in a power encounter. Since that time there have been no more physical attacks.* Regarding what was formerly the 'devil's hill,' God alone knows how many of His servants have been taken out of the battle because they did not recognize this device of the enemy" Timothy M. Warner, (*Spiritual Warfare*) p. 90.

A "power encounter" is a direct confrontation with satan, in which *a Christian gives orders to satan* as to what he *must do* or is *forbidden to do.* The order is given in Jesus' Name. Then if the Christian knows to do it, he prays the Blood of Christ's protection over himself and the situation.

CHAPTER SEVEN

ANIMISM/SPIRITISM

Definition of Animism

ANIMISM AND SPIRITISM are related, yet different. Animism means the *belief* that everything on earth, animate and inanimate, has a spirit in it. Spiritism is *contact* with demonic spirits. In most animist/spiritist areas of the world, the two overlap.

Dr. Timothy M. Warner explains the animistic worldview, the belief that *everything has a "spirit" in it*. It is not a world religion like Islam or Hinduism, but it is widespread. (Possibly because demons inhabit objects and cause people to theorize that the object itself is alive.) Most of the non-Western world, as well as large segments of the Western world, have a folk-level set of religious beliefs akin to animism. Animism has common elements:

1. The belief that everything in the world—animal, vegetable, and mineral—shares the same kind of spiritual power. It might give you good luck or it might kill you.

2. The common belief in animism is that there are spirit beings here on earth that involved in all aspects of life on earth. Dr. Warner calls them "described demons." The people of the world have always been aware of the existence of "spirits." That's why Hindus worship three million "gods" (spirits) hoping they aren't leaving one out that might take offense and harm them. Animistic spirits may be associated with natural objects, with people, or with the dead, and they may be good or evil in nature. To the animist, *physical and spiritual are inseparable* Warner (*Spiritual Warfare*) p. 26.

Example #32
Victory! Cutting Down the "Evil Tree"!

"Be strong and of good courage; the Lord shall fight for you."
(Deuteronomy 31:1 and Exodus 14:14)

At separate times, three Muslim Indonesian men had attempted to cut an "evil tree" down. Within 24 hours each of those men was dead. In desperation, a man from that village came up to our ministry headquarters in Jakarta and asked if we had any men who could cut the tree down. Two of our Christian men went. The villagers expected that they, too, would die. But the Christian men prayed the Blood of Christ's protection over themselves and *in Jesus' Name they cut the tree down.* Nothing bad happened to them. In that area of Indonesia, that victory was a powerful witness to the reality of Christ and Christianity. (A tree itself is not "evil," but Indonesia has a history of occult masks [housing powerful demonic spirits] being buried at the base of large trees, giving those demons a "home.")

Example #33
Indonesia: The "Rice Goddess" Hinders Harvest

Indonesia's rich volcanic soil and a hot, wet climate make it perfect for growing rice. However, rice harvesters' *fear of "the rice goddess"* makes harvesting slow. Because of that, farmers don't have time to plant a second crop during the growing season. The result is that Indonesia can't grow enough rice to feed her people; the nation has to import rice. What are rice harvesters afraid of? They believe that the top leaf on each stalk of rice, the "flag leaf" has the "eyes of the rice goddess in it" and she will be angry if she sees them cutting her down and will cause something bad to happen to them. Attempting to avoid her anger, harvesters stand behind whichever way the flag leaf on the rice stalk is drooping, and "cut her down" with a small, curved knife blade hidden in the harvester's hand. That way the rice goddess "can't see" who did it. Indonesians fear that if they don't adhere to that time and labor intensive harvesting routine the rice goddess will be angry and retaliate in some way; possibly cause crop failure the next year or sickness in harvesters' families, or cause of their water buffalos to get sick and die. Those are things that happened in the past when Indonesians had tried to harvest more efficiently.

Is that foolish thinking? There is no "rice goddess," but demons are active and always working to harm people. If harvesters don't obey that harvesting pattern they have experienced demonically caused problems that they attribute to having offended the "rice goddess." Only Christian farmers in Indonesia are free from that fear. They can grow rice abundantly and prosper.

India: Fatalism Hinders Progress

Every animist/spiritist belief and pagan ritual harms the welfare of the people. That is satan's plan. India sometimes suffers a shortage of wheat because of adverse weather conditions and because rodents and other vermin are not killed. Why aren't they killed? Because India is primarily Hindu, and Hinduism teaches reincarnation, coming back to earth in a different body. Hindus fear to kill animals, including rats, because a deceased loved one might have been reincarnated into that animal. Grandmother might have been reincarnated as a rat. So not even rats are killed. Because rats eat such a large amount of the grain that is produced in India, at times people suffer hunger. One year when India suffered a wheat crop failure, merciful America sent an entire shipload of wheat and unloaded it on a dock for Indian authorities to distribute. But none of them took responsibility to do that. The load of grain went undistributed and became so fouled by rat urine that much of it could not be eaten.

It is virtually impossible to bring about lasting progress in a spiritist/fatalist culture such as Hinduism produces. During Roy's time in India, he and other Project staff worked in various aspects of village development. They spearheaded the installation of clean water wells in about a hundred villages within the 50 mile radius of Project headquarters. The Indians were *thrilled to have clean water to drink.* Roy taught them how to maintain the wells, and a nurse from the project taught villagers the importance of sanitation, so they could avoid deadly water-borne diseases like hepatitis. But even though the medical information was given, and maintenance of the wells was explained, *the Indians did not make the effort to maintain the wells.* Each person thought someone else should do the job. The wells became fouled and villagers went back to drinking polluted water. People contracted hepatitis and other diseases and considered it "fate." Babies died and parents were sad, but they dismissed the deaths as "fate." Hinduism *keeps the people down by locking them into the inertia of "fate,"* the belief that their lives are predestined. Because of that belief, they think it doesn't much matter what they do or don't do, the outcome is *set.* That mindset cripples progress.

Roy upgraded the poultry because he was concerned that village children weren't getting enough protein in their diet. Native Indian chickens are very small, and lay only three to five eggs *a month.* So Roy imported American "white leghorn" chicken eggs and incubated them at the foot of his bed in his little mud hut, using a kerosene lantern to keep them warm. Roy raised hundreds of the white leghorn chickens and distributed them to the farmers, who were thrilled to get them. The purebred white leghorns laid 25 to 30 eggs a month. And even when they cross-bred with the native banty hens, the new generation of hens laid 20 to 25 eggs per month. That gave Indian farmers protein for their entire family, as well as eggs to sell. It was an immense boost.

But the day after a Hindu festival there were *no white chickens to be seen.* What had happened to them? The Indians had sacrificed *all* the white leghorn chickens to their Hindu gods. Why? They told Roy it was because "the gods demand their best" (or they might retaliate). *The Hindu religion had destroyed progress.* Roy loved the Indian people, but he said he would never again go anywhere to try to help people unless he could also present Christ to them.

Example #34
Victory! Christ Inspires Progress in Indonesia: Muslim Mayor Transformed!

"Today if you hear His voice, do not harden your heart."
(Psalm 95:7, 8)

Later, as a missionary in Indonesia, Roy saw that when people became Christians, they progressed. In Java, as in many places in the world, community leaders tend to be proud and lead easy lives, avoiding menial work, and are continually waited upon by servants. On a trip to East Java, Roy and his team went into a village to visit some Christians there, but first it was good manners to meet the mayor and ask his permission to be in the village. Roy and some team members did that. The proud Muslim mayor quickly asked Roy to "get money from America" for his village; to build a school, build a church for the Christians, and get seed and fertilizer for his farmers. Instead, Roy listened respectfully, but then asked, "Pak Lurah," (Mr. Mayor) has anyone ever told you how you can know God personally?" "No, I have never heard of that." Roy asked, "May I share this little booklet with you that tells how you can know God personally?" "Yes, please." So, communicating through an Indonesian Campus Crusade for Christ man who spoke Javanese, Roy led the mayor to Christ. Afterward, Roy asked the man if he would come and meet with the Christians and other villagers and tell them what he had prayed. "Yes." And he did, with genuine enthusiasm.

First, the formerly proud mayor apologized to his people for having been a selfish man. He said, "I and my father before me (who had been the former mayor) are very wealthy. You can see the size of my big home in comparison to your little homes. Everything we did was to benefit ourselves. I am very sorry. Today I invited Jesus to come and live in me. With His help I want to be a better leader." It was unheard of for a proud Javanese leader to apologize to people considered his social inferiors. But he did apologize, genuinely. It was *instant evidence that the man had gained new life in Christ.*

The mayor became filled with energy and concern for his people. He himself led the committee to build a school, help the Christians build a church, and help the farmers get better crops. All Roy needed to do to help the village was introduce the mayor to a local government official, to get a loan of seed and fertilizer for his farmers. He did that and the village prospered. *Christ moves people forward!*

Roy had many wonderful witnessing experiences in Indonesia, talking to people in all walks of life. In a parking lot in East Java, taking a break with the team of Indonesians he was training, Roy saw a middle-aged gardener tending the lawn and began talking to him. "Did anyone ever tell you how you could meet Jesus and live forever in heaven?" "No, but I would like to meet him. Is he in your car?" And Roy explained who Jesus is and how to know Him. The man bowed his head and asked Jesus to come and live in his life. Roy saw the man a few times after that and he was rejoicing. He had found a Christian church to attend and he "only had to walk two kilometers to get there." (Not quite two miles. To an Indonesian, that wasn't far. Many Indonesians walk everywhere.)

CHAPTER EIGHT

OVERCOMING TRAVEL DANGERS

Example #35
Victory! God Helps Robin Solve Car Trouble!

"You O Lord, only, make me to dwell in safety."
(Psalm 4:8)

YEARS AGO, GOD helped our daughter Robin when her little red convertible overheated on a lonely highway one evening, after Thanksgiving dinner at my brother's house. She pulled off to the shoulder and stopped, wondering what could be wrong. It was November, the weather was cool, and Robin knew her radiator had water in it and that the car's thermostat was working. What could be wrong? Since this was before cell phones, she prayed that someone would come along and help her. Then, a bit fearful of that on the lonely road at night, she prayed that no one would stop. She asked God to show her what was wrong with her car. Then it came to her mind (from God) that it might be a trick. She didn't know for sure, but on the *chance* that it was, she whispered, "satan, if you're making my car overheat, in Jesus' Name, *stop it!*" The *temperature dropped immediately.* Robin drove safely home.

Example #36
Victory! Flight Protection!

I will lie down and sleep in peace, for you alone,
O Lord, make me to dwell in safety."
(Psalm 4:8)

Many years ago, the night before I was to fly to a Campus Crusade for Christ conference in Colorado, Robin phoned and begged, "Mom, don't fly tomorrow! I have such a bad feeling about it." The next morning, on a day that looked "too beautiful for anything to go wrong," my plane had taxied out onto the tarmac and was waiting for clearance to take off. It was in the era when cockpit doors were left open, and from my aisle seat I could see the pilot and co-pilot happily laughing and talking together. It was about 10 minutes before I remembered Robin's warning. I whispered, *"satan, if there is anything wrong with this plane or the pilots or anyone on board, in Jesus' Name I forbid you to hide it."* Immediately *a panel of red lights flashed in the cockpit.* Soon the pilot announced that the flaps weren't working and we would all have to take other flights. He taxied back to the gate and everyone got off. Robin's warning had been a merciful message from God that saved at least 100 people, as well as the airplane and ground damage if the plane had crashed.

Now, before any flight, in Jesus' Name we quietly forbid satan to hide it if anything is wrong. We encourage you to do the same. *And always whisper the Blood of Christ's protection over yourself afterward.* It will protect you from any demonic strike-back.

Example #37
Victory! God Saved the Jumbo Jet!

"I led them with cords of human kindness, with ties of love."
(Hosea 11:4)

On one of his trips to Africa to participate in the Nairobi International School of Theology graduation in Kenya, Roy and about 250 other passengers were boarded at LAX, the Los Angeles International Airport, awaiting take-off to Detroit and Amsterdam, with Roy then to fly Kenya Airlines to Africa. Because of what he had learned from Robin's warning to me, as he waited in the jumbo jet Roy whispered that command. *In Jesus' Name he forbade satan to hide it* if anything was wrong with the plane or the crew or anyone on board, and he prayed the Blood of Christ's protection over the flight. Within a few minutes, the pilot announced that *the plane had a malfunctioning valve* and the passengers would have to take other planes. Roy had to wait eight hours to get a KLM flight to Amsterdam, which threw off his flight to Kenya, but *all 250 passengers and crew of the original plane were safe!* Most people have no idea how real and powerful a friend the *Lord Jesus Christ* is.

As you cooperate with God in ways like that, *you must let Jesus use your voice*, if only a whisper. That way *He* is giving voice to the command through you, and His army of angels obey *Him*. God has complete power over everything in the universe, and acts independently in whatever ways He chooses. *On earth He has chosen to let humans cooperate with Him.* As people pray, or don't pray, "so goes the battle." Humans are God's high creation, intended to make life better for the people around them. Part of that involves prayer for situations that seem to need prayer. Flying is one of them. Roy and I like to quietly pray the Blood of Christ's protection over people around us as well as for ourselves, and in other situations also, such as on a busy highway.

Example #38
Victory! Roy Outwits (Outwaits) Corrupt Police!

"Do not fret because of evil men."
(Psalm 37:1)

On a teaching trip to Nigeria, Roy landed in the capital city of Lagos at about midnight, and was met by a young Nigerian Campus Crusade for Christ staff man. But as soon as they stepped out of the airport, onto the sidewalk, they were arrested by two Nigerian policemen. Roy suspected it was going to be an extortion attempt, and it was. The policemen drove them into deep jungle about 25 minutes away, took them into a hidden little hut, and motioned for Roy and the young man to sit on chairs. Nothing was said. The police just sat across the room and stared at Roy and waited. They doubtless had done this before and frightened visitors had begged to be returned to the airport. And paid. Roy sat peacefully, pretending he had no idea what they wanted. He quietly prayed, in Jesus' Name forbidding satan to harm them, and he prayed comfort for the frightened young Nigerian who accompanied him. (Of course, that young man had to live in the same country as those crooked police.)

Finally, three hours later, at three a.m., the disgusted police gave up and took Roy and the young staff man back to the now-deserted airport and dropped them off. At that hour the airport was closed, so no taxis were out front. Like most airports, it was far from the city, so they were stranded. They waited and prayed and finally a taxi drove up. By the time they got to the hotel and to sleep it was five a.m. It had been a long flight and a long night, but Roy and the young CCC staff man were safe and thanking God.

Example #39
Victory! Roy Escapes Ethiopian Tour Trap!

Every country seems to have good people and bad people. After a night flight to Nairobi and Jordan, Roy and another seminary professor had a layover in Addis Ababa, Ethiopia. The airline provided hotel vouchers so passengers could rest in the morning if they wished to, but because Addis Ababa is the capital of Ethiopia, Roy and the other professor decided to take a tour instead. Right outside the hotel door they hired a taxi driver to show them around. It was a very interesting tour, and after two hours of seeing the sights the driver headed back toward the hotel. But he stopped two blocks from it and wouldn't go on. Suddenly suspicious, Roy looked around and saw four Ethiopian men coming toward them from a side street. He told his friend, "Run!" They jumped out of the taxi and ran as fast as they could to the hotel. They barely got through the doors in time. The would-be thieves piled up against the doors but didn't try to come in. It had been a trap. *But God let Roy see the men in time to escape.*

SECTION TWO:

GOD'S ANGELS: HELPERS OF HIS PEOPLE

CHAPTER NINE

ANGELS

THE BIBLE HAS *more than 250 references to angels.* Google: "Strong's Exhaustive Bible Concordance Online" to access the list.

WHERE THERE IS REVERENCE FOR GOD,
THERE IS ANGELIC PRESENCE.

That was true in the Old Testament and it is true now. Angels are servants of the Most High God, the army of the Lord Jesus Christ, *assigned as guardians and helpers to all people God knows will love Him and inherit eternal life.* That includes helping people God knows will receive Jesus in the future, as they did in saving Roy's life in the Himalayas before he knew Christ personally.

Example #40
Victory! Roy Saved by an Angel in the Himalayas!

"Sing praises to the Lord, proclaim among
the nations what He has done."
(Psalm 9:11)

When Roy was 23 years old, doing technical assistance in India, he was able to join an Indian Department of Anthropology expedition into the Himalayan Mountains. Three university anthropologists were seeking to find a tribe of Tibetans that had vanished somewhere between Tibet and India in the vast snowy passes of the Himalayas a number of years before. Thirty-nine men were in the expedition: the anthropologists, Roy, and thirty-five sherpas who carried food and gear. ("Sherpa" is the name of the mountain tribe that carries climbers' gear.) Roy carried his own 80 pound pack and occasionally helped tired sherpas, swinging one of their 80 pound loads atop his own. Even though sherpas have bulging calf muscles, many of them lack endurance because they eat very little protein. (Roy was a powerful 6 foot 3 farm boy who had been raised on plenty of milk and meat.)

The team got up to almost 18,000 feet (27,000 meters) but had not found evidence of the Tibetans they were seeking. They had to stop their search because they didn't have enough oxygen masks for the thin air, or sufficient ice-climbing equipment to cross the deep crevasses (splits in the ice). The group was resting on a high mountain pass when Roy, sitting on his jacket, *suddenly heard a loud voice to his mind command,* "Move!" He jumped away just as a huge boulder rolled silently down the slope and *stopped right on his jacket.* It would have killed him. That experience was before Roy knew Jesus personally. The warning voice was *God's mercy, shouted to his mind by an angel.*

Dr. Timothy Warner states, "Among other functions we see angels protecting [people] from danger" (Genesis 32:1–2; 2 Kings 6:17).

Description and Function of God's Angels

Angels are the army of the Lord Jesus Christ and carry out His commands of protection and mercy toward people who love God. They have been seen as tall, clean looking, luminously bright, powerful young men, and the largest angels seem to have greater responsibility than smaller angels. God's angels can appear as unknown, helpful humans when needed, a phenomenon experienced through the centuries. People in crisis prayed and were helped, sometimes by a "kind stranger." Angelic ability to take human form is confirmed in the book of Hebrews 13:2 as Christians are admonished to show hospitality to strangers, "for by this some have entertained angels without knowing it." God says that each person who will inherit eternal life has a "guardian angel" (Psalm 34:7). Sometimes people have felt comforted by an angelic presence they could sense, and sometimes they were saved from catastrophe when they weren't even praying, helped by the angel assigned to guard them. God uses angels to carry out His purposes in the world He created. The chapters about Angelic Help and Miracles have some wonderful, true stories of angelic help.

If you love Jesus, there is never a time that He and His angels are not with you.

What the Holy Spirit brings to every Christian's lips when that person is in trouble is a desperately whispered, "Jesus!" or "God help me!" The act of genuinely calling on the King, the Lord Jesus Christ, brings angelic help. "The angel of the Lord *camps* around them that fear Him [reverence Him] and rescues them" (Psalm 34:7). Power from God's angels is released in response to the obedience and faith and prayers of God's people. Accordingly, people's circumstances in life can be changed. Because of God's great mercy, angels have also helped people who didn't yet know God and even were unaware of imminent danger.

Angelic Responsibility

Dr. Timothy Warner states that "Angels perform a wide variety of functions in the universe of which our world is a part. This is a God-created and God-sustained world—there is a scientific orderliness about the world, but it had its origin in God's act of creation, and is maintained by His sustaining power. And although satan is the temporary 'prince' of earth, angels are here to counter satan's destructive power. When Jesus returns, which could be soon, His angels will destroy satan's earthly empire and reconstruct the earth. Among other functions—we see angels doing such things as giving guidance to people (Genesis 22:11, 15; 31:11, 12), protecting them from danger (Genesis 32:1, 2; 2 Kings 6:17), delivering them (Daniel 3:28; Acts 5:19; 12:7), destroying enemies (Genesis 19:13; 2 Chronicles 32:21; Acts 12:23), providing food for a weary prophet (1 Kings 19:5, 7), and other acts of ministry to 'those who will inherit salvation' (Hebrews 1:14). We are not given a full-blown theology of angels in the scriptures, but we are told enough to assume that *God uses angels to carry out His purposes in the world He created.* Far from being an impersonal, material world operating by 'natural' law, the world is functionally upheld by the power of God exercised by His authority through angels" (*Spiritual Warfare*) pp. 28–30.

Example #41
Victory! Angels With Flaming Swords!

"The Lord has become my fortress, and my
God the rock where I take refuge."
(Psalm 94:22)

"Near a village in Thailand where the Jesus film was being shown, a gang of thugs decided to rob the film team of their equipment and sell it for some quick money. They crept into the village during the night and scouted out the hut where the team's equipment was being stored. Security was simple, so it looked like an easy job. But as they approached the entrance, they were startled by *two brilliant white beings filling the doorway!* Both were over eight feet tall [almost three meters] and brandished flaming swords. The robbers, not raised with Bibles or Christianity, had never heard of 'angels' or 'flaming swords.' They fled into the jungle. Hiding there, they convinced themselves that what they had seen were ghosts. They decided to try again. This time they went around to the back door, but the same huge figures appeared there. One of the robbers cried out, 'If this is the power of their God, we don't dare steal from them.' Later, some of the gang members saw the 'Jesus' film and became Christians. It was one of the converted gang members who reported this story to the film team" Eshleman, (*I Just Saw Jesus*) p. 113.

Example #42
Victory! Protected By an Angel!

"I will be with him in trouble. I will deliver him and honor him."
(Psalm 91:15)

Guideposts magazine reported the experience of a young woman who witnessed a murder as she took a shortcut home from her evening job as a waitress. She attended college in the daytime and worked at night, so she was very tired. And she had to walk home. The safe way was long, so she decided to risk using a back alley shortcut. She knew it wasn't as safe, but it would get her home quickly. However, going through the alley *she witnessed a stabbing, and saw the face of the man who did it.* Unfortunately, the man had turned and looked right at her after he did it. She was filled with fear. "Oh Jesus, what should I do?" If she *ran,* he would know she saw him, and if she didn't run, he might chase her and kill her, too, so she couldn't report him to the police. "Oh God, help me!"

She decided to walk slowly, like she didn't know anything, although she was shaking with fear the whole way. When she reached her apartment she telephoned the police, and gave a description. They called her in to identify the man and he was tried and convicted. After the trial, she asked to speak to him. "You knew I saw you—why did you let me go?" "Are you kidding! With that big guy you were walking with! No way!" The young woman thought she had walked alone, but she hadn't. In response to her cry to Jesus for help, her angel made his huge presence visible to her enemy. In time of trouble every Christian wishes he or she could see their defending angel, but it *is often only the Christian's enemy who sees the angel and is frightened off.*

Example #43
Victory! Saved From Attack!

"O Lord my God, I take refuge in you."
(Psalm 7:1)

Jeanie Ganssle, a close friend of our daughter Karen and also a campus minister at Yale University, told me of an experience she had in her teens, shortly after receiving Christ into her life. She was driving her car when a guy pulled up beside her and pointed to her front tire, saying something was wrong with it. Puzzled, Jeanie pulled over to the side of the road and the man stopped behind her. Fortunately, she had the presence of mind to lock her doors and roll her window up most of the way, leaving just enough room to talk to him. He came to her window and ordered her to roll it down. She did not, and he forced his arm into her car, trying to reach the handle. Jeanie, without forethought, said, *"In the name of Jesus, please leave me alone!"*

The man jerked back like he'd been *electrocuted*, raised his arms in a surrender gesture and said, "I was just kidding!" Then he hurried back to his car and sped away. What had frightened him? *Was he afraid of Jesus? Or had he seen an angel in Jeanie's car when she spoke Jesus' Name?* The man had seen something, because *he was badly frightened and fled.* As in the previous story, it probably was a situation in which the person's *enemy* saw the angel, but the person being protected did not. Much relieved, Jeanie was safe. Speaking about "Jesus" had not been premeditated; she was a brand-new Christian. God must have prompted her to say His Name and His angels defended her.

God's angels act in great numbers when Christians pray, individually and in groups. The Bible tells us to "pray without ceasing" (1 Thessalonians 5:17). By sincere prayer we cooperate with God and His angels to bring mercy to people on earth. I think the most important things to know about angels is that *they exist, are the army of the Lord Jesus Christ, and we are to be fellow laborers with them to accomplish Christ's purposes.*

Example #44
Victory! Angel in a Motorcycle Jacket!

"Let all who take refuge in the LORD be
glad; let them ever sing for joy."
(Psalm 5:11)

The Bible lists many references of angels talking to and with humans, the angels appearing both in human form and angelic form. Our Christian friend Dr. Bravo, the former Director of Mountains Community Hospital at Lake Arrowhead, was clinically dead. Doctors wanted to remove his life support, but his wife, Heidi, refused. She stayed beside his bed and prayed. Three days later Dr. Bravo woke up. When he was able to speak, he told Heidi that two angels were with him in his hospital room, encouraging him. Were they dressed in glowing white robes? No. One of them was wearing a black leather motorcycle jacket! What a surprise! (He probably appeared like that so Dr. Bravo could be sure he was really back on earth!) He said they were clean-looking young men who spoke encouraging words. Over the days, the angels took turns sitting with Dr. Bravo, vanishing and reappearing. One of them even told jokes to keep Dr. Bravo cheered up! And they laughed as they told him not to bother to tell the nurses they were there, "because they wouldn't believe it anyway." Doctors say there is no question that Dr. Bravo had been dead.

Example #45
Victory! Angel Starts Dead Battery in Sumatra!

"For the Lord is good; His loving kindness is everlasting
and His faithfulness to all generations."
(Psalm 100:5)

Roy's exploratory trip to Indonesia in 1968 was a search for land on which to grow rice to sell to support the fledgling Campus Crusade for Christ ministry in that country. Through an official in President Suharto's government, Roy had a 2 p.m. appointment to meet with the Governor of South Sumatra about locating suitable land. (Sumatra is a huge island, as large as California and Oregon put together, so it has two governors.) Roy took a ferry from the northern tip of Java, above Jakarta, to the southern tip of South Sumatra, then a train north to Palembang, the capital of South Sumatra. In the train, he was sharing the Gospel with an English-speaking Indonesian when a patrolling English-speaking Indonesian soldier came by and asked what he was showing the other man. Roy said, "I'm sharing some wonderful news about how to know God personally." The soldier listened, and he was the one who prayed to receive Christ.

In Palembang, a former missionary Roy had met on an earlier trip took him in his jeep to check out some land. It was a 20 mile drive (30 kilometers) along a raised road, with swamp on each side. Wet, but not suitable for growing rice. Then the jeep ran out of gas. The man's driver was able to get a gallon of gas from a passing car, but couldn't get the jeep to start. Roy and his friend pushed the jeep, but it wouldn't start. Finally the battery was dead and the friend gave up. Roy urged, "Let's try *one more time*, and let's pray." *"Lord Jesus, please make this engine run. Engine, in Jesus' Name, start!"* Another push, and *the engine started up.* They got back to Palembang in time for Roy's appointment with the Governor. His friend was amazed, and Roy thanked God for starting the motor. That kind of physical intervention is done by angels, in response to commands given in the Name of their King, the Lord Jesus Christ.

Example #46
Victory! Our Home Rescued From Smoke!

"My shield is God most High, who saves the upright in heart."
(Psalm 7:10)

In a distant city, our daughter Robin *felt a sudden strong alarm that "something is wrong at home!"* She jumped into her car and raced the 60 miles to our house. When she arrived, she found the house *filled with the smell of smoke.* She threw open all the doors and windows and hunted for the source of the trouble. It was the private guest bedroom upstairs, black with smoke. Roy and I were out of town and had allowed friends to stay in that room. They had made a fire in the fireplace and closed the damper before they left, seemingly not realizing that a closed damper keeps the smoke from going up the chimney, forcing the smoke into the house. It was a nuisance to have to clean the room of soot and smoke smell, but at least our house was still standing. We knew that God's angels had spoken the warning to Robin, and we were very grateful.

A few years ago our home was in jeopardy from a wind-driven fire blowing strongly north-to-south, *straight toward us.* In the pre-dawn morning, police wakened residents with a bull horn, ordering them to evacuate. The sky was red. Roy walked down to check the status of the fire and found it was burning only a few blocks from our home, shooting embers in our direction. In the mountains, burning embers can ignite trees and wooden shake roofs far in advance of the fire itself. We had experienced God turning the wind in a previous fire, so out on our deck I asked Roy to please, "tell the fire to turn, in Jesus' Name." He did that. Roy "spoke against the fire" in a normal voice, telling it to "go back," and in Jesus' Name forbade satan to destroy our home. He prayed the Blood of Christ's protection over our house and property. We were required to leave, so we couldn't see what the fire was doing, but a week later, when residents were allowed to return, we saw that the fire had come *no closer* to our home than it had been when Roy "spoke against it" in Jesus' Name. The wind had turned, taking the fire west. We wish Roy had told it to reverse direction, snuff itself out, but we didn't think of it. At least not as many homes were lost as would have been if it had continued south. Roy and I think angels turned the wind. Please remember that, in case, God forbid, you ever have a similar emergency. And if you ever are in that situation, in Jesus' Name *tell* the wind to put the fire out.

Example #47
Victory! An Angel Guards Karen's Wallet!

"Because he loves me, says the Lord, I will rescue him."
(Psalm 91:14)

After our daughter Karen graduated from the University of California at Riverside, she worked in Washington D.C., first for our local congressman and then for President Reagan. Those were good experiences, but she wanted to help change lives by leading people to Christ. So she joined the staff of Campus Crusade for Christ (now known as CRU) and was assigned to Dartmouth University in New Hampshire as a women's ministry chaplain. New Hampshire is very far from our home in southern California, and we were glad when Karen returned for a little vacation. She wanted to drive along the beautiful Pacific Coast, so we stayed overnight at a motel in Dana Point and then drove south on "PCH," the Pacific Coast Highway, stopping for breakfast at a little coffee shop close to the highway. Then on to beautiful La Jolla ("la hoya").

When we got there and were enjoying the view, Karen reached into her purse for something and exclaimed, "My wallet! I must have left my wallet in the coffee shop!" It contained not only her money, but her driver's license, her credit card, and her Dartmouth Chaplain's identification card. And there we were, 45 minutes away from that busy coffee shop! My heart sank. By the time we got back, we would have been gone for an hour and a half! It would take a *miracle* for the wallet to still be there. It seemed so hopeless. We prayed together as we started back, but I didn't feel hopeful. I whispered, "Oh, Jesus, please tell me how to pray!" Very clearly to my mind He said, *"Pray as though it just happened."* So I prayed as though we had just walked out of the coffee shop. Knowing that God had spoken to me, I fervently asked that an angel guard Karen's wallet.

When we got back to the coffee shop I ran inside. *To my immense relief and gratitude the wallet was safe in the kitchen.* The baker told me she had gone into the dining room for a cup of coffee right after we left, and seeing the wallet she put it in her kitchen for safe keeping. *"An angel used you to rescue it!"* I exclaimed. "I know!" she beamed. She told me that when she checked the wallet for identification and saw that Karen is a Christian chaplain, *she knew God had sent her into the dining room to rescue the wallet.* We rejoiced together (and I was able to press some reward money into her hand). Would that way of prayer be effective again? Yes. I used it in another situation to locate a "hopelessly" lost earring. Would that way of prayer *always* be effective? I don't know. But keep it in mind. You have nothing to lose by trying it.

Example #48
Victory! Water From "Nowhere" Saved Our Truck!

"My tongue will speak of your righteousness
and of your praise all day long."
(Psalm 35:28)

As Roy and I drove a big load of our watermelons down to the Los Angeles wholesale market in our stake truck, we had to climb the barren Ridge Route, the 60-mile-long dry mountain pass between the San Joaquin Valley north of the Ridge, and the San Fernando Valley on the south side. Our truck began to heat up and Roy discovered that the radiator was leaking. What could we do? Roy stopped at a little service station to refill the radiator, and knowing that there were *no more service stations on the barren route,* I picked up all the discarded paper cups and bottles I could find and filled them with water. In the truck I balanced them at my feet, not minding the bit of sloshing. But we couldn't make it to the top of the ridge. We had used all the water from the cups and bottles and *the temperature gauge registered red.* We prayed for a miracle. "Oh Jesus, please help us."

Roy had to pull over to the shoulder and stop, so he wouldn't blow the engine. It was *where* he "happened to stop" that was so amazing. On those long miles of high barren hills Roy had "happened" to pull over *right in front of an unmarked Forest Service exit* that curved out from behind a hill, and our truck almost blocked the exit. A Forestry Service jeep came around that little road, needing to exit onto the highway. "Are you having trouble?" the friendly Forest Service man asked. "Yes, our engine is hot; we need water." He went to his jeep, brought over a big container of water and filled up our radiator. He also filled my cups and bottles, "just in case." That got us over the highest point of the Ridge Route and we made it safely down to Los Angeles, unloaded our watermelons, and got the radiator fixed. Thank you, kind Forest Service man, and thank you God and our angels for *causing Roy to stop the truck at possibly the only place on the barren Ridge Route where we could get water.*

Example #**49**
Victory! Steaks

"Your love, O Lord, reaches to the heavens,
Your faithfulness to the skies."
(Psalm 36:5)

The next two stories are not about emergencies, but about how God does extraordinary things when people care about each other and are willing to share what they have. Wherever there is love, kindness, and freedom in sharing, you can be sure that God is there. Angels are aware of even *unexpressed* or *hidden needs* and are able to intervene by prompting people to do things that bless and meet the needs of others.

I stopped teaching right before our son Michael was born and it was my joy to stay home with baby Mike and three-year-old Karen. But we felt the lack of my salary. Roy attended seminary and farmed only part time, so we didn't have much money. But we were happy and we weren't starving. Roy had brought up a big freezer from his family's ranch in Yorba Linda, but we had no extra money to buy food to store in it. We only had a couple of loaves of bread in there. Roy swung open the little freezer at the top of our refrigerator and shook his head. "Forget the big freezer. *What I would like is this little freezer filled with steaks!*" We quietly gave our big freezer to friends who had several children, entertained a lot, and had access to fruits and vegetables to preserve in it.

The next day something very wonderful happened. A man from our church *who knew nothing about the freezer,* came walking up our long vineyard driveway, bringing a *box of steaks!* He had just butchered a steer. The steaks filled up our little freezer, *just what Roy had wished for!* It felt like an angel had prompted that dear man to bring them to us. It was a wonderful lesson in not holding tightly to what we don't need, but sharing it with someone who does need it. *We had given the freezer, and someone else gave Roy what he desired.* And the woman who got the freezer even put some of her wonderful pies in there for us! Through the years we have seen God work in that pattern. We hope the dear smiling man who gave us the steaks received something wonderful that he desired!

Example #50
Victory! Skis for All the Kids!

"Bless the Lord, O my soul; and all that is
within me bless His holy name."
(Psalm 103:1)

At the beginning of the school year when Mike and Robin were in Junior High, I asked what they would like God to help them with that year (instead of my usual prayer for good behavior, good friends, good teachers and good grades). Mike said he would like to ask God to help him get skis. He had saved $20, but that amount wouldn't go far toward buying skis. So we prayed, and *Mike asked God "to give him skis in a way that would bless the other kids."* Privately, while I thought that was a sweet attitude, I couldn't imagine how one boy's prayer for skis could bless the other kids. Little did I know.

I was in a PTA board meeting at the Junior High and heard the comment that Snow Valley, the ski resort, was getting new ski equipment. As soon as my meeting was over I took Mike and Robin up there to see if I could buy some of the old equipment for them. The owner was known to be brusque, so I dreaded asking him, but...all he could say was "no." It was worth a try. Yet at first I drove past the ski lift for a while, trying to crank up my courage. Then I parked near his office and got out of the car whispering, "Jesus, please help me." He spoke strongly to my mind, "Eleanor, ask for *all* the children. Ask on behalf of the PTA." What a great idea! (I think I even said that out loud as I began to walk toward the ski shop office.) With new confidence I went up the stairs to the man's office and smiled, "Hello, I'm Mrs. Rosedale from the Lake Arrowhead PTA and I understand you are replacing your ski equipment. Would you consider donating the old equipment to the school children? Then more children could take ski lessons up here and keep coming." "Of course. How many hundreds of skis and boots could you use?" "As many as you can give us."

It took the big school stake truck two trips to load up the 500 pairs of skis and about 350 pairs of ski boots. (No poles, but those were not expensive.) Roy and Mike helped turn the cafeteria-auditorium into a *gigantic ski shop.* Parents outfitted their children with free ski equipment, and after that the adults could pick out free equipment for themselves. Roy and Mike and Karen and Robin got skis and boots and Roy is still using his. *It was a phenomenal answer to a boy's prayer.* God honored Mike's unselfish prayer and used His angels to orchestrate the whole wonderful thing. *God turned it all around, to "bless the other kids," just as Mike had prayed.*

Example #51
Victory! Stopping a Dog!

"Keep me safe, O GOD, for in you I take refuge."
(Psalm 16:1)

I was walking on a quiet street on my way up to see my friend Sharon, when a stocky bulldog-looking dog roared out at me from a driveway, barking angrily. I felt fearful, and wasn't sure what to do, but from habit I whispered, "Dog, in Jesus' Name go back to your house! Satan, in Jesus' Name get that dog away from me!" The dog immediately dropped his head and slunk back to his house. He was afraid of something. Had he seen an angel? Or hadn't I combed my hair? Something had scared him. Whatever it was, the dog was no longer a threat. Please remember that if you are ever in danger from some kind of animal: a dog, a bear in the forest, an aggressive human. *You have Jesus!* His angels can protect you. But you must *speak your command,* if only in a whisper. The Christian friend I was walking up to visit had an interesting experience. Her husband had worked most of the day on their car, but couldn't get it to start. Sharon came out, saw his frustration, and said, "Let me pray." "That won't help." But she quietly prayed anyway, "Car, in Jesus' Name I tell you to start!" *And it started.* Would it always? I don't know, but it was wonderful! None of us are Peter or the Apostle Paul, but the same Holy Spirit was operative.

Example #52
Victory! Laughing With Our Angels!

"Trust in the Lord and do good; so shall you dwell
in the land and surely you shall be fed."
(Psalm 37:3)

This is about the amazing way God got our family home from Indonesia. We hadn't saved money for our return trip because Roy used most of our $400 a month salary for ministry. It was his goal to move the new Campus Crusade Indonesia ministry forward as fast as possible. So he got our evangelistic and discipleship materials translated and printed in the two major Indonesian languages and took Indonesian CCC staff around Java to train them. Roy paid for all the printing and food and lodging because even though lodging didn't cost much by Western standards, and the team often ate at roadside stands, it was still more than the Indonesians could have afforded. Roy said he wanted to *invest in the people. He developed the ministry faster than anyone except he himself had imagined possible.* It was his "plan."

Dr. Bill Bright, founder and President of Campus Crusade, was thrilled with the progress and came to Indonesia to speak at a big evangelism and discipleship training conference Roy and the Indonesian CCC staff had organized in Malang, East Java. Eleven hundred Indonesian pastors and missionaries attended. It was the biggest Christian conference ever held in that country. What meant most to Roy is that *missionaries and pastors told him that finally they had learned how to lead people to Christ personally.* Most had never before been taught how to do that. One missionary told Roy that he had been in Indonesia for six years and only knew how to "do church" because that is what he had been trained to do. He said he had never introduced anyone to Christ, but after learning how to do it at the conference, within a month he had led thirteen people to Christ. He was a happy man! And Roy was happy for him!

Dr. Bright asked Roy to return to America and train missionaries for Campus Crusade. By the time we left Indonesia, he had trained 80 Indonesians to conduct lay training for evangelism and now, thank God, there are about 400 national workers, sharing the Gospel on all the major islands of that vast archipelago of islands. And before we left Indonesia, we also wanted to help our translator and household helpers get into homes of their own, or at least repair the ones they had. With just $500 extra, each of them could do that. We felt if we didn't help them they might not have another chance. They were thrilled. *We would always have regretted it if we hadn't helped them.* Sometimes in life you have only one chance to help.

But furlough time was coming and we didn't have enough money to get home. We had saved just enough to travel a little in Europe to see Eleanor's family in Germany, but not enough to get back to California. Roy figured it would take $1900 more to get the five of us from Europe to America and home. He wasn't worried. He said, "When it's time to go home, the money will be here." The way God did it still makes us smile. An English friend came to Jakarta and was hunting for Roy and found him—not always easy to do in that busy city. We didn't have a phone so I didn't know Roy was bringing the man up to our home for dinner and overnight. It was my helpers' day off so I especially thank the dear Lord that I had made a good dinner! Homemade bread and a hearty beef stew called "borscht." We had a wonderful visit and in general conversation Roy mentioned that we would be going on furlough. But he said nothing about needing money. Yet the next morning our guest told us that as he was shaving, God spoke to him that he was to pay our way to England, and we were to stay at his estate in Brighton. Later, after Roy had taken our friend to his appointment in Jakarta and returned home, I expressed delight at the prospect of seeing England. Roy responded, "It's great that he wants to do that for us, but God knows we don't live in England. Let's see what else God is going to do."

Shortly afterward, our home church in California sent a letter saying they wanted to help us come home, and asked how much it would cost. Roy figured out that it would cost $1900 to get from England home. But *before that information could even reach them,* two letters arrived on *the same day.* One was from the Englishman, containing air tickets to Singapore and England, and the other was from our home church with $1720 for the trip. It was a very generous amount and "close enough." We were thrilled. It felt like a special present from God that the travel money from all these dear people came on the same day! We had a wonderful time in England and then in Germany with my family. Coming home, at our stop in Chicago, a ministry supporter who wanted to continue talking to Roy insisted on driving us to Iowa, where Roy visited aunts and uncles.

Then, back in California, Roy got a phone call from our travel agent. He said Roy had a rebate of $180 coming because we hadn't flown the entire way. When it registered with Roy what that meant, he started laughing. $1720 from our church plus $180 rebate added up to *exactly* $1900! Roy started laughing and felt sure his angels were right there with him, laughing too! *The amount was to the penny!* We had helped Indonesians, and God had used generous Christian friends to help us! And it's fun to know that God and His angels have a sense of humor. Heaven will be filled with laughter and good spirits. Do the best you can for each other, work hard and be kind, and tell God your needs. If you have Jesus in your life, *God is responsible for you.* He will use His angels and people who love God to help you.

CHAPTER TEN

SHARED POWER—GOD'S, MAN'S, AND ANGELS'

D R. GREGORY A. Boyd made this profound analysis: "If the cosmos is not something of a free democracy under the ultimate ruler-ship of God, it has to be something of a tyrannical monarchy. Either some power is shared or it is not. If not, all the blame for all the evil in the cosmos has ultimately to rest squarely on the lap of the monarch whose will is purportedly never thwarted. But if power is shared, the blame rests with demons and people, the biblical view" paraphrase of Gregory A. Boyd (*God at War*) p. 118, 119.

God Shares Power With People

As Holy Scripture and history make clear, God has chosen to allow His power to be shared with people, His high creation. Sometimes the results have been messy, but God is developing sons and daughters for eternity. You might wonder, "But doesn't God have total control over everything?" *Yes and no.* God has total authority over the universe, power to control everything that He chooses to control. But within the parameters of His absolute power God *has chosen to share some of His power with men and angels.* They are His *highest creations,* His family.

God is sovereign, but He has chosen not to be a dictator. He allows angels and humans *freedom* to make their own decisions about many things. "Love involves freedom and that freedom involves genuinely open alternatives and thus genuine risks. This dimension of significant self-determination and power, shared by angelic and human society, opens up the possibility of conflict in the spiritual and earthly realms" Gregory A. Boyd (*Satan and the Problem of Evil*) p. 212. We highly recommend Dr. Boyd's perceptive books for deep study. "*Satan and the Problem of Evil,* and *God at War.*"

Personal freedom is what God has chosen to give men and angels. God is *love* (1 John 4:16) and *love cannot co-exist with tyranny.* Therefore God has given His highest creatures, humans and angels, a portion of what He Himself enjoys: *freedom of thought and action and self-determination.* With action of any kind in the natural or spiritual world, there are results. They might be good, bad, or neutral, but humans and angels are accountable. Demonic former angels misused their freedom and were expelled from Heaven. Humans have freedom to progress on earth in two major ways:

1. by what they accomplish *physically* by their faithful work

2. by what they accomplish *spiritually,* through prayer and kind treatment of others

By their God-given ingenuity, people have created marvelous inventions, written beautiful music, healed wounds, painted lovely pictures, taught children, built magnificent structures, and learned secrets of the universe. By what they have accomplished spiritually they have helped establish God's love in many millions of lives as they have led people to Christ, developed churches, taught God's Word, gained God's help for people and nations, and provided care and food for millions of people in need.

God has ordained that humans have a personal relationship with Him. "The essence of any interpersonal relationship is mutually influential communication. God set things up so that we need to communicate with Him and He needs to communicate with us. God wants us to mediate this love to the segment of the world under our jurisdiction. He has chosen that His people be 'co-regents' to reign with Him on earth (2 Timothy 2:12; Revelation 5:10; 20:6). He wants it [His will] carried out in cooperation with us. He could have created a world in which He did not need prayer, or any creaturely decisions, to carry out His will. If God *needs* anything it is because He chooses to...*He chose to create a somewhat risky world in which some things genuinely hinge on what free agents do, both physically and through the power of prayer"* (Boyd, *Satan and the Problem of Evil* p. 232). *Does that mean God's will can be thwarted? Yes, but only if He permits it.*

The Bible says, God is *not willing that any person would perish* (2 Peter 3:9) Yet many people *will* perish. Not because God wants them to, but because humans are free moral agents. His people either didn't talk to unbelievers about Jesus, or they did, and the people rejected Him. Neither is God's will, but it occurs.

Example #53
Hearing God and Praying

Angels work as a team with people who pray in the name of their King, the Lord Jesus Christ.

Years ago, our daughter Robin, a kindergarten teacher, had an experience that illustrates that. She had been in a kitchen shop looking for a shower gift for a fellow teacher who was to be married. As she went up and down the aisles considering various gifts she noticed that she was being followed. The man stayed about ten feet away from her, didn't look at her or attempt to talk to her, but he persistently kept close, following her all around the store. When Robin was leaving the store she reported the incident to the manager and asked for an escort to her car, which he gave her. He told her that a number of women had complained about the man, but he couldn't report him to the police because he hadn't done anything illegal. Robin put the unpleasant incident out of her mind.

But about two weeks later, in her apartment in the evening as she was washing off her eye make-up, she heard God speak loudly to her mind: *"Pray! Now!"* And she knew it had something to do with the man she had seen in the store. The command was so intense that she immediately stopped washing her face and ran to get on her knees and pray, half her makeup still on. She knew instantly that the man she had seen in the store was about to attack a woman somewhere. She prayed hard for God to rescue whatever girl the man intended to attack or was attacking, and in Jesus' Name Robin was forbidding satan to use him to harm the girl. It was such a strong burden to pray that Robin told me she was weeping as she prayed, begging God's angels to protect the girl. She thought to call Roy and me to pray too, but God said to her, "There isn't time!" She prayed earnestly for about 15 minutes and then suddenly the burden to pray was gone, lifted, as though God said, "It's OK now, that's enough." She didn't know what was happening, or to whom, but there was no question in her mind that something terrible was about to happen and she had to *pray* in order to stop it. It was a war in the unseen realm and her prayer enabled God's angels to intervene.

Cooperating With God and His Angels By Prayer

Prayer is the human part of God's triune force for good; the Christian praying in Jesus' Name and angels responding to the command given in the name of their King, the Lord Jesus Christ. It isn't that we, as humans, are the ones actually stopping the problem, but our prayer is the necessary cooperation with God's angels, so they are authorized to act. God wants those who love Him to be co-workers *in bringing mercy to people on earth.* That is the way God chooses to work. If people don't pray, then it is possible that what God wants to do in a given situation won't come to pass. He has chosen to limit Himself to work in tandem with His people. That is an awesome responsibility for every Christian. As we pray, or don't pray, so goes the battle on earth. We are either blessed and bless others, or evil rises and disturbs the peace.

As Christians, *we are fellow laborers with angels* to accomplish Christ's purposes. Demons harass sinners and the world in general, but *they cannot be where Christians have forbidden them, and righteousness excludes them.* God's angels are assigned to help those who want to obey God; angels respond to their cries. They guard over people who love God and they intervene on earth when God's people pray. We all need to pray more: for our families, community, and nation.

WITHOUT PRAYER, PEOPLE ARE NOT AS PROTECTED AS THEY COULD BE, AND SHOULD BE, AND WOULD BE, IF THEY PRAYED OR IF OTHERS PRAYED FOR THEM.

Example #**54**
Ten Demonic Strongholds Broken By Prayer!

In two of his books, *The Third Wave of the Holy Spirit*, and *How to Have a Healing Ministry*, Dr. C. Peter Wagner summarizes *ten spiritual warfare victories that have been gained as Christians have prayed in groups.* The following list gives some of Dr. Wagner's examples of demonic strongholds broken by prayer.

1. **Thailand**
   "A wave of conversions followed when the missionaries set aside one day a week for spiritual warfare." (Spiritual warfare means waging direct war on satan by *commanding him in Jesus' Name* to do or not to do a certain thing.)

2. **Uruguay-Brazil border**
   "People who were closed to the gospel on the Uruguay side of the town's main street become open when they crossed over to the Brazilian side." (That indicates that demons have assigned territories.)

3. **Costa Rica**
   "Symptoms of mental illness left a patient when she traveled to the United States, and they reappeared when she returned to Costa Rica. Christian psychologist Rita Cabezas was told by one of the demons that they were limited to their territory and could not go to the U.S."

4. **Navajo Reservation**
   "Herman Williams, a Navajo Alliance pastor, suffered serious physical symptoms which left him as he crossed the reservation boundary for treatment in the city, and recurred when he entered the reservation again. The spirits causing this were traced to a witch doctor on the reservation. When the witch doctor died [was killed], the problems stopped."

5. Philippines

"Lester Sumrall cast a spirit out of an inmate in Bilibid Prison, which was followed by a dramatic change in the receptivity of Filipinos [in the prison] to the gospel."

6. Argentina

"Omar Cabrera by prayer and fasting exercises a ministry of identifying the spirits controlling certain cities, breaks their power, and finds little subsequent resistance to God's power for salvation and healing."

7. Korea

"Paul Yonggi Cho attributes the contrast in receptivity to the gospel between Germany and Korea to the victories in spiritual warfare gained through the ministry of prayer of Korean Christians."

8. Argentina

"Edwardo Silvoso reports the accelerated multiplication of churches within a radius of 100 miles of the city of Rosario after a team broke the power of the 'spirit of Merigildo' in 1985." (Merigildo is a high ranking demonic spirit of the area.)

9. Greece

"Loren Cunningham of YWAM (Youth with a Mission) tells an incident that happened in 1973. As 12 co-workers were praying and fasting for three days in Los Angeles, the Lord revealed to them that they should pray for the downfall of the prince of Greece. On the same day, similar groups of Christians in New Zealand and Europe received the same word from God. All three groups obeyed and came against that principality. Within 24 hours a political coup changed the government of Greece and for the first time YWAM workers could preach the gospel in the streets."

10. **Evanston, Illinois**

John Wimber gave this report: "After 6 years of ministry in Evanston, Vineyard pastor Steve Nicholson had seen little fruit. They prayed for the sick and few got well. Then he started to fast and pray seriously. At one point, a grotesque being appeared, asking, 'Why are you bothering me?' [Demons can change their appearance to frighten people or please them, according to the demon's purpose. But their true appearance seems to be unpleasant, distorted by sin.] The demon eventually identified itself as a demon of witchcraft that had supervision of that area. In the heat of the confrontation, *Steve named the city streets and claimed them for God.* The spirit said, 'I don't want to give you that much.' Steve replied that *through Jesus he was commanding the demon to give up the territory.* The demon argued some more and then left. *Immediately, the sick began to get well.* In a little over three months, the church more than doubled, from 70 to 150, most of them new converts from witchcraft. Almost all of them had to be delivered from demons as they were being saved."

Binding and Loosing By Prayer

In his book, *Engaging the Enemy*, Dr. Wagner teaches about "binding and loosing" in the spiritual ream. "Whatever you bind on earth shall have been bound in heaven, and whatever you loose on earth shall be loosed in Heaven" (Matthew 16:19). Our nation needs us to bind evil and loose burdens, releasing God's mercy on people, in Jesus' Name.

Roy and I have used some terminology that resembles sports equipment:

- Your *offensive weapon* is the NAME of Jesus. That drives evil away and/or brings angelic help in your situation.

- Your *defensive weapon* is the BLOOD of Jesus. That keeps evil away.

- *Your continuing weapons* are a cleansed life and knowledge of the Bible, God's Word to you, so He can talk to you and you will understand.

CHAPTER ELEVEN

THE POWER OF GROUP PRAYER—WINNING BATTLES IN WORLD WAR II

I T IS NOT coincidental that when the Lord's servants commenced openly to challenge the power of darkness and, in the name of our victorious Lord command the demons to come out of the possessed ones, the gates of hell began to yield and captives were set free... *We are commissioned to invade his territory, not just wait for him to attack us*" Robert Peterson (*Are Demons for Real?*) p. 8. God's angels wage the war against demons when Christians pray. When cities or territories or institutions are involved, *it requires group prayer to overcome many demons.*

Rees Howells: Man of Prayer

Rees Howells was called by God to be a man of prayer. He had a Bible College in Wales and during World War II *his entire student body prayed together earnestly about specific problems England faced* against Hitler, and what God told Howells the battle strategy needed to be. The enemy threats, unusual victories, and *official British acknowledgement of the effectiveness of the men's prayers are a matter of record in England.* Howells kept a meticulous daily diary of prayer concerns and victories that formed the basis of the book "*Rees Howells, Intercessor*" by biographer Norman Grubb. It was as a result of reading that book that Roy asked Jesus to come into his life.

During the four years previous to the outbreak of World War II, the Lord was changing the burden of Rees Howells from local concerns—development of the Bible College—to national and international countries and nations." Howells and the men of his Bible College prayed earnestly for the defeat of Hitler's powerful armies.

Allied forces gained victories that British political leaders acknowledge to be miraculous.

World War I Set the Stage for Hitler

The unjust Treaty of Versailles after World War I set the stage for the rise of Hitler. WWI began in 1914 in Sarajevo, the Austro (Austrian)-Hungarian capital of Bosnia, when a dissident student in a Serbian secret society called the "Black Hand" assassinated the heir to the throne of the Austrian-Hungarian Empire (*World Book Encyclopedia*). That single act marked the outbreak of a pointless, widespread war. Austria-Hungary declared war on Serbia in 1914. Neighboring nations Germany and Bulgaria, and then Turkey, joined them, making an alliance of four nations. Serbia recruited *twenty-three* other nations from around the world to defend them, and finally all of Europe was involved. Five million soldiers died. In 1918 the smaller group of nations lost, and the "Peace Treaty of Versailles" (France) insisted that Germany accept all blame for the war. The terms were deliberately punitive. It was France's plan to keep Germany from ever rising again. America's President Woodrow Wilson signed the treaty, but only reluctantly. He warned that the harsh treaty would cause another war. It did.

Hitler's Early Occultism

Howells recognized that Hitler was an "anti-Christ" and was determined that he be defeated. He said, "Mussolini [the Italian leader] is a man, but Hitler is different. Hitler knows the moment the spirit [satan] came into him" (p. 231). "Hitler was only 15 years old, but had been studying medieval occultism and black magic. He was with a friend, August Kubizek, when suddenly he [Hitler] began to speak in a voice that was loud, hoarse, and raucous." Kubizek felt that some strange being had seized control of Adolf, and was inhabiting his body. His mesmerizing oratory was not recognized as his normal voice by people who knew him. He had become demon possessed" (Google: Satanism of Hitler).

Germany's Financial Distress

To punish Germany, the Versailles Treaty required that Germany forfeit land, people, livestock and a tenth of its factories, cut down their merchant fleet and abolish their navy. In addition, heavy taxation was imposed. It was severely punitive, intended to keep Germany from ever rising again. Rampant inflation made Deutsche marks, the German paper dollars, worth almost nothing. My parents were still in Germany at that time, and said inflation was so severe that if you wanted to eat in a restaurant you had to carry a big bag (or wheelbarrow) full of Deutsche marks to pay for it. And before you finished eating, the *price of the meal might have gone up!* Prices rose *more than fivefold (500%)* each week. It was an extremely difficult time. And a world-wide depression in the early 1930's made the situation even worse.

Hitler's Rise to Power

Hitler emerged on the German political scene with such thundering oratory that he gave the discouraged Germans *hope*. With his powerful satanic voice he convinced them that Germany *would rise again!* I've heard that Hitler's voice could mesmerize people who didn't even understand German! It was to be "Deutschland uber alles;" "Germany over all!" (Like Americans might say, "America is #1!") The German people followed Hitler, and German engineers with metal from the vast Ruhr Valley mines built a war machine capable of "blitzkrieg," (lightning strikes) that could *overrun entire countries in a day*. Hitler's goal was to unite all of Europe under *his* control. It was to be the "Third Reich," the "Third Kingdom." The Roman Empire had been the Second Kingdom. Ironically, years later the nations of western Europe did unite, but not under one man's control.

The Power of Group Prayer

Following are some of the *amazing war victories* gained in answer to the prayers of Rees Howells and the men of his Bible College in Wales, *as they prayed in groups.* Howells set his Welsh Bible College to *earnest prayer,* sometimes praying all day and into the night. A newspaper headline read, "Director of Bible College Urges Prayer to Stop War" (*Rees Howells, Intercessor*) p. 233. Britain was not well armed, and in 1940 Howells said, "From a worldly standpoint there is no hope of victory; *but God has said it: 'The enemy will not invade Christian England.'*" Many in Britain recall the terror of those days. British citizens didn't have guns, nor did even their policemen. Many Americans air-mailed their guns to English citizens, but there wasn't a supply of ammunition for the various calibers of guns. It was a tense time. The men of the Bible College were praying earnestly, but the situation in England was so grievous that Howells said, "I would be willing to die, but I cannot afford to die, neither can we afford that Hitler should live" (p. 236). May 26 was a day of public prayer in Britain. Winston Churchill, England's Prime Minister, said, "I could feel the fear, not of death or wounds or national loss, but of defeat and the final ruin of Britain" (p. 238).

Continually, through all the years of the war, Howells and the men of his Bible School in Wales prayed ceaselessly. Many times they prayed through the entire night.

Example #55
Victory! The Miracle of Dunkirk!

When Belgium fell to the Germans, about 350,000 retreating English troops were rescued at Dunkirk (Dunkerque), France's northern-most beach, and transported across the North Sea to safety in England. About a thousand English and French ships and boats of all kinds took part in the rescue (*World Book Encyclopedia*). Acknowledged by various leaders to be an intervention from God, the miracle of Dunkirk was that *the normally rough North Sea was calm, allowing even rowboats to cross.* The calm seas held, and the rescue continued for a week. It was an almost complete evacuation of English troops. "Dunkirk" means "church among the dunes." It must have felt like that to the young men being rescued.

And then Mr. Churchill said, "How thankful we are that God had this company of hidden intercessors whose lives were on the altar day after day as they stood in the gap for the deliverance of Britain" (*Rees Howells, Intercessor*) p. 239–240.

Example #56
Victory! German Army Moved Away From England

When Germany invaded Britain by air, in the midst of an air raid God gave Howells an assurance of victory. He was speaking at a meeting in England and told the group what God had said. Together they praised God in advance for what He was going to do. In his *War Memoirs*, Mr. Churchill gives September 15 as "the culminating date" in the Battle of the Air. Churchill asked the British Air Marshall, "What other reserves have we?" "There are *none*." British citizens were demoralized. Howells and his students prayed that God would move Hitler away from England and toward Russia (p. 248). *Suddenly, there was a continuous eastward movement of German bombers and fighters.* No new attack appeared in England. The Luftwaffe (German Air Force) that had flown bombing raids over England *suddenly turned and left*.

Example #57
Victory! "Lord, Turn the Enemy to the Mediterranean"

In Howell's journal was the petition, "Lord, turn the enemy down to the Mediterranean." On April 6 Hitler declared war on Yugoslavia and Greece, then Crete and North Africa. The immediate crisis for Britain passed. Then Hitler swung around and invaded Russia, which Howells and the men of the Bible College saw as an intervention of God to help the Allies. That decision of Hitler was reckoned as one of the great acts of divine intervention which spelled the "doom of the Nazis" (pp. 247–248). After the war, Air Chief Marshall Lord Dowding, Commander in Chief of Fighter Command in the Battle of Britain, said, "At the end of the battle *one had the sort of feeling that there had been some special Divine intervention* to alter some sequence of events which would otherwise have occurred" (p. 245).

Example #58
Victory! Hitler's Troops Perish in Russian Snow

The main prayer of the College became: "Lord, bring Russia into the war and deal with communism." Six weeks later Russia had come in. The Russian armies disintegrated and Hitler's armies were almost at the gates of Moscow. Mr. Howells said, "Thus saith the Lord: 'He [Hitler] is wintering in the Russian snows.'" Goering, a high-ranking German officer, lamented that "Three million of the flower of the Nazi army perished in the snow." Victor Kravchenko, in his book *I Choose Freedom,* said: "The Germans could have taken Moscow those days virtually without a struggle... Why they turned back is a mystery only the Germans themselves can solve for history" (pp. 248–249). *It was because the men of Howell's Bible College prayed.*

Example #59
Victory! El Alamein, North Africa!

With German Field Marshall Rommel ("the Desert Fox") and the Italians growing strong in North Africa, prayer began to be centered on the Bible Lands. "Unless God will intervene on behalf of Palestine," said Mr. Howells on July 4, 1942, "there will be no safety there for the Jews. Is this prayer we prayed this afternoon of the Holy Ghost, (the Holy Spirit) that the enemy is *not* to take Alexandria?" The following week the tide turned at El Alamein, saving Alexandria, Egypt.

In his book, *Pipe Line to Battle,* as quoted in the magazine of the Merchant Service Officer's Christian Association of April 1944, British Major Peter W. Rainier recorded that between Rommel's men and Alexandria were the remnants of a British army: 50 tanks, a few score field guns, and about 5,000 soldiers. The sides were equally matched, but the Germans held the advantage because of their superior 88 mm. guns. Both armies were near exhaustion from heat, dust and lack of water. The battle was grim. In the words of Major Rainier: "The sun was almost overhead, and our men were fast reaching the end of their endurance when the Nazis broke.

"Slowly, sullenly the Mark IV tanks lumbered back from their battle smoke. And then an incredible thing happened: 1,100 men of the 90th Light Panzer Division, the elite of the Afrika Korps [German desert troops] came stumbling across the barren sand with their hands in the air…their swollen tongues blackened and protruding. They had been 24 hours without water when they overran the British defenses and found a 6-inch water pipe. They shot holes in it and drank deeply. *It was sea water. Two days later it would have been full of fresh water.* The surrender of those 1,100 elite German soldiers may have been the *deciding incident* in the battle for Alexandria." Major Raines wrote, "Ten minutes more and it might have been us" (*Pipeline to Battle*) pp. 251–252. The editor's comment: "Such an incredible happening as this cannot be treated as a mere coincidence. Assuredly the hand of almighty God is in evidence once more, coming to our aid when weighty issues are in the balance" (Google: *Pipeline to Battle*).

Hitler was furious that Rommel had surrendered at Al Alamein. Rommel did not apologize. He told Hitler that he valued the lives of his men; he wanted them to live to become old men. Many Germans recognized that Hitler was evil and several groups of German leaders sought to kill him. Rommel was implicated in one of those plots in July 1944. Rommel was popular with the German people, so Hitler had him secretly hung.

Example #60
Victory! Stalingrad

The prayer attention of the College then turned again to the Russian campaign. The Nazi army continued to advance toward Stalingrad and then, *"to the wonder of the world, was driven out again utterly broken and demoralized.* Howells exulted, *"It was a mighty triumph of the Holy Spirit"* (pp. 248–249).

Example #61
Victory! The Miracle of Salerno!

Germany had invented machine guns, and in Italy in September 1943 in the invasion of Salerno, "the enemy artillery was advancing rapidly with ceaseless firing. The noise was terrible and it was obvious that unless a miracle happened, our troops could never hold up the advance long enough for the beachhead to be established. Suddenly, for no accountable reason, the firing ceased and the Nazi artillery stopped its advance...We waited, but still nothing happened; and nothing happened all that night, but those hours made all the difference to the invasion. By morning the beachhead was established" (*Rees Howells, Intercessor*).

Example #62
Victory! Saved From Submarines!

In the last great prayer battle of the war, Howell's College prayed for the young Americans coming to fight on "D-Day." "We have a perfect right to ask God to come and fight with our young men. Groups prayed, and Howells told God, "If you hadn't intervened at Dunkirk, not one of us would be here today." Beseeching God in prayer in Jesus' Name brought powerful angels into the battle (p. 253). On April 6, 1944, 156,000 Allied troops invaded Normandy with 4000 ships and 11,000 planes. The miracle was that it was the *one night*, the *only night* that German U-boats did not patrol the channel. If German U-boats had patrolled the English Channel that night, they would have been able to sink Allied battleships, with the loss of many more thousands of lives. Still, it was a terribly fierce battle on the beaches of Normandy, with great loss of life. But Allied Forces were able to overpower the Germans and drive them out of France.

Rees Howells and the people of his Bible College had prayed for six years, against evil and for the victory of the Lord Jesus Christ and His Gospel. Norman Grubb, (*Rees Howells, Intercessor*) p. 217–257. *The major victories of WWII trace directly to the prayers of the men of Howell's Bible College*, a fact acknowledged by British military men and politicians.

PRAYER IN JESUS NAME BROUGHT ANGELIC
WARRIORS TO JOIN THE FIGHT AGAINST HITLER.

Satan sometimes gives egotistical people power and wealth and prestige, the things they crave, but he *never does it for that person's benefit.* Satan is incapable of love or altruism (doing something for the benefit of others). Any gift of "power" that satan gives comes with an evil motive: *to use that person to destroy other people*; hundreds, thousands, millions, as Hitler did until he himself was defeated in answer to prayer. But not before many millions of lives had been shattered by his war.

Personal note: I know from German relatives that Hitler's rule was a terrible time for German citizens also. Christian pastors who opposed his persecution of the Jews became Holocaust victims. When the Allied Forces invaded Germany and it was clear that Germany was losing, Hitler was desperate. Roughly eight million Germans (both soldiers and civilians) had already died and weapons were depleted. My uncle, a German officer and a Christian, was ordered to send fifteen-year-old youths into battle *with painted wooden guns,* to make it appear that Germany still had weapons and fighting men. He refused, and was executed as a traitor. To me he was a hero. Before Hitler committed suicide, he ordered groups of his own personal troops killed, saying, "Germans who can't win don't deserve to live." German citizens in bombed-out ruins were hungry and cold and ill from wounds, yet Hitler bitterly ordered all remaining blankets and food supplies burned. It was to be Gotterdamerung, dramatic Wagnerian destruction. *If he couldn't win, let everyone die.* He was demonic.

Mercy From America!

Example #63
Victory! "Food Boxes With Wings"!

"Blessed are the merciful, for they shall obtain mercy."
(Matthew 5:7)

Along with most other people in war-torn Europe, my German relatives in Tuttlingen were hungry. All over Europe, people who lived in cities were especially desperate, because the ancient way of constructing city dwellings in long, adjoined walls left almost no space for gardens. So city people didn't even have a place for a few chickens to provide eggs. My grandmother prayed for what seemed impossible: *"Dear Jesus, please send us food."* God *gave her a dream in which she saw "food boxes with wings" flying to her.* And they did! Wonderful, merciful America arranged for "Care packages" of food to be shipped free air freight to Germany and other war-torn countries. Thousands of Americans of German background sent Care packages of food to loved ones. My two uncles in Detroit sent more than a hundred Care packages, and my mother sent many also. They were the "food boxes with wings" that flew to my grandmother, just as Jesus had shown her would come.

Example #64
Victory! The Berlin Airlift!

All over the world, Christian America was known for deeds of mercy. After World War II, there was an emergency in Berlin. Post-war Germany had been divided into four sections. The huge capital city of Berlin was located deep inside the quadrant of Germany that was controlled by Russia. The huge, capital city of Berlin was divided into West Berlin and East Berlin. West Berlin was controlled by America, England, France—and East Berlin by Russia. Russia did not want the other three powers to be in any part of Berlin, so they blockaded all rail, water, and highway supply routes that led into West Berlin, *cutting off the food supply.* The Germans in West Berlin would have starved and been without heat in wintertime.

America and England and a few other nations organized a *massive airlift.* For *almost a year,* until the blockade ended, they *flew* deep inside Russia's German territory to get supplies *over* the blockade and into the hands of Germans in West Berlin. Cargo planes filled with supplies landed every three minutes: *land, unload; land, unload; land, unload;* bringing food, coal, heating oil, medicines, and machinery. A few other allied nations helped. Two million, 323 thousand, 738 mercy flights were made into West Berlin, keeping the Germans alive.

What they did for the desperate Germans was *amazing!* (*World Book Encyclopedia*, and Google: "Berlin Blockade") The Berlin Airlift was a monumental act of mercy and the people of Berlin never forgot it. After about a year, the blockade ended. Later, the communist Russians built the heavily fortified Berlin wall to keep East Germans from fleeing into the freedom of West Germany. The wall was finally torn down in 1989–1990.

CHAPTER TWELVE

WEAPONS OF OUR WARFARE— THE NAME AND BLOOD OF JESUS

ND THEY OVERCAME him [satan] by the *Blood of the Lamb* and the [spoken] *word* of their testimony" (Revelation 12:11). If you are a Christian, the Blood of the "Lamb," Jesus, washed you clean in God's sight.

Background

Sin is "thoughts or behavior that conflict with the nature of God," who is constructive, loving, and morally pure. Sin is destructive, an offense to God. Here are three critical facts about sin:

1. No human is without sin. "For *all* have sinned and fall short of the glory of God" (Romans 3:23).

2. Sin is not allowed in heaven. Yet to be excluded from heaven would be "death" in the sense of separation from God and all that is good.

3. Sin gives satan the right to harass us. God doesn't protect us from the consequences of our sin.

Those three problems are mankind's continuing dilemma. God loves people so much that He sent His son, Jesus, the only perfect person who ever lived, to die in our place so those who trust Him can live. Our acceptance of that gift resolves all three of those major problems: God's forgiveness, inclusion into heaven, and power over satan.

HOW DID GOD SOLVE THE PROBLEM FOR PEOPLE? Before Jesus came, God provided people with "the law," not only that they should earnestly try to obey it, but to help them realize that they couldn't. God's standard is higher than they could consistently obey. Only Jesus was able to obey God's high moral standards perfectly. Yet disobedience was "sin" and "the wages of [penalty for] sin is death" (Romans 6:23a, KJV). How could God harmonize His righteousness with His love and mercy? He instituted an *atoning sacrifice for sin; a perfect lamb as a substitute for us, paying the wage (penalty) of "death for sin."* And because the lamb died instead of them, if people were genuinely repentant, they could go free, accepted by God. That was the spiritual "picture" of what was to come when *Jesus, God's "perfect lamb" would sacrifice His blood, His life, for all mankind, so that those who sincerely ask His forgiveness are made completely clean in God's sight.*

God's Perfect Lamb

That is why Jesus is called "the Lamb of God; God's lamb." When John the Baptist introduced Him to the people he said, *"Behold God's lamb, who takes away [bears] the sin of the world"* (John 1:29). "For the wages of sin is death, but the free gift of God is eternal *life* through Jesus Christ our Lord" (Romans 6:23). Jesus, who hadn't sinned, was the perfect "sacrificial lamb" to take the place of people who *had* sinned. *Because Jesus had not sinned, death could not hold him;* He was able to rise from the dead, overcoming physical and spiritual death on behalf of all people who believe in Him and receive Him into their lives. The benefits of Jesus' life and sacrifice come to all people who sincerely ask God's forgiveness for sin. *Then Jesus bonds with them and stays with them to help them.* Because Jesus will live forever, *they* will live forever. *His eternal life becomes their eternal life.* Many people don't have theological words for that, but they know within their spirit that it is true, because they have experienced that Jesus is with them, *in them.* He said He would never leave us nor forsake us (Hebrews 13:5) and He does not lie. That is part of why He is "perfect."

Why can every Christian command satan and demons to leave, in the Name of Jesus? Because Jesus *is superior* to satan. Jesus is the powerful *Son of God*, without sin. Unlike the rest of mankind, He never cooperated with satan in any way. Satan *fears* Jesus, knowing He is destined to rule eternally. The *Blood* of Jesus and the *Name* of Jesus are known and feared in the entire unseen realm. Speaking it in your defense protects you from evil.

But don't mistake that for a magic formula. Those are major weapons with which Christians can drive evil away, but we must also sincerely desire to avoid sin. We want to keep our lives morally clean, refraining from words and deeds that grieve God and invite demonic harassment. Reverencing God forms a link to Him. Immoral talk or behavior forms a link to evil forces; but when we sincerely ask God's forgiveness, that link is broken. Then we are able to "pray the Blood" over our lives, gaining protection from evil. Are we perfect? No. Forgiven, yes.

Example #65
Victory! The Weapon of His Name!

After Jesus demonstrated casting out devils, He assigned His twelve disciples to do the same. In Matthew 10:1 He gave them authority to do that. He said, "These signs will accompany those who have believed [in Jesus]: in MY NAME they will cast out demons..." (Mark 16:17). He appointed twelve [disciples], so that they would be with Him...and *have authority to cast out demons*" (Mark 3:14–15). "And He [Jesus] gave them power and *authority over all the demons...*" (Luke 9:1). "Jesus summoned His twelve disciples and gave them *authority over unclean spirits, to cast them out...*(Matthew 10:1). Then Jesus gave his larger group of disciples the same authority to cast out devils. They returned with joy, saying *"Lord, even the demons are subject to us in your name."* He said, "I have given you authority to tread on serpents and scorpions [symbols of demonic evil] and over all the power of the enemy..." (Luke 10:17–19).

From the time the Holy Spirit was poured out upon the Church at Pentecost (Acts chapters 1, 2), Christians everywhere in the world have been empowered by the Holy Spirit to cast out devils, just as Jesus and His disciples did. Were those mighty works to cease? No. Jesus commanded His disciples to *do the same things until the "end of the age,"* when He returns to earth to rid it of evil (Mark 1:18–20, paraphrased). Jesus told His disciples, "All authority has been given to me in Heaven and on earth. Go therefore and make disciples of all the nations…*teaching them to obey everything I have commanded you.* And lo, I am with you always, even to the very end of the age" (Matthew 28:16–20 KJV and NIV).

Example #66
Victory! Demons Flee!

"And after the demon was cast out, the mute man
spoke; and the crowds were amazed and were saying,
"Nothing like this has ever been seen in Israel."
(Matthew 9:33)

In her booklet, *Spirit Wars*, p. 27, Christian author and former "psychic" Johanna Michaelson relates her experience of being involved in "psychic healing" in Mexico before she came to the L'Abri Christian study center in Switzerland and received Christ into her life. A counselor at L'Abri explained to her the reality of Christ, and the difference between occultic wonders and genuine Christianity. Johanna was very interested to hear it.

It was November 1972, and Johanna decided to leave psychic occultism and trust Christ completely. She was on her way to talk to Birdie, her counselor, about receiving Christ, when Johanna had a very frightening experience. It was evening, but not yet dark, and as she walked toward Birdie's chateau, jet black darkness suddenly swirled around her and demons knocked her down hard and pummeled her. In hideous screeches they told her they were going to kill her. Johanna was terrified, and struggled to get away from them. When she reached the safety of Birdie's chateau, ugly demonic faces peered at Johanna through the windows. She was distraught and asked Birdie, "Can't you see them?" Birdie responded, "No, I can't, but I can get rid of them." Birdie "spoke against" the demons, giving them orders: "In the Name of *Jesus Christ* of Nazareth, I command you to be gone. I *forbid* your presence here. I claim the protection of the Blood of Jesus upon us. Go where Jesus sends you!" *Instantly the faces vanished and the room was filled with peace.*

The Name of Jesus is our weapon and His Blood is our shield. "One of the marks of spiritual maturity is the confidence to resist the enemy with the authority of Christ—indeed, to be *confident that the authority is effective against all the hosts of hell"* Timothy M. Warner (*Spiritual Warfare*) p. 72.

What is called "psychic" healing is healing done by demonic spirits. The practitioners with whom Johanna had worked in Mexico displayed Christian religious pictures on their walls, so Johanna thought psychic healing must be an aspect of Christianity. But it was a trick and a trap. Her participation in the occultic activity *gave demons the right to attach to her life and attack her.* Thankfully, prayer in Jesus' Name set her free.

In 2 Corinthians 10:3 the Apostle Paul says, "For though we walk in the flesh, we do not war according to the flesh." The real battle is a spiritual one. Paul continues: "For the weapons of our warfare are not carnal [according to the flesh], but *mighty through God to the pulling down of strongholds of evil,* casting down arguments and every high thing that exalts itself against the knowledge of God, bringing every thought into captivity to the obedience of Christ" (2 Cor. 10:4, 5). A *"stronghold"* is just that; a place in a person's life where satan has a "strong hold;" a place where demonic spirits are entrenched. Pulling down strongholds is a direct action against evil.

In his book, *Warfare Prayer* (pp. 64, 65), Dr. C. Peter Wagner teaches that there are *three kinds of spiritual encounters:* truth encounter, allegiance encounter and power encounter. The phrase that most directly addresses the demonic is 2 Corinthians 10:5; "every high thing that exalts itself against the knowledge of God." The Greek word for "high thing" is *hypsoma,* which is a term that relates to "astrological ideas," "cosmic powers" [New Age], and "powers directed against God, seeking to intervene between God and man." Those are forces we see in our cities: crime, violence, gangs, poverty, abortion, racism, greed, rape, drugs, divorce, false religion, social injustice, child abuse, and more.

Example #**67**
Victory! Overcoming Spiritism in Brazil!

"The assumption that believers [Christians] have automatic protection from demons has been proved wrong again and again" Warner (*Spiritual Warfare*) p. 109. A missionary to Brazil reported that the problem of "Macumba Lover Spiritism" [a form of witchcraft] is "running away with the country." The spiritists [witches] will cast plagues on anyone for money, and *the plagues are thrown on Christians as well as non-Christians.* Missionary wife Mrs. Carl Taylor reported that "Just two weeks ago a woman who practices this kind of thing went across the street to another woman I had led to the Lord about eight months ago, and accused her of saying bad things about this neighbor. The [new] Christian did what she could to prove it was a false report by taking that neighbor with her to testify to the falsity of it. But the Macumba woman was furious and shook her fist and said, 'You'll suffer for this, you just see.' *And it happened.* Her 8-year-old boy began crying night and day with rheumatic pains in his legs. They swelled so badly that the mother rushed him to the doctor. It was a strong, demonic attack.

"The doctor prescribed medicine but the legs got worse. Then the father had a terrible fall and hurt his leg. When I saw the mother, she looked terrible. I went to give her the customary Brazilian hug and she backed up and said, 'Oh, Dona Cora, don't touch me! I'm burning up with fever.' *I knew that all that sickness couldn't be normal* so I went to the woman's house the next morning. The woman said, 'I feel wicked in telling you about my [Macumba spiritist] neighbor, but we have had no rest since she threw that plague on us.' We read the Bible together and then broke the powers of this [demonic] plague, in the name of Jesus, pleading *His precious blood.* The woman's fever *left right away, and the little boy had no rheumatic pains from that hour on*" Reported by Mrs. Carl Taylor, Brazil (*Demon Possession in Many Lands*) p. 180.

Not all difficulties are a result of an evil person sending demons to trouble us. Many adverse situations are just part of living in an imperfect world. But if you face a *cluster* of difficulties, it probably *is* a demonic attack. Or, if personal sin has allowed evil to attack, ask God for forgiveness and restoration. You won't have to wonder; He will put it uppermost in your mind. Then you can sincerely ask forgiveness and be cleansed (1 John 1:7). When you have done that, you can stop the troubles by commanding them to *stop*, in Jesus' Name. Do it *out loud*, if only in a whisper. Then *pray the Blood* of His protection over yourself and your family. *Tell satan to get out and stay out!* If you are a Christian, you have the greater authority, because Jesus is *in* you.

I like to think of it the way we all stood behind our mother or father when we were threatened as children. If you did not have loving parents, that is more difficult to imagine. But mentally think of Jesus as your strong defender. Demons tremble at Jesus' presence, just as they did when He was on earth. They whimpered, "Have you come to destroy us before the time [of God's judgment against them]?" Forbid satan to trouble you in any way. Read your Bible, draw close to God, obey Him, and *refuse to accept severe problems as normal.* Pursue the possibility that they could be stopped in Jesus' Name.

Example #**68**
Victory! Learning to Command satan to Leave!

When our son Mike was only three months old, he suffered a strangulating hernia that required emergency surgery. I remember carrying his dear little self across a lawn to the hospital, teary, praying for his recovery. I gratefully remember the compassionate older nurse as she reached out her arms to tenderly take Mike from me. It was nick-of-time surgery. However, Mike came home from the hospital sick with an intestinal problem he hadn't had before being in the hospital and nothing the doctor prescribed stopped it. Roy and I prayed and prayed, but poor little Mike continued to have intestinal trouble day and night. I comforted him and fed him liquids, lots of liquids, to prevent dehydration, and washed lots of diapers. It was winter, and my wash tubs and washing machine were out on the cold screened porch. We didn't have a clothes dryer, so diapers hung all over the house. I was very tired and very worried. On a Saturday night, after Mike had been ill for almost a week, I was ironing a Sunday shirt for Roy and felt tears run down my face. "Why, Lord? Why?" I whispered. "We're trying to do what You want us to do."

God spoke so clearly to my mind that it seemed audible: "This is *not* from Me. *I will contend with him that contendeth with thee and I will save thy children.*" Hope filled my heart! I ran to check my Bible. That verse is Isaiah 49:25. *God was talking about contending with the devil!* It made me so mad that satan had attacked my baby that I wasn't even afraid. I ran into Michael's room and whispered strongly, *"Get Out! Satan, in Jesus' Name, get out!"* The diarrhea stopped immediately! We were thrilled. We had learned something very important.

But the next morning in our adult Sunday School class as we held Mike and joyfully told our class what had happened, there was suddenly a loud "bubble, bubble, bubble." (Like satan mocking, "Ha, Ha, Ha, I'll fix it so no one will believe you.") How could it be? We were bewildered. "Lord, please tell us what to do." After class He put it on both our minds at the same time: "You didn't forbid it to return." That's right, we didn't! We didn't know we needed to. So in Jesus' Name we forbade the illness to return. That ended the trouble! I learned since that in Mark 9:25 Jesus said to a demon, "I command you, come out of him *and do not enter him again.*"

It was a wonderful thing to have learned, that in Jesus' Name we could order the enemy to "go," and "forbid his return," and he had to obey! That helped us on the mission field, and at home, and it has enabled us to help others, as we hope and pray it will help all of you. This is the full verse of Isaiah 49:25: "Thus saith the *Lord,* Even the captives of the mighty shall be taken away, and the prey of the terrible [satan] shall be delivered. For I will contend with him [satan] that contends with thee, *and I will save thy children.*" And He has kept that promise all these years!

You might wonder, "Why didn't God just drive satan away Himself, in answer to my prayer?" He *did* do it, as He spoke through me. I had no power to drive satan away. But Jesus did. It was Jesus *in* me who drove satan away. God has chosen to let His people be cooperators with Him. That means you, too, if you are a Christian.

I have to smile as I think about God talking to me in "King James" English. He did that because I had a King James Bible. Using words from the kind of Bible I was familiar with, God knew I wouldn't question that He was speaking to me. *He can talk to anybody in any language on earth, spoken or written or even just thought.* He understands the thousands of languages of earth, not only what people speak, but what they are thinking and feeling in their hearts. He can communicate with anyone about anything, in just the right way.

Jesus Christ: Centerpiece of the Human Race

Why is Jesus' Name great? *Because He is the Son of God,* who was willing to sacrifice Himself to save others. "And being found in appearance as a man, He humbled Himself by becoming obedient to the point of death, even death on a cross. Therefore God has highly exalted Him and given Him a name that is above every name, that at the name of Jesus every knee should bow, of those who are in Heaven, and those who are on earth, and those who are under the earth, and that every tongue shall confess that *Jesus Christ is Lord,* to the glory of *God the Father*" (Philippians 2:9–11, NIV).

The Weapons of Our Warfare

"They overcame him [satan] by the Blood of the Lamb [Jesus] and the Word of their testimony" (their words about knowing Christ) Revelation 12:11. Dr. C. Peter Wagner lists six weapons of spiritual warfare in his book (*Engaging the Enemy*) pp. 7–11. All the weapons are geared to defeat satan.

1. **The Name of Jesus**
    Mark quotes Jesus as saying, "In *My* name they will cast out demons" (Mark 16:17). John quotes Jesus as saying, "If you ask anything in My name I will do it" (John 14:14). Paul says that God gave Jesus "the name which is above every name" (Philippians 2:9). And there are other references. What is so important about a name? *It is the*

authority that the name bears. When Jesus invites us to use His name, He transfers divine authority. It [His Name] is an awesome weapon. No one has the authority of Jesus unless Jesus is truly their Lord. At the Name of Jesus, demons flee.

2. The Blood of Jesus

When Jesus shed His blood on the cross, Satan's power was broken. It was on the cross that Jesus "disarmed principalities and powers" and "made a public spectacle of them" (Colossians 2:14–15). Satan hates nothing more than to be reminded of the Blood of Jesus. He cannot stand against the blood of Jesus. The Blood of Jesus is the banner of Satan's defeat (*Engaging the Enemy*) p. 10.

History of the Blood As a Shield

In the spirit realm *"the Blood" of Jesus gives a shield of protection.* That is why we "pray the Blood" over people after praying with them, or when we feel they might be in trouble. It annoys satan when a Christian is helped, and if we haven't prayed the Blood of Christ's protection over our lives, we have experienced that satan will often try to strike back at us. The retaliation might be a physical or emotional difficulty or an expensive inconvenience, like the car or dishwasher breaking down, but if you have "prayed the Blood" over yourself satan cannot strike at you. The Blood makes you "off limits" to him. It is the symbol of our cleansed life and satan's defeat, and every demon knows it. So as you pray for yourself or someone else, quietly "pray the Blood" over both of you. *The Blood is your impenetrable shield.* It cost Jesus His life to gain that for you. Never think "Jesus," or "the Blood" without reverence. And never think a person can "claim the Blood" and "live like the devil." We all need to be careful to avoid sin, because it offends God and tears us down. And if a person ever actually had received Jesus into his life, and willingly sins, Jesus is there, but displeased. Satan wouldn't own that person, but he would have the right to harass him.

Why Is Physical Blood Symbolic of Life?

Because a person's physical *life* is in his blood. It contains the DNA of his life: molecular instructions to grow the body, renew the body, defend the body from infection, heal wounds, carry food to nourish the cells, get rid of waste and other poisons, keep the person alive, and much more. The blood sustains the *life* of the body. *The Blood of Jesus does those things for a person spiritually.* It cleanses from sin, overcomes evil, and gives life forever. When the Blood that Jesus shed for all mankind has been applied to our lives in forgiveness and cleansing, we have life forever and satan has no sin-claim on us. We will *not die eternally*, facing punishment for sin. *Rather, we will live forever,* as God has promised. When John the Baptist saw Jesus coming toward him he said, "Behold, "God's Lamb," who takes away the sin of the world!" (John 1:29). It makes us perfectly clean in God's sight. It is worth repeating: never think "Jesus," or "the Blood" without reverence.

Satan is a bully and will attempt to deceive and discourage you, but you can back him down by pleading the *Blood of Jesus.* When Roy and I were missionaries in Indonesia, an evil woman set a "death curse" against me. In the midst of it, as soon as I prayed "the Blood, Lord, the Blood," the demons backed away and left. *Against the Blood of Jesus, evil spirits cannot win.* All demons know what it represents, and fear it.

There is a wonderful old hymn, *"There Is Power in the Blood,"* written by Lewis E. Jones around 1900. "Would you be free from the burden of sin? There's pow'r in the Blood, pow'r in the Blood; Would you o'er evil a victory win? There's wonderful pow'r in the Blood – the precious Blood of the Lamb." *It is true.* It is God's plan!

Weapons of Our Warfare, continued
(Dr. C. Peter Wagner)

3. **Agreement**

The greatest day in the history of the church was the day of Pentecost, when "they were all of one accord" (Acts 2:1). The accord was "in prayer and supplication" (Acts

1:14). We agree on what we see the Holy Spirit doing.
Jesus said, "If two of you agree on earth concerning anything that they shall ask, it shall be done for them by
My Father in heaven" (Matthew 18:19). When numbers
of believers in one local church or from many churches
in the same area get together to *agree in prayers, power
against the enemy increases dramatically.*

4. **Fasting**

I am referring to voluntarily abstaining from food for
a given period of time. Some forms of spiritual warfare
require fasting as a prerequisite for victory. When Jesus
was explaining to His disciples why they couldn't cast the
demon out of the epileptic boy, He said, "This kind does
not come out except by fasting and prayer" (Matthew
17:21). With the right attitude and with God's timing and
guidance, fasting is one of our most useful weapons.

Power Gained By Fasting

When there is a "stronghold of evil," a powerful force holding or
oppressing a person or a community or a nation, *it takes more than
one Christian to break that demonic hold.* That's because there are
many devils at work and it takes more than a few angels to contend
with many devils. What can we do? *Either gain additional prayer help,
or fast and pray, or both.* Throughout history, all religious groups
have known that fasting brings strong help from whichever power
the person is aligned with. The men of Rees Howell's Bible School in
Wales fasted and prayed in groups, and gained victories in World War
II (Examples #55–62).

Example #69
Victory! When Daniel Fasted

In the Old Testament in Daniel chapter 10 is the powerful account
of the Prophet Daniel's vision. After the disturbing vision, Daniel
fasted and prayed. An unknown heavenly being came to visit him and

encourage him. It is an account of angelic *war*. God's angels fighting against demons in order to get an answer through to Daniel.

Daniel was a captured Hebrew, taken from Jerusalem to Babylon (now southeastern Iraq) in 604 BC. There he rose to high rank in King Nebuchadnezzar's court. Then, when Babylon fell to the Persians (Iran), Daniel served Persian King Darius. In his vision, Daniel saw the troubles that are to come upon Israel right before Jesus returns as *King* and rescues them. Daniel was so grieved, he fasted and prayed for 21 days. Then a heavenly person appeared to Daniel and assured him of victory (Daniel 10:16). He told Daniel he had been trying to reach him but *had been detained by a strong satanic spirit power* (just as there are still demonic strongholds over places on earth today). In response to Daniel's fasting and prayer, the powerful Archangel Michael blasted through the Persian lines (the satanic forces controlling Persia) so Daniel's prayer could be answered.

The prayer principle is the same in today's world. If we are worried or grieved about something, and have prayed and had other people pray, and we don't have an answer, it is good to fast and pray, because fasting brings extra angelic help. Fasting is not easy to do. Our stomachs always remind us that we are hungry. Yet that is good, because it *reminds* us what we are serious enough to fast about. Just why fasting brings extra help from God, I don't know, except that it shows we are very serious about the need. We are willing to "deny our flesh" in order to gain special help from God. If you fast, do it as secretly as possible, just between you and God. Don't make a "show" of it. Tell only God what you need.

Spiritual Weapons

The Bible instructs us to "put on the whole armor of God" (Ephesians 6). All the armor is valuable, yet all but one piece of it is for defense. The Apostle Paul wrote, "Put on the whole armor of God, so you will be able to stand safe against all the strategies and tricks of satan. For we are not fighting against people made of flesh and blood, but against persons without bodies—the evil rulers of the unseen world, those mighty satanic beings and great evil princes of darkness who rule this world; and against huge numbers of wicked spirits in the spirit world. So use every piece of God's armor to *resist* the enemy whenever he attacks, *and when it is all over, you will still be standing up."* Paul lists the armor: truth, the willingness to spread the good news of peace with God, faith, the helmet of salvation, and the sword of the Spirit, which is the Word of God.

The Weapons of Our Warfare, continued
(Dr. C. Peter Wagner)

5. The Word of God

In Ephesians 6 the full armor of God is described in detail. Of the six pieces of armor, five are defensive weapons; only one of the weapons is for offense: *the sword of the Spirit is the Word of God.* "The sword of the Spirit" is hearing from God like Daniel did. It is knowing what God's will is for a certain time and place. Knowing God's will by receiving the "word of God" and acting accordingly is a crucial aspect to effective spiritual warfare. [Dr. Wagner refers not only to God speaking to you from the Bible, but also what He speaks to you in your mind in present situation.] *Speaking God's words in Jesus' Name functions like a sword that cuts down evil.*

6. Praise

Our praise, under any circumstances, blesses God (Psalm 145:2). In Philippi, Paul cast a high ranking "spirit of divination" out of a fortune teller, and her masters were angry. [She had made money for them.] Paul and Silas were beaten and thrown in jail. They were in an inner prison with their feet in stocks. What did Paul and Silas do? They praised God! A divine earthquake loosened their prison doors. The jailer was saved and a church was planted. The secret? They praised God even *before* they saw the victory.

I am continually amazed that all of us who love Him can call upon Jesus any time of the day or night and He is there. How can He possibly care for each of the millions of people who belong to Him? It is because He is *not limited in the ways humans are.* God is everywhere at once (omnipresent), and all powerful (omnipotent). He knows "everything about everything," all the time (omniscient).

SECTION THREE:

GOD'S HATRED
OF WITCHCRAFT

CHAPTER THIRTEEN

WITCHCRAFT

Witchcraft is a ruthless effort to gain power by employing demons.

Preface

G OD HATES WITCHCRAFT today as He has hated it through the ages. Witchcraft and genuine Christianity are *opposites*. Witchcraft wants power over others, with various kinds of gain regardless of the harm it causes. Christianity wants the welfare of others, and is generous. "Witchcraft" is the collective term for any deliberate contact with evil beings and is called a "craft" because it has patterns and rituals that can be learned. That is very different from Christian power, which is God Himself, working through you to accomplish good.

What Is a Witch?

A witch is someone who *contacts demons in order to get something*; information, or money, or "love," or revenge, or to use demons to cause events, good or bad. *"Black witches"* are the most hated people in every nation; senders of demons to harm, kill, affect weather, crops, people, animals, cause disasters. No wonder God said, "Do not permit a witch to live" (Exodus 22:18). With an ordinary criminal there is the possibility of bringing him to justice. But not a witch, because no matter how terrible the results of a curse she sets, she cannot be convicted in a court of law because she wasn't physically present when the demonic attack occurred. She might be suspected, but there is no way to prove "she did it," particularly in a secular society that denies that witches and demons even exist. Men deeply involved in witchcraft have other names, such as "warlock."

Where people have had the luxury of growing up in a society made spiritually peaceful by Christianity, yet ignore what the Bible says about witches, and ignore what the world has experienced with witches, they tend to be naïve and spiritually insular. They base their beliefs on what they have personally read or heard or *not* experienced, rather than upon what the Word of God says about the subject. Roy and I have known such people. Many of them are fine people, but they make the mistake of basing their ideas upon what the secular world teaches rather than upon *what God says is the reality.* Perhaps they think the problem stopped at some indeterminate point in history past. It won't stop until Jesus returns to earth as King and strikes it down. Denying the reality of witchcraft might cause some people to feel comfortable and spiritually safe, but *their misperceptions will not make them immune from demonic harassment,* nor will it eradicate witchcraft or the evil effects of it. On the contrary, ignorance allows witchcraft to spread unimpeded, to the point where now it has taken open root even in formerly strongly Christian America.

God forbids *any kind* of witchcraft. In the Bible, He says, "Let no one be found among you who practices divination or sorcery, interprets omens, engages in witchcraft, or casts spells, or who is a medium or spiritist or consults the dead. Anyone who does these things is *detestable* to the LORD" (Deuteronomy 18:10–12). God would not have forbidden those damaging practices if it were not possible to do them. "You shall *not* practice divination or soothsaying" (Leviticus 19:26). "Do *not* turn to mediums or spiritists; do *not* seek them out to be *defiled by them.* I am the *Lord* your *God"* (Leviticus 9:31).

Witchcraft: Employing Demons to Get One's Own Way

Witchcraft Mindset

Example of a "witchcraft mindset:" When my father was a reliability control engineer on the "Minute Man" missile project (America's first defensive missile, hidden in deep silos across the Midwest), a fellow engineer quietly called him aside and said, "Gene, come with me to a secret meeting tomorrow night. I used to go to church but it didn't help me; I was always poor. But at this meeting we worship devils and now I have lots of money." Dad considered the man profane and avoided him. In one way or another, all people involved in witchcraft are like that man, without reverence for God, willing to contact evil spirit power in order to acquire gain.

Demons are everywhere that God is not honored. They are particularly active where there is great sin; such as violence, immorality, greed for money and power, or a family heredity of seeking contact with demonic spirits. Many people are vulnerable, because humans have troubles on this earth, and if they don't have God's help they can feel desperate. That can lead to the temptation to seek information from witches, who use demons to know things, do things, "give help" of various kinds, and perhaps provide an explanation of "why" something happened, such as sickness or an accident. But not only is it the sin of seeking help from demons, but it is a *false hope*, because some of the problems people experience are *caused by demons,* and if they seek help from witches to solve those problems, the witch uses *other* demons to attempt to explain "who or what or why." So there is a strangling circularity about it. What you can be sure of is that whatever demons a person gets involved with will end up harming him. And the extent of the harm might not even be known until Judgment Day.

Witchcraft Danger to Missionaries

In years past, Christians who knew the Bible knew that Jesus had consistently confronted evil and defeated it. But to many of them, what Jesus did seemed so far removed from their own daily lives that they thought it "was only for then," not for now. So when modern-day churches sent missionaries into pagan areas of the world, the missionaries were usually well taught in terms of Bible knowledge, but woefully unequipped in terms of knowing how to contend with the evil spirits they would encounter. Many didn't even understand that the activity of evil spirits was the *main* thing that held people back from understanding and receiving the Gospel. Or if the missionaries did know it, most of them had not been taught how to contend with it. In America, the prevalence of Christianity had caused this nation to exist so spiritually peacefully that beyond living clean lives, there didn't seem to be the need for defense against evil. So that aspect of Christian ministry wasn't taught to missionaries who trained in the U.S. *And many Christians, then and now, falsely believed that a Christian cannot be harmed by satan or demons.* Not true. Now that evil has risen so openly in America, Christians need to know how to recognize it and combat it in Jesus' Name.

Missionary Casualties

Years ago a missionary from California had to be sent home from the mission field because he began to behave in bizarre ways. At that time in our lives, Roy and I didn't understand that demonic enemies are real. We could only speculate as to what might be causing the former missionary's odd behavior. His home church was wonderful and caring, filled with people who loved the Lord and prayed for the man, but nothing helped him. He was considered a psychiatric case and institutionalized. A tragedy. *One missionary off the field.* Later, as we learned more, Roy and I realized that the man must have been "demonized," physically and mentally harassed by a strong demon that was set against him in the Latin American country in which he had worked. But he wasn't "possessed" in the sense of demons "owning" him. "A Christian may be attacked by demons and may be affected mentally and sometimes spiritually [and physically], but he cannot be owned by demons" Timothy M. Warner, (*Spiritual Warfare*) p. 80.

And some children of missionary friends who served in a Latin American country were so harassed by evil that the family had to come home. Even several years after they returned, the children continued to behave strangely, and the parents didn't know what to do. It is false to think a Christian can't be oppressed by evil. The tragedy was that they had never been taught to give a command against evil in Jesus' Name. *A family off the mission field.*

In another country, a missionary mother confided in me that she had become afraid of her teenage son because he was threatening to kill her. Teenage sons the world over tend to be hostile toward their mothers when they begin to come into manhood; they want to sever the "apron strings" of female control. But this teenager's behavior had become so violent and bizarre that the mother was afraid of her son.

The circumstances were so strange that I suspected witchcraft. Who would profit from that family having to leave the mission field? The entrenched evil powers! Can I prove that the boy's hostile attitude was a result of witchcraft? No. But if someone is bitten and his behavior changes abruptly, you look for the snake. Nothing else in their lives had changed. Because witchcraft was so strong in the area where they ministered, it seemed very possible, even probable, that a "spirit of murder" had been sent into the boy's mind to drive the family out of the area. *Another missionary family attacked.* Satan targets missionaries because they get people out of his evil kingdom and into Christ's kingdom. They are *a threat to the entrenched witchcraft culture.* But if missionaries don't know how to defend themselves spiritually, they are vulnerable. And they can become very discouraged. Over our years in ministry Roy and I have tangled with a few of those worst witches, but mercifully, God protected us. I love the chorus: "Thou, Oh Lord, are a shield about me, You're my glory, and the lifter of my head." The words are *true.* God didn't promise that His children would never feel "down," "discouraged," but He did promise to be the "lifter of our head." Missionaries feel that.

Lack of Spiritual Warfare Skill

All the distressed missionaries I've told you about seem to have been victims of witchcraft. They all lived in spiritual *war* zones. Missionaries have to be able to defend themselves and their families and their message spiritually. They need to know how to "bind the strong man" (satan) as God's Word instructs them to do (Matthew 12:29). Tie him up! Make him unable to interfere or strike back! You want to be able to rescue the people satan has captured. Or, if missionaries did know that satan and witchcraft were their direct foes, many had not been taught how to contend with them. *They didn't know they could directly triumph over evil in the Name of Jesus.* Most missionaries have been taught the conventional western misunderstanding that because Christ lives within them they couldn't be attacked. Then, in the middle of an attack their minds reel; it isn't supposed to be happening! They discovered that what they had been taught wasn't true, or at the very least, was not sufficient. That left them at an alarming disadvantage.

Example #70
Missionary to Amazon Tribe Defeated

A Wycliffe Bible Translator wrote: "I went to the Amazon Jungle in 1963 in order to begin our ministry among the Apurina people—so far as I know I was the first one to challenge Satan's dominion over this people, a total domination down through the centuries. My basic purpose in being there was to see if I could remove that people from Satan's house and take them to Jesus' house; if I could transfer them from the kingdom of darkness to the kingdom of light. But unfortunately, in spite of a Master of Theology degree and having read the Bible through several times, I was not aware of these truths [about spiritual warfare]. I got *clobbered!* I got it without mercy, until I had had enough! *Satan wiped the floor with me. I didn't know how to defend myself*—actually, I didn't really understand what was happening.

"You see, I was skeptical about the activity of the demons. Oh yes, I knew that satan and the demons exist, because the Bible is clear and emphatic on that score, but I knew very little about how they operate and virtually nothing about the use of our weapons, whether for defense or offense. My theological background, both formal and informal, was strictly traditional—My professors transmitted the idea that a servant of Christ was untouchable, or exempt from demonic attack; that sort of thing wouldn't be a problem for us" Timothy M Warner (*Spiritual Warfare*) p. 78, quoting from Wilbur N. Pickering.

I'm sure God's angels have protected missionaries from many dangers, *yet with Christ's Spirit in them, they had superior power they might not have been using*. Not knowing to *speak* Jesus' Name and Blood against evil is like having a high-powered rifle to combat a slingshot, but not know how to pull the trigger. Because of that, many missionaries either gave up attempting to contend with satan, or they settled into other kinds of ministries that wouldn't draw so much opposition. If Christians think the time for using the spiritual gifts promised by Jesus is past; that missionaries only need a "loving message about Jesus," they are mistaken. People appreciate the missionary's kindness, *but it takes spiritual power to overcome so much spiritual opposition.* People in pagan areas who have witnessed the power of evil don't feel safe to turn away from it unless they are convinced that Jesus is the *greater* power. They might even want to, but they wouldn't dare. There could be a strike-back from witchcraft that even jeopardizes their lives. On most mission fields of the world, the nationals' *minds are so blinded* by satan that they don't even "hear" the message the missionary preaches.

Yet virtually all Christians, at some point in their life, were spiritually blind until the light of Christ shone into their hearts. In Christian countries it was *easier for them to receive Christ;* Christianity had protected them from the degree of demonic pressure and deception that satan exerts in pagan countries. "The god of this world, [satan] has blinded the minds of those who don't believe, lest the light of the gospel of the glory of Christ, who is the image of God, shine into their hearts, and they be converted" (2 Corinthians 4:4). *The missionary has to be able to overcome listeners' spiritual blindness,* in the Name of Christ. Roy did that in Thailand when he spoke against satan, forbidding him to blind the minds of the two Buddhist leaders (Chapter 6, #29). Roy's prayers were an example of Revelation 12:11; *"And they overcame him [satan] by the Blood of the Lamb [Jesus] and the word of their testimony* [what they spoke]".

Example #71
Victory! Missionaries to Kalimantan Triumph!

Dr. Warner quotes Robert Peterson's report in *Are Demons for Real?* p. 8, on the effectiveness of the OMF (Overseas Missionary Fellowship) ministry in West Kalimantan (formerly Borneo). "There was a breakthrough in ministry and 'more than 1500 men and women came into a personal saving experience in the grace of God...Young people joined together to form evangelistic bands and responded to urgent invitations to come and bring the Gospel to country villages. Other young people dedicated their lives for full-time service and sought training in Bible schools and colleges. Some have gone to other islands as missionaries. West Kalimantan became one of the bright spots in OMF work, and the Church flourished.' When asked what accounted for this, the reply was, '*We believe it is not just coincidental that when the Lord's servants commenced openly to challenge the power of darkness and, in the name of our victorious Lord, command the demons to come out of the possessed ones, the gates of hell began to yield and captives were set free*'" Warner (*Spiritual Warfare*) p. 132.

Example #72
Marco Polo, Kublai Khan
Almost a Christian

Kublai Khan (1216–1294) was the great Mongol ruler of China, grandson of Genghis Khan. In 1271 when Marco Polo made his second trip to China, Kublai Khan appointed him his trusted envoy around the Mid-East and South-East Asia, down to Singapore and Indonesia.

The Khan's contacts were so broad, and China so large, that Kublai Khan allowed various religious groups to live in China and allowed the four major groups to have a yearly parade: the Moslems, the Buddhists, the Christians and China's witches. But he had a reverent attitude regarding Christ. He *would not permit Christians to lead their parade with a cross, because he considered the cross an insult to Jesus, the "ignominious symbol of the unjust torture and death of the most perfect man who ever lived."* Kublai Khan regarded the Christian faith "as the truest and the best; nothing, as he observed, being enjoined to its professors that was not replete with virtue and holiness."

Then why didn't Kublai Khan conform to it and become a Christian? His wrote his reasons for not doing so to Nicolo and Maffeo Polo, Marco Polo's uncles. His reason was that he was afraid of the witches in his court and wanted a demonstration of superior Christian power to restrain them. "When I am witness of this, I shall place them and their religion under an interdict, and shall allow myself to be baptized. Following my example, all my nobility will then in like manner receive baptism, and this will be imitated by my subjects in general; so that the Christians of these parts will exceed in number those who inhabit your own country." Polo commented, "From this discourse it must be evident that if the Pope had sent out persons duly qualified to preach the gospel [and counteract evil] the grand khan would have embraced Christianity, for which, it is certainly known, he had a strong predilection" (quotations from a very old book, *The Travels of Marco Polo*). We don't know if Kublai Khan ever received Jesus into his life in the conventional way, but he certainly was an intelligent and rational and noble-minded man. I hope Jesus appeared to him in a dream or vision, the way He appeared to my mother many years ago, and has been appearing to Muslims and other people hungry to know God personally in this age. I hope we will meet Kublai Khan in Heaven.

In later centuries evangelical missionaries did go to China and led many Chinese to Christ. Now China has many millions of Christians. Those early missionaries must have known how to defeat satan in Jesus' Name and taught their Chinese converts to do the same. *Each generation needs to know how to stand against evil* and feel confident in doing so. When Roy taught our Chinese Campus Crusade for Christ staff in Hong Kong, he presented the same truths we are presenting in *God Wins*, and the Chinese Christians were grateful to learn them. They said witchcraft is still strong in China. As strong as in Kublai Khan's time? We don't know. But Christianity has turned multiplied millions of Chinese hearts and minds to Christ. Kublai Khan would have been pleased.

Example #73
Witchcraft in San Clemente

Roy got a phone call from a Campus Crusade for Christ worker in San Clemente (a beach area above San Diego in southern California), asking for advice. A family in the man's church was frightened and asked for help because objects were moving around in their house, just as Kublai Khan experienced in his palace 700 years ago. That means the family moved into a home in which severe witchcraft had been practiced. Roy told the man that the family would either have to vacate that home, or find the physical "thing" or "things" that gave strong demons the legal right to be there, and *burn* those objects. How did that problem get into California? Sin is not new anywhere in the world, but in recent decades southern California has had an influx of immigrants from countries where witchcraft is openly practiced. It can be assumed that unless those people become Christians, (like the Cambodians of Examples 10 and 11) they would practice their witchcraft in America, too. And there has been a surge in the media glorifying witchcraft. That is *demonic "mind-bending," reversing truth,* an insidiously evil trend.

None of us like to think about evil people, but remember this: *witches, past and present, are afraid of Jesus and His Blood and His angels.* If you ever sincerely asked Jesus to forgive you and come into your life, He is there. You can name His Name against evil. Christians can *bless people.* They can gain *angelic help to assist people* in their need.

Lack of Spiritual Warfare Training in Churches

Angels congregate where righteousness is; demons congregate where sin is. So when America was strongly Christian there was a sense of God's presence. Only occasionally in America was there a sense of evil, or only in certain places or among certain people. There was a general sense that America was a God-fearing country. "Where the knowledge of Christ is, demons do not come" (*Demon Experiences in Many Lands*) p. 25. It could be added that where there is some knowledge of Christ, but it is shallow, demons do come but not always very openly. Where knowledge of Christ is suppressed or attacked, demons are free to flood in. Unfortunately, that seems to be occurring in America at this time. Only renewed churches will be able to stem that tide.

In most of America's churches there is little or no teaching about how to overthrow evil because there hasn't seemed to be the need. The need exists, but until recently evil seemed hidden. And *there has been a major theological error.* Most of Western theology assumed that for the Christian, everything, including bad things, all come from God, all work for God's good, and are under His direct control. That post Augustinian error is *soundly refuted* by Dr. Gregory A. Boyd in *God at War,* and *Satan and the Problem of Evil.* Chapter Ten of *God Wins* deals with that issue. Because of that error, in most Christian churches the need for direct overthrow of evil is dismissed or not often discussed. Another part of that problem is that because most Christians have not been taught how to oppose satan, they fear him rather than fight him. In contrast, Jesus and the Apostles and the Early Church did *not* fear talking about satan or *to* him. And they fought him. They gave direct orders against his activity, *and satan fled. Jesus should be the role model of ministry in our churches.*

It is not only pastors and missionaries who need to know these things, but *every Christian.* It is an absolute necessity for Christians to be able to contend with evil, especially as we have seen evil rise in our society. We aren't Christians just to sit in church and hear sermons and sing and have fellowship with friends, as pleasant as those are. We have to be aware of where spiritual battles are and be able to contend with them in Jesus' Name, *and win.* It is our high privilege as Christians that we have *authority* from Christ to do that.

Only Christians can overcome all demons. In witchcraft, stronger spirits can overcome lesser spirits, but *only Christians can overcome all demons.*

God's Hatred of Witchcraft

GOD WOULD NOT HAVE LISTED THIS CONDEMNATION OF WITCHCRAFT IF THOSE EVIL ACTIVITIES DID NOT EXIST.

(Scriptures from King James and New International Bibles)

Isaiah 47:11	"Disaster will come upon you and you will not know how to conjure it away. Keep on then, with your magic spells and many sorceries" (and reap destruction).
Micah 5:12	"I will destroy your witchcraft and you shall no longer cast spells."
Exodus 22:18	"Do not allow a sorceress to live." (Sorcery is magic done by demons.)

Nahum 3:14	"Woe unto the city of blood and full of lies, all because of the wanton lust of a harlot, mistress of sorceries."
Malachi 3:5	"Be a swift witness against the sorcerers." (workers of demonic magic)
2 Kings 9:22	"How can there be peace, as long as all the idolatry [worship of demonic spirits living in carved objects] and the witchcraft of Jezebel abound?"
Leviticus 30:31	"Do not turn to mediums or spiritists; do not seek them out to be defiled by them. I am the Lord your God."
Isaiah 47:12–15 (Paraphrased)	"Stand fast now in your spells and in your many sorceries with which you have labored from your youth; Perhaps you will be able to profit, Perhaps you may cause trembling. You are wearied with your man counsels; Let now the astrologers, those who prophesy by the stars, those who predict by the new moons, stand up and save you from what will come upon you. Behold, they have become like stubble, fire burns them; they cannot deliver themselves from the power of the flame...There is none to save you."
Jeremiah 27:9	"Do not listen to your mediums or sorcerers...they prophesy lies."
Malachi 3:5	"I [God] will be quick to testify against sorcerers, adulterers and perjurers." (A perjurer is a liar, harms people by giving false testimony.)
2 Kings 9:22	"What peace? so long as the harlotries of your mother Jezebel and her witchcrafts are so many?"
Leviticus 30:31	"Do not turn to mediums or spiritists; do not seek them out to be defiled by them. I am the Lord your God."

1 Samuel 15:23	"Rebellion is like the sin of divination." (Knowing things from demons.)
Acts 8:11	"He [Simon the sorcerer] had bewitched them with sorceries."
Isaiah 2:6	"They practice divination like the Philistines."
Revelation 22:15	"...outside [the Gates of Heaven] are dogs [unbelieving Gentiles and cruel, filthy-minded people] and sorcerers."
Daniel 2:27	"No wise man, enchanter, magician, or diviner can explain; but God in heaven reveals mysteries."
2 Chronicles 33:6	"She has a familiar spirit" (demons tell her things about other people's lives).
Leviticus 20:27	"A man or woman that has a familiar spirit or is a wizard must be killed."
Numbers 5:14	"A spirit of jealousy came upon him." (Spirits have the specific names of their destructive assignment against mankind.)
1 Samuel 28:7	"...woman has a familiar spirit." (Familiar with the details of people's lives.)
1 Samuel 28:8	"Divine unto me [inform me] by the familiar spirit." (Spirit of divination.)

Names and Definitions: Witchcraft Objects and Activities

The following objects and activities are an attempt to know and control events, using demonic spirits. Demons *inhabit* objects used by witches. *These are witchcraft practices that God forbids. This list will help you know what objects to avoid, and what kind of people to avoid.*

Amulet	An ornament, gem, or scroll worn as a charm against evil; often inscribed with a magic incantation: a "fetish."
Astrologer	Attempts to tell the future by consulting position of planets. (Not to be confused with astronomy, the scientific study of stars.)
Augury	To tell the future by divination. Chinese use tea leaves, some Africans use goat intestines and other means. Whatever the means, the intent is the same: to open a line of communication with the spirit world and gain information.
Charm	Anything worn to avert ill or secure good fortune: an amulet. Also, an incantation; action or process believed to have magic power; a talisman or spell. (A missionary in India reported that unless you remove the charms from a demonized person, the devils won't leave.)
Conjurer	One who summons a devil or spirit by invocation or incantation.
Coven	A group of witches meeting together who made an agreement, a "covenant," with satan.
Divination	Foretelling future events or gaining hidden knowledge by demonic help.
Diviner	One who gets hidden knowledge by demonic help.
Enchanter	Casts spells by demonic power.
Enchantment	A spell cast by a sorcerer or witch.
Fetish	Sorcery, a charm. An object supposed to possess magical power, as in saving its owner from harm or curing disease or repelling evil spirits or to attract their opposites. (Demons have no interest in humans' welfare, but will fight each other to gain worship from them.)

Incantation	To chant a magic formula. The use of spells or verbal charms, spoken or sung, as part of the ritual of magic. Also, a verbal formula that is chanted or recited.
Magic Arts	Witchcraft able to work demonic magic.
Magician	One who works magic by demonic power.
Medium	A "go-between" the living and the dead, carries messages back and forth.
Wise Men	Not all "wise men" contacted demons for information. Some were learned astronomers, like the Magi who followed the bright star when Jesus was born. From their study of the Hebrew scriptures the wise men knew a King had been born.

Note: NASA, America's National Aeronautic and Space Administration research station developed software that shows what happens in the heavens on any night in history. *At http://bethlehemstar.net/ you can see the "star" that the magi saw. It was a super-bright conjunction of three planets. You can also place yourself on the moon and view earth at the time "the sun was darkened" when Jesus died. You see the gray curved shadow of the solar eclipse over the entire Mid-East. (It gave me tears in my heart to see it, knowing what it represented.)You can request past, present and future dates.*

Witch	A woman who worships devils in order to gain favors from them.
Witchcraft	The study of how to contact demons, pay homage, gain demonic favors.

Please note: If any of you are involved in witchcraft, *I beg you to stop.* God doesn't want to have to destroy you, but that will happen to every person who pursues contact with demons and doesn't turn away from it. Turning away won't be easy; satan and evil people will try to hang onto your life. Please get prayer help to break away from any form of occultic activity.

This is what God says will happen to all witches: *Those who practice magic arts will be in the fiery lake of burning sulpher* (Revelation 21:8). That is where satan and all demons will be going, along with all humans who willingly cooperate with them in doing evil.

You don't want to be there.

CHAPTER FOURTEEN

WITCHES AND SÉANCES

What Do Witches Do?

Overview

As CHRISTIANS, WE don't really want to know about witches, yet to some degree we need to know, so we can guard our families and help defenseless children when we realize they are in trouble from witchcraft.

Roy and I have two women friends (unrelated to each other) who were raised in secret witchcraft homes and as girls suffered terribly. Separately, in different cities, God led kind Christian neighbors to befriend the girls and lead them to Christ. Both women deeply appreciate the kindness of those neighbors, and appreciate knowing Jesus now, but the cruel experiences left painful memories.

Like satan, many witches enjoy being cruel. In the basement of the home of one of the girls, during coven meetings she was tortured; repeatedly burned, and then was plunged into ice water to hide the abuse while the witches laughed. Sadly, her own grandmother was one of those cruel witches; smiling in church, cruel in the basement. So evil, and so different from a normal grandmother's love for her grandchildren (or even for *any* children). The other friend has flashbacks of being forced to participate in the ritual killing of an infant when she was only three. It was a "blood sacrifice" to satan. She was so horrified by the experience that until the day she went home to heaven, she was emotionally fragile and couldn't bear the color of the dress she was wearing when the murder took place.

Witches meet secretly in dark, hidden places (like sewer rats) to call upon evil spirits. They like to meet in places that are "down, and dark," where they can't be seen. That is the opposite of going *up* into church where music praises God and light streams through beautiful windows. Most commonly, witches meet in a basement or other underground area, or in a hidden forest or other dark, *hidden* area, because what they do is shameful. A "black witch" might work alone, but usually several witches gather together to form a "coven," a group of witches, and call upon evil spirits. (The word "coven" comes from the word "covenant," the agreement witches make with satan.) In league with demonic spirits, witches' minds are invaded by increasingly evil thoughts, and they commit evil deeds.

"Black witches" of all countries are worse than ordinary witches. Black witches make blood offerings to satan of a human baby or a small animal because in order to carry out the black witch's "spells," satan demands blood and cruelty. *He knows that the death of a valued living creature offends God the most; therefore those deaths please the evil side.* A blood sacrifice brings the most powerful demons to carry out the witch's "spells." Through them, the witch can cause grievous harm, even death, to people she (or "he" if it is warlock) dislikes or is paid to kill. It is the same thing the Canaanites and Aztecs and other evil groups did thousands of years ago. And we can assume that people who practice black witchcraft in today's world still do it, but more secretly, in order to avoid being arrested.

Other kinds of witches are less dangerous than a "black witch," but *God forbids contact with any witch.* That is because *every kind of witch-craft involves contact with demons.* Witchcraft spirits hate Christians because they hate Jesus. They know He is destined to rule earth as its eternal King, and they will be punished. *That is why when Jesus appeared on earth, demons cried out, "Have you come to destroy us before the time? We know who you are—the Holy One of God!"* (Mark 1:24). That time of their destruction is coming. They knew it then, and they know it now.

All black witches have several attitudes in common: they are selfish, profane, deceived, and without pity. Unless they repent, they will be in hell. Don't be deceived by their "gifts." The fact that "spirits" can sometimes reveal future events indicates that those spirits, demonic and ancestral, *possibly/probably have a hand in causing those events,* working to make their predictions "come true." People in Asia are aware of that and go to great lengths to avoid offending the family's departed members, for fear they will suffer harm from them (from demons posing as those relatives).

Example #74
Séance on a College Campus

When we had our cotton farm in California, many young people from our church attended a Christian college sponsored by the denomination. But not all the students were from our denomination or were Christian. One year, for "excitement," a group of students secretly conducted a "séance" in the basement of their dormitory building in the middle of the night. They wanted to see if they could contact a demonic spirit. It was going to be a spine-tingling thrill. It turned out to be "worse than they hoped."

On their first attempt, because a Christian was with them, the "séance" didn't work. Apparently, with a Christian present it couldn't work. (Isn't that interesting; just one person with Jesus in him and demons couldn't show up!—But don't try it!) So the Christian guy left. The next time the group performed the witchcraft ritual to summon spirits, evil spirits *did* show up, *and scared the kids out their wits!* Up in the dorm rooms other students heard their screaming and called paramedics and the Dean of Students. A girl who'd been at the séance was so traumatized that she had to be in a psychiatric ward for many weeks. All the participants were sent home and the ringleaders expelled. But the terrible memories remain. Whether the demons' excessively ugly appearance at the Christian college was the way they normally look, or contrived as a slap at the kids, I don't know. Perhaps it was both. But through the ages demons have been seen as ugly. They can change their appearance to accomplish their goals, but their actual appearance has been distorted by sin (Note Chapter 10, #55, "Demonic Strongholds Broken by Prayer: Evanston, Illinois").

The students were foolish and blasphemous to contact evil beings. That gave demons the legal right, spiritually, to continue to harass them. It will take genuine repentance on their part, and the help of Christians who know how to pray effectively against evil, to set them free from the extended consequences. Then they can ask God to heal their terrible memories, so the frightening images won't continue to haunt their minds or ever appear again. *And they need the Blood of Christ's protection over their lives.* Recently a woman who knows some of the (formerly young) people who were students at that time said it seems to her that many of the former students' lives are *still negatively affected*, not just the students who actually sought contact with evil. A tragic result.

Some powerful universities have occult fraternities. A young man who declined membership in the most prestigious one at a top Ivy League school told me he would have had to swear an oath of allegiance to the devil. He said he told the guys, "I can't do that! I'm a Christian!" And he walked out. Good for him! What a person "speaks," matters. People who pay homage to the devil, whether seriously or just as a prank, have invited evil influence into their lives. Avoid establishing bonds with such people, or making such a pledge.

Angels of both kinds, angelic and demonic, can change their appearance to suit their purpose. To gain allegiance from men in occult fraternities, if demons show up at all, it would probably be in the form of golden-robed princes of earth. Students hungry for earthly power would feel that honoring demonic "rulers of earth" would help them gain earthly power. However, once anyone pays any allegiance to the devil, evil powers gain some control and use that person to harm others.

Importance of Rejecting Evil

"Resist the devil and he will flee from you" (James 4:7). *How can we bring God's angels into our communities? Righteousness brings them in.* Power from God's Angels is released in response to the obedience and faith and prayers of God's people. That is why individuals, collectively as a community and nation, need to aspire to be merciful and prayerful and righteous, because the choices people make to pray or not to pray, to obey God or not to obey Him, determine their own destiny and corporately the destinies of their communities and nation.

Example #75
Victory! Demon-Possessed Teen Set Free!

Roy travels to various countries as a seminary professor, and in that capacity he taught a class on Missions to our Campus Crusade for Christ staff in Rangoon, Burma (now called Yangoon, Myanmar). Part of what Roy taught was a section on Spiritual Warfare; how to recognize and overcome demonic spirits. Harassment by demons is widely known in Asia (and many other areas of the world). The Burmese wife of the CCC National Director of the Myanmar ministry asked Roy if he would go with her to a village to pray for the suffering daughter of Burmese Christians. The girl had been demonized ever since she visited a cousin in Thailand.

While in Thailand, for unknown reasons a "black witch" put demonic spirits into the Burmese girl (who probably was not yet a Christian). Afterward, the girl had such a terrible time that her parents had to go to Thailand and bring her home. The parents were desperate for help. When the demons were "in the girl," she writhed on the floor and made guttural sounds that were a different voice. It was a demonization straight out of the New Testament, just as Jesus and His Disciples confronted. The demon—or demons—entered the Burmese girl and left her at *their own will*, the same way the dog demon went in and out of the little Mexican girl (Chapter 1, Example #1).

When Roy and his team arrived, the girl was lying on the floor, making the guttural sounds. Roy told the demons to get out of her, in Jesus' Name, but nothing changed. That meant there were multiple demons in her, strong ones, and they would fight to stay in. The six Christians prayed: Roy and the girl's parents and three people from the Burmese Campus Crusade team. It took a long time to set her free. For two hours all of them prayed and sang gospel songs and told the demons to "Get out and stay out! In Jesus' Name." Finally, whatever spirits were in the girl gave up and left. She sat up, finally peaceful, and spoke in her normal voice. In Jesus' Name, Roy and the group forbade the demons to *ever* return, and prayed the Blood of Christ's protection over her. The girl's peace was the strong indication that the powerful demons were gone.

Roy didn't know what had actually taken place in Thailand, whether the girl had dabbled in the occult, or whether it was strictly a malicious attack against her Christian family. If she had been dabbling in the occult she would need to ask Jesus to forgive her or the demons would have the right to return. Only a cleansed life and the Blood of Christ's protection can guard her. *Demons cannot be where Christians have forbidden them and righteousness excludes them.*

Example #76
Victory! Puerto Rican Witch Receives Christ!

A friend of a young couple in Roy's CCC International School of Theology Missions class led a Puerto Rican witch to Christ. She had been involved in Santeria, a satanic cult that has manifestations of demonic possession and thinks it has "power" to "order the Saints of the Church to do their bidding." Laughable if it were not so evil and pathetic. In Santeria, demons take "possession" of people's bodies during trances, causing them to writhe around in mud like *snakes*; totally debased as humans. That keeps on-lookers in awe and fear and belief in the wickedness.

In his book, *Biblical Demonology,* Merrill F. Unger states: "Cases both of spontaneous or involuntary and voluntary possession [by evil spirits] are practically universal in extent, there being no quarter of the globe where such phenomena have not been authenticated nor any class of society, primitive or civilized, where they have not occurred, nor any period, ancient, or medieval, or modern, in which cases may not be cited. Usually demon possession is accompanied by 'gross superstitions, unbridled sensuality, and widespread phenomena of possession'" (p. 84). It could be added that the human spirit is inviolate unless that person, or that person's family had let down the barrier against evil. Only then might there occur an "involuntary" possession.

The Puerto Rican witch had been what is called "demonized," under the strong influence of demons that stayed around her. But she had not been "possessed" in the same base way as the people who writhed around in the mud like snakes. They were possessed. Her form of witchcraft was tarot cards. She sought demonic spirits to give her information as she told fortunes, and through information from demons she could give accurate prophecies. (That indicates that demons know the future, or cause it, or both.) But the witch said that her heart was sad, empty. When the student in Roy's seminary class shared the Gospel with her, she prayed the "sinner's prayer," asking Jesus to forgive her and enter her life. But then she began to have many problems, one after the other, more than ever before.

So the woman who led her to Christ brought her to Roy's office for counseling. Roy knew immediately what was wrong, because it is common when people leave evil and trust in Christ, that at first their lives seem worse. That is because satan is angry at having lost them, so he attacks them. *New Christians need to be instructed about how to defend themselves.* In Jesus' Name, Roy commanded satan to leave the woman alone, and not cause any more bad things to happen to her. He *prayed the Blood of Christ's protection over her and told her to burn her tarot cards and other paraphernalia because devils were in them and would oppress her until she burned it all,* "burned up their house," and she would not have a free heart until she did that. The woman didn't feel any better when she left his office, but she and her husband bought a big metal washtub anyway, piled her witchcraft stuff into it and set it on fire. *As it burned, they felt their spirits lift so high that they began to sing with joy!* It was the end of their troubles. After that, things went well for them.

Note: People who are led to Christ are often not instructed about the importance of getting rid of the satanic baggage that had attached to their lives. It can come from deep sin, or sin in their family, or family background, or damaging friendships or practices. The items used to contact evil *must* be gotten rid of—occult objects, occult games, idols, charms meant for witchcraft, witchcraft books, etc. or the demons that accompany them will persist in harassing them, and make converts feel continually discouraged. People from an occult background will not be able to experience the abundant Christian life until they are freed from the bondage of those things.

Example #77
Victory! Jungle Witch Becomes Evangelist!

In a Thai jungle, when a New Life Training Center ministry team came through, a woman who was the respected chief witch in her village received Christ. This witch was not a "black witch." She attempted to help her people by predicting events, telling fortunes, locating lost objects, and using spirits to heal people. She told Roy (through an interpreter) that when she received Christ she was so happy to have found Him that she gave up "the old ways." She was given a Bible and earnestly studied it and attended the New Life Training Center discipleship classes given by Thai staff of Campus Crusade for Christ. Right away she began teaching a Bible study up in her bamboo stilt house, and led so many villagers to Christ that the group outgrew her upper floor. She and her husband cleared the area under their stilt house, and by placing mats on the ground they had room for the house church they were leading. Eventually a large stilt church was built. (People in that area need stilts because the river floods periodically. The river is valuable for water and fish and canoe transportation, but it floods.)

Example #78
"White Witch"

Most women who openly admit to being witches insist they are "white witches" who don't hurt anyone, and they insist that there is no such thing as demons. Yet they set out exactly the same kinds of "offerings" that demons everywhere require: candles and flowers and food to honor the demons, and they meet in a forest or other dark place and call on the demons. These supposed "non-witches" carry out virtually the same rituals as witches who admit they seek contact with demons. Others insist that they are just "calling on the powers of the universe." Not true. *There are only two spiritual "powers:" God and satan, and it is not God they are calling on.* Possibly some novice witches are just naïve. And some witches like palm readers consider themselves to be "good witches." Some even have a religious statue in their room. They are aware of both God and evil, and possibly some of them think their information comes from God. But it doesn't. God isn't in the "fortune telling" business. However, using demons, satan can make such a "fortune" come true, and then people think the witch has God's power to tell fortunes. God forbids people to go to witches for guidance or information.

On a TV talk show I heard a self-described "white witch" give seemingly accurate answers to questions about people's departed loved ones. That kind of witch is also called a "medium," going between the living and the dead; something God forbids. She was an older woman, grandmotherly, yet "tough" in her words and behavior. She responded to questions from women in the audience who asked about their departed loved ones. When the program went to break she apparently didn't realize her microphone was still on, because when the interviewer leaned close and asked her what to do about a certain problem he had, her answer was broadcast all over the country. In an ugly voice she growled, "You curse him to hell!" Her mild manner was a lie.

Note: Neither humans nor demons have power to "curse someone to hell." They are not in charge of hell, and unless the witch repents, she will find that out. God tells what will happen to witches: (Exodus 22:18; Deuteronomy 18:10–12; Leviticus 9:31).

Witches like the "white witch" get their "secret information" from demons. But the *opposite is also true.* By His Holy Spirit, God gives secret information and inspiration to people who love Him. *God's inspiration is always about what will help us, or warn us, or enable us to help others. It is never a trick or deceitful.*

Example #79
Demonic Information

A student in Roy's Spiritual Warfare class made a startling discovery. While attending a conference of magicians (his mother being a practicing magician), he videotaped the session where a "psychic" on the stage would tell the numbers that had been written on a paper by someone in the audience. The man was 100% accurate every time. Then Roy's student whispered, "satan, if you are giving the man the numbers, in Jesus' Name I command you to stop. *Immediately the man on the stage could no longer get the numbers right.* In frustration the "psychic" left the stage. The video documented the situation. Satan communicated the numbers to the man's mind *until, in Jesus' Name, satan was forbidden to give him the numbers.* Then the man's mind went blank and the show was over.

Example #80
Young Witches in Church

Witchcraft covens recruit disaffected, unhappy or profane young people. Then with drugs and the thrill of the "wicked and mysterious," they are hooked. Some covens send witches into church services to disrupt the pastor mentally, or in other ways disturb the service. I have a copy of a letter from a witchcraft coven, found on the floor beside a public copier in Pasadena and picked up by a Christian. She gave it to a Mission leader and he gave me a copy. It instructs the witches "how to look" when they go into a church to disrupt the service. They are to "dress modestly and be sure to carry a big Bible." They consider Christians stupid and naïve, and I suppose sometimes we are. Not stupid, but perhaps too accepting. Christians are glad to see new people in church and like to think the best about them. Ask God to give you a warning in your spirit if any would-be disrupters come in.

One Sunday morning as Roy and I were attending church near our home, we were sitting way over on the right side of the sanctuary. Off to our left I saw two teenage girls I hadn't seen before, perhaps sixteen or seventeen years old. There was nothing unusual about their appearance, and normally I would have been glad to see new faces in church. But as the service began I noticed a quick sneer go between the girls, so I felt uneasy about their motives. I wasn't sure, but I knew how to find out. Under my breath I whispered, "satan, if those are your girls, in Jesus'

Name I tell you to get them out of here." The girls jumped up and rushed out of church. They must have been from a coven, sent into our church to disturb the service in some way. Ask God to help you notice if such people show up in your church. Covens usually send teenage witches because they look innocent. You don't have to do anything openly; just whisper what I did, and if they are evil, they will have to leave. It was interesting to me that *in response to the Name of Jesus, satan had to order them to leave.* That was a small illustration of the power of Jesus being stronger than the power of satan. Roy has had similar "quiet confrontations" with possible witches in church, protecting the pastor and the congregation.

For the most part, Christianity kept demons out of America (*Demon Possession in Many Lands*) p. 25, but *in the aggressive attack on Christianity in recent years, evil has risen,* Movies featuring witches as heroines have become public fare, the producers either ignorant or uncaring or deliberate about the mind-bending effects such movies have on young people. Satanism, satanic cults, and many other occultic groups now flourish in America and other nations of the Western world in similar ways as they have flourished in non-Christian countries for centuries. *We, as Christians, need to counter it around the world by fasting and prayer and by actively resisting it, forcefully objecting to it, and teaching spiritual truth wherever we can, in whatever venue we can,* whether to large groups, small groups, or individuals. And always pray the Blood of Christ's protection over yourself when you have anything to do with witches or speaking out against them.

CHAPTER FIFTEEN

WITCHCRAFT DEFEATED

Example #81
Victory! Toddler's Curse Rash Healed!

THE FOLLOWING EXAMPLE is an account of a severe problem caused by witchcraft that Roy and I encountered in Africa. I went to Africa with Roy on one of his teaching trips to the Nairobi International School of Theology in Kenya (NIST, a school he helped start 30 years ago, in 1981). His great interest and expertise is in Missions and he teaches Mission History and strategy all over the world. Spiritual Warfare is part of the course he teaches, and on that trip he taught men and women in the Master's Degree program.

Preliminary to teaching spiritual warfare, Roy tells his class: "Before I discuss the overthrow of the demonic, I have learned it is wise to pray the Blood of Christ's protection over myself and my family and the people I'm speaking to. Satan is not pleased to have Christians learn they can circumvent his devices, and he attempts a retaliatory or 'don't try it' strike. If I have 'prayed the Blood,' nothing happens. *While some theologians might dispute the efficacy of 'praying the Blood,' I know of no person with actual experience against the demonic who did not learn very quickly that he had better do it.* As the blood over their door posts protected Israelites from the 'death angel,' so satan couldn't harm them, *Christ's Blood over our lives is the symbol that we are in His Kingdom, under His protection.* The Blood is the symbol understood, respected, feared, and unchallenged in the entire unseen realm. In a situation of extreme evil in Indonesia, when not even the name of Christ pushed the adversary back, pleading the Blood did" Roy Rosedale (*Missions Tomorrow*, Spring/Summer 1989).

While Roy was teaching, I taught a similar class for wives who were not in a degree program. After my class, a pastor's wife from Uganda asked me for advice and prayer. Her eighteen-month-old baby girl had been *born with painful weeping lesions all over her body,* and not even the finest doctors in Uganda could cure her. The woman's husband was the senior pastor of a big church in the capital city of Kampala, so they were able to afford the best medical help, but nothing the doctors could do had helped their daughter. Because of that, and because curses are common in Africa, the mother wondered if perhaps her baby had been cursed. I told her I didn't know, but it is always good to pray. And if the lesions were caused by a curse, the problem could be stopped by "speaking against it," in Jesus' Name. I suggested we talk to Roy about it.

As it turned out, the baby's father had attended Roy's class on spiritual warfare and had also asked his help. The father wanted Roy to come to their home and pray for their little girl. Roy would have gone, *but he wanted the father to experience for himself that he didn't need Roy.* Roy assured him that because he and his wife had Jesus in their lives, THEY could speak against the problem, and if *it was demonic it would have to stop.* So that evening the couple "spoke against the enemy." They told satan if he was causing the lesions, to "Stop it! In Jesus' Name, and get away from our little girl and never bother her again." They prayed the Blood of Christ's protection over themselves and her, just as we taught them to do.

THAT EVENING THE BABY'S SORES BEGAN TO DRY UP. IN THREE DAYS SHE HAD NEW SKIN!

There was great rejoicing on campus! The approximately 70 African graduate students were thrilled for the baby and the parents. And they were thrilled for their own lives also, because *it meant that they, too, could have victory over curses.* Curses are a widespread evil in Africa, very much feared. The baby's skin was *visual proof* that in Jesus' Name, evil could be stopped, just as it was stopped when Jesus walked on this earth. It was a time of great rejoicing at the seminary! The Africans, many of whom are pastors, are extremely appreciative that Roy has taught them how to overcome evil. They say Roy is the only missionary they know who ever acknowledged the problem of curses and could tell them specifically *how to overcome them.*

But sadly, there were two Western professors in the seminary who were not happy about the baby's fresh new skin. In their U.S. seminary they hadn't been taught to "speak against satan" so they thought it wasn't biblical to do so. But in Mark 16:17 *Jesus clearly taught, "In My Name cast out devils."* Jesus *has never rescinded that order.* In fact He enlarged it by sending the Holy Spirit to help Christians *continue* those great works. Jesus *rejoiced* that 70 of His disciples had healed the sick and cast out devils. That was *exactly what the African baby's parents had done.*

The American professors were good men, but stubborn in their refusal to accept that a Christian today could cast out devils in Jesus' Name. *Jesus Himself said we are to do that until He returns.* It was saddening that the two men were willing to deny the truth of what had taken place *even though the evidence of victory was right in front of their eyes!* Did the professors think that satan, who clearly had afflicted the girl, had then decided to heal her? Or that the rapid healing after 18 months of misery and ineffective medical treatment was accidental? Impossible! The healing began *immediately when her parents told satan to get away from their little girl, in Jesus' Name!* That was *proof* that the affliction had been demonic. The African students were disgusted with the professors. It was the same prideful defense of their religious training that caused the Pharisees to disbelieve the miracles that Jesus accomplished right in front of *their* eyes. We must all be careful not to fall into the trap of being so religiously prideful or insecure that we are willing to deny truth, deny evidence, in order to protect our pride. What Jesus had done for the little girl was *wonderful and undeniable.* The Africans were very displeased with the professors' attitudes, which harmed their standing as teachers. It was recommended that the two men be dismissed from the NIST faculty and sent back to the US.

Example #82
Victory! Woman's Curse Rash Healed!

In the Philippines our seminary is The International School of Leadership, located in Manila. It has students from many countries.

A student from Burundi, Africa came to Roy for help. He and his wife had been married less than a year, and the wife's face, which had always been beautifully clear, was now covered by ugly pimples that had been there several months. As with the baby in Nairobi, no medical treatments had helped. After Roy taught on spiritual warfare, the young husband asked if the problem might be demonic, perhaps a curse set by someone jealous of their marriage or that they were able to attend seminary. Roy didn't know. But he told the young man that if the rash was demonic, it could be stopped by speaking against satan in Jesus' Name, forbidding him to cause that problem or any other. They prayed that way, rebuking satan, and in three days the young wife's face was clear, just as the toddler's skin in Nairobi was clear. That indicated that the problem had been sent by someone involved in witchcraft. Thankfully, Christ's power is *greater* and the curse was broken. Roy and I praise God for His love and His power to dispel devil.

Proof that the attacks on the baby and the Burundian woman were demonic is that *in both cases the problems stopped when the Name of Jesus was used.*

Western Misconception

Westerners and many Western missionaries erroneously think the people's fears are "just superstition." Not so. Superstitious aspects emerge, because people cannot see what is actually happening, so they can only extrapolate from "causes" to "consequences." Evil spirits reinforce that, making people afraid. Because actual demons are involved, it is an error to think of people's fears as "superstitions," belief in things that don't exist. The things they are afraid of do exist. The people in those cultures think Westerners are ignorant of spiritual realities, and to some extent they are right. It was the same complaint we heard in Indonesia and other places about Western missionaries; that the Christian God is unable to contend with the "spirits" that Africans and other nationals have experienced the reality of. It's because Western missionaries are not usually trained to recognize and overcome demonic problems. If God hadn't taught us Himself, we probably wouldn't have learned how to do it either.

Example #83
Victory! Angels Save Eleanor From Death Curse!

In the following account, an Indonesian "black witch" was hired to set a death curse on me, Eleanor. This was the background: When Roy and I were fairly new in Indonesia, I discovered that Bipin, the Indonesian woman we had hired to do the laundry, was stealing the new towels I had brought from America. I noticed the diminishing supply and then noticed that Bipin, in her wrap-around batik skirt, came to work slender and went home fat. No one could eat that much rice! Realizing what she was doing, I confronted her out on the patio. I then insisted that Roy take her home on his motor scooter and retrieve our towels. He did that, and sure enough, our towels were at her house, except for the ones she had already sold. Bipin's dishonesty was especially disappointing because we treated all of our helpers very well and paid them well. Because Bipin was a thief, Roy had to fire her. I am sure he spoke kindly, because he always does, but he did have to fire her.

Bipin's rage at being caught must have festered, because two years later she contracted "Omi" (a black witch) to kill me with a death curse. It could have taken those two years to save up enough money for such a "big" curse—one that also required a blood sacrifice of some kind, a small animal or an infant. We knew of Omi, but at that time didn't know she was a witch. By day she was the "jolly" cook employed by some missionary friends.

One mid-morning when Roy was away on a ministry trip to East Java, I saw Omi walk around the side of my house, cross the patio and go to our open-air kitchen. I thought she had come to have a cup of tea with our cook, although she never before had come to our house. When I saw her I greeted her with "Selamat Siang," the appropriate mid-morning greeting, and she nodded but didn't smile. I did notice that my helpers appeared uncomfortable, but I had no idea why. Then Bipin came around the corner of the house a little later and joined

Omi and the other women. She had not been on our property since we'd had to fire her. I thought it odd, yet didn't suspect malicious intent. In retrospect, I'm sure my helpers knew what was going on and were afraid for me. Since Westerners don't generally think in terms of "curses," I had no idea that Omi and Bipin walking around my property was part of a curse ritual they had to carry out, a physical thing they had to do as "their part" of carrying out the death curse.

Earlier in the day another part of the ritual had been carried out. They, or someone connected with them, threw a dead rat in a plastic bag on our lawn close to the street. I just thought "somebody's trash" and had it removed. We learned later that the symbolism was known to Indonesians and would frighten them, thinking they were marked for death. But I was unaware of those things at the time, so it had no effect on me.

That night, after I went to bed, I got up to get a drink of water from our clean water supply in the living room. As I stepped through the doorway I was suddenly aware of tall, invisible, evil beings in the room, in a semi-circle advancing slowly toward me. I couldn't see them physically, but in my spirit I *felt* their overwhelming presence. I knew their locations in the room and where they were moving, and that they were *tall*. I've learned since then that in the angelic realm, whether evil angels or good angels, "tall" means powerful. I knew the tall evil beings were there and slowly advancing toward me and I was *very afraid*. Roy was gone, and the children were asleep. I whispered loudly, "Get out of here! In Jesus' Name, get out of here!" But they didn't leave; they kept slowly advancing. Then I was terrified. I didn't know what else I could do, because my "big gun," the Name of Jesus, hadn't stopped them! What could I do? *"Oh Jesus!"* I cried out, *"Tell me what to do!"* Suddenly I found myself kneeled over on the tile floor, my head down, arms over my head, praying, *"The Blood, Lord! The Blood!* Over me, over Roy wherever he is, over the children, Oh I don't know what's happening, but *the Blood, Lord, the Blood!"* Immediately God saved me! *When I "prayed the Blood," the evil beings slowly receded and then were gone.* I remember that prayer like it was yesterday. *I thank God that the Blood of Jesus dispels demons.* I have since learned that the symbolism of "covered by the Blood" means that in the spirit realm I was "sinless" and therefore satan could not attack me. The room was peaceful again. I sat up and quietly wept with relief. I think it must have been God's angels who pushed me down, in response to an order from God, and His Spirit had me speak exactly the thing that drove the evil beings away.

The next morning each of my helpers peeked apprehensively around the corner of the living room window instead of walking happily toward the kitchen as they usually did. I knew they feared I would be dead. It was gratifying to see them *beam* as they saw me alive. They were astonished and overjoyed. I pretended nothing had happened, because I wanted Omi to have to be shamed and embarrassed in defeat, and for my helpers to realize that *Jesus is stronger than Omi's evil.* In Jesus' Name I have forbidden satan to *ever* do that to me again or to any member of my family. However, God had saved me, and through the difficult experience He taught me to "pray the Blood." I had never done that before, never "prayed the Blood," never had known the importance of it. But I've done it ever since, as I've realized what a *powerful weapon of defense "the Blood" of Christ is.* With that knowledge I've also been able to help other people, as I hope you will be helped. There is spiritual power in the Blood of Jesus. In direct conflict with evil, the Blood was the shield that evil could not penetrate.

The *Blood* and the *Name* of the Lord Jesus Christ are the words *most feared by satan's realm.* Through them, satan lost his spiritual stronghold on mankind. As Christians, on that basis aren't we "sinless" all the time? No, and in our hearts we all know it. Saved, yes. Sinless, no. It is a mistake to think that because we have salvation, we are free to live carelessly and there will be no consequences on earth. In Indonesia, I hadn't been "sinning" that I knew of, so I think it also has to do with the strength of the evil spirit forces that are arrayed against you. The almost palpable strength of those evil spirit enemies was so great that it was necessary to *plead what they could not overcome: the Blood that defeated them at the cross.*

Comments About Death Curses

I learned that a death caused by a curse is usually one of two things: a fear-induced heart attack or suffocation by demonic spirits. As far as we have ever heard, no Christians have ever been killed by a death curse. God always saves them. *But non-Christians have been killed by such curses.* People who do not have Christ must be unprotected from having to see the demonic beings and literally die of fright, their heart failing them. Or, there can be respiratory failure caused by the demons. If the doctor acting as coroner lives in a witchcraft area, he might suspect a death curse, but how could he prove it? He can only report the medical reality, that the person's heart stopped or he suffered respiratory failure. Even if he suspects that it was a curse death, what could he say? And how would it help? He would have no way to prove it was a demonic attack or be certain "which witch" did it. And he might be afraid to even delve into it, because he doesn't want to be attacked. If I hadn't been protected from seeing my attackers, I might have died also, as many people have. *But Christians have the protection of angel guards, and the powerful shield of the Blood of Christ. Above all people, Christians are blessed!* Obey God in day-to-day life, and pray the Blood at any time, but especially when you are in danger. Use your voice if just in a whisper.

African Syncretism

In 2003 Roy taught a class on Missions at the African Center for Theological Studies in Lagos, Nigeria (another seminary he helped start). All twenty-five of his students were pastors of churches in Lagos, and one of the assignments for the class was to write about the effect of witchcraft on the African Church today. Every one of the pastors knew of other pastors who would go to witch doctors for power, greater attendance and more money for their church. Most of the pastors in Roy's class had never had any teaching about spiritual warfare. Roy kept their papers on file for reference and will list just a few of them. Combining unrelated religious practices like Christianity and spiritism in an attempt to gain extra benefit, as the pastors in Roy's class reported was being done in Nigeria, is called "syncretism." It is an effort to harmonize Christianity with tribal occultism, in hopes of benefitting from both. The supposed Christians who go to church by day and witch doctors by night are either spiritually immature, or they have no true relationship with Christ at all.

Example #84
Effect of Mediums and Witch Doctors on the African Church: A Few Pastors' Reports

1. From a pastor's report about the spiritual difficulties Africans face: "How all these affect the Christian Church today: Even after people have prayed to receive Christ, some are still bound to their fear of the spirits and its powers. Some of our people are still bound by the fear of retribution for forsaking their ancestors and their customs, rituals and taboos or the worship of spirits. So people are in our local congregations who are supposedly Christians, but are still tied to their cultural roots. They have prayed to receive Christ but they are not converted."

2. One African pastor wrote: "The biggest challenge posed by the phenomenon is that consulting these mediums is not limited to unbelievers. So called Christians are caught in the act most of the time. Even Christian ministers have been found to be involved [in this] diabolical practice. What makes this possible is the fact that the consultations are in secrecy and no record is kept for people to know who has been visiting them. In fact the mediums hold it a duty to protect the identity of their customers. Most of the people that come to church still find it easy to go to the medium when they have problems. They believe that the Bible can take care of their heaven while the medium helps them sort out their earthly problems. The result of this is a lack of commitment."

3. An African pastor's analysis of missionaries' inadequate theology: "Church leaders, especially expatriate missionaries, have presented evil inadequately. As far as the African is concerned, God is our Father and we are His children. He does not cause evil, sickness or death. It is a known fact that missionaries, the early church leaders, and some contemporary leaders dismissed spirits, and witchcraft as mere superstition. At this point, though we acknowledge with deep appreciation the role missionaries played in transforming the African society through the gospel, we must also add that *missionaries and early African church leaders failed in understanding the worldview of the African.*"

Warwick Montgomery speaks to that issue in his book, *Demon Possession, Demonology in Anthropological Perspective* (pp. 180–181): "The Western missionaries do not understand the suffering of the Africans. When Africans complain...of being tormented by an evil spirit, they answer that the spirit torments the body but not the soul and that there is no reason to be upset. However, the Gospel is clear on this point. *Jesus DID give his disciples the power to expel demons. If the missionaries do not use it, they are either refusing to put it at the service of the Africans or they have lost it.*" The reason people go to "witch doctors" or "shamans" anywhere in the world is that *they have problems they can't solve,* and if the missionary lacks the spiritual power to help them, they go to the witch doctor.

God's powerful Holy Spirit is Christ's side of the spiritual spectrum, demonstrating God's love and power. Unfortunately, too few Christians have been taught about the Holy Spirit's power, *so to the African, demons hold the power.*

If Christians don't have the strength of God's Holy Spirit within themselves, then they have *less* power than the witch doctor, and the nationals know it. Now Campus Crusade's Jesus FILM is overcoming that barrier. People in other countries "see Jesus" and believe Him. In fact after a Jesus film showing in Africa recently, the camera staff saw that *the audience had gathered in a circle, looking at something. But the cameramen couldn't see anything.* Going down to the group they asked what they were looking at. *"The man in white from the film is standing here talking to us. Can't you see him?"* No, the missionary cameramen could not see the vision.

Example #85
Victory! 31 Miraculous Results of "JESUS" Film!

Campus Crusade for Christ has used the film "Jesus" to present the Gospel to people around the world. As of Spring 2010, the film has been *translated into more than 1,000 languages.* God is bringing knowledge of Christ to millions of people even in closed and semi-closed countries, accompanying the showing of the Jesus film with miracles of healing, visions, and other extraordinary demonstrations of mercy. Jim Green, the current Executive Director of the Jesus Project, has published a beautiful prayer guide called "The Power of Jesus." It has photos and thrilling, miraculous stories from many countries where the Jesus film is being shown. I encourage you to send for it. "Jesus Film Project," 100 Lake Hart Dr., Orlando, Florida 32832. (800) 387–4040, or e-mail:info@Jesusfilm.org. Website: Jesusfilm.org

Following are abbreviated accounts of some of the wonderful results reported in the booklet. How could it be that they could gain those miracles? The people saw Jesus do wonderful things in the film, so they *expected* Him to do the same for them. And He did! Jesus must have been *delighted* with their faith.

Thirty one victories are listed below!

- Malawi, Southeast Africa....angels on the bridge

- Nigeria, West Africa...a special travel mercy for bus carrying the Jesus film team

- Iraq, Middle East...two Muslim leaders have visions of Jesus

- India...idol-worshipping leader dreams of God, sees Jesus film and is converted

- India...Malto villagers see Jesus walking in the clouds, weeping over dead missionary
- India...600,000 villagers reached, including Hindu priest
- Tanzania, East Africa...victory over demonic interference
- Nigeria, West Africa...fed by an angel
- Nepal, South Central Asia...deaf-mute healed
- Central Asia...a dream from God
- North Africa...a powerful dream
- China...grateful shop owner
- West Africa...gravely ill child healed
- Egypt...a dream, then ministry to converted clerics
- Jordan, Middle East...Jesus appears in a taxi
- Mauritius, South and East Africa...300 viewers listened in the cold
- Lebanon, Middle East...a circle of threats
- Ethiopia, East Africa...demonic snake apparition banished, 2,000 people saved
- North Africa...vision of Jesus
- Africa, rural...saved by sound of Jesus film
- Mozambique, southeast Africa...salvation and healing
- Ivory Coast, West Africa...rebel leader converted
- Jordan, Middle East...religious leaders watch Jesus film
- Taiwan, Republic of China...Jesus appears
- Israel, West Bank...26,000 orders for Jesus film in Arabic

- West Africa...prisoners converted

- Brazil, South America...deaf man healed

- Iraq...mission team protected by helicopters

- Philippines, southeast Asia...conversion of rebels

- East Africa...mass response to Jesus

- Central African Republic...witches converted

There are only two spiritual powers in our universe from which people can choose their allegiance: God the Heavenly Father, or satan, the prince of darkness. There are many non-Christian religions, yet all of them (even the belief that "there is no God," or "everything is God"), fall under satan's realm as he encourages and gives power to anything that promotes defiance of, or denial of, God the Father and Jesus. In his book, *Spiritual Warfare, Today and Tomorrow* (p. 22), Dr. C. Peter Wagner writes, "Occult level spiritual warfare deals with demonic forces released through activities related to satanism, witch-craft, freemasonry, eastern religions, new age, shamanism, astrology and many other forms of structured occultism."

You might wonder how it can function, that evil and good are both on this planet and affect people. As a simple illustration, stretch your arms out wide to each side, and wiggle the fingers on both hands. Pretend one hand represents God, and the other hand represents satan. Physically opposite. But they are both alive, both can "wiggle fingers." Just for illustration, say the fingers on the left are satan and demons. They don't stay out at the end of your arm; they want to wiggle "in your face," in your life, causing trouble, inciting to sin. Your other arm represents God's power. It is immensely more powerful, with big muscles and strong hand, but you have to ask for God's forgiveness in order to gain His help. God isn't trying to prove anything. He is "sifting the hearts of men" (Luke 22:31) to see who will be sorry for sin and seek Him. Then He will remain close to that person, helping them, letting them know He is close, and giving them life that will never end.

CHAPTER SIXTEEN

NEW AGE WITCHCRAFT

Example #86
Victory! Woman Escapes New-Age Witches!

AVOID ANYTHING CALLED "New Age." It is demonic witchcraft, presented with a smiling face as the best thing to bring happiness and success. Instead, it is a one-way ticket into demonic deception.

One of Roy's former seminary students married a lovely young starlet who had naively gotten involved with New Age in Hollywood before she was a Christian. She was lonely for friendship and the people at a New Age meeting seemed kind and friendly, so she joined. (She learned later that people who didn't join saw the smiles vanish, and expressions on the faces of the New Age witches become hostile.) But at the early stage, this young woman had no idea it was witchcraft.

A woman was assigned to be her human "spiritual guide" and told her that when she got home "two very nice women spirits" would be in her room to "keep her company and help her." Sure enough, two spirits in the form of transparent women were in her room moving around (demons in the form of female spirits). They smiled at her, and at first she tolerated them. But when they came close and wanted to touch her hair it "freaked her out." She complained to her "human guide" that she didn't want spirits in her room! "Oh, no problem, just sprinkle salt around your bed and they can't approach you." (Roy and I almost laughed at that, because salt was considered an ancient "demon repellant." Nothing new about witchcraft. Advising the young woman to use salt was an admission that the female spirits were demons in the form of departed humans.) She sprinkled salt around her bed, and sure enough, the see-through women disappeared. But the next day something *worse* appeared in her room; a frighteningly ugly male spirit in clothes from the 1800's who looked as though he had been hung. The young woman fled her apartment screaming, jumped into her car and raced away crying, begging God to help her, determined to turn in at the first church she came to. Fortunately, it was "Church on the Way," an excellent church. She zoomed into the parking lot and ran into the office. The staff led her to Christ, and in His Name they forbade the evil spirits to bother her any more. *The trouble stopped.* She began going to that church, and met and married Roy's former seminary student there.

Please note: It is Jesus, and only Jesus, who can stop the demonic harassment caused by New Age. Was the ugly male apparition a departed human spirit? *No,* it was a demon sent to frighten her, probably as retaliation because she rejected the female spirit demons in her room. In the realm of involvement with evil, situations go from *bad to worse.*

Mid-East Demonic "Goddess" Idols

A prominent female TV personality involved in New Age said to the women who listen to her program, "You are the only God you will ever need" (or something similarly absurd and blasphemous). New age followers are "up to their eyeballs" in demonic witchcraft. Remember, *demons aren't around anyone to be "nice."* They hate even each other.

Women are often spiritually sensitive but I think they also tend to be more easily deceived than men, and both their vulnerability and their hunger for dominance has fed that deception. Female involvement in witchcraft is a very old problem. In the Mid-East, the ruling demonic spirits are predominantly female. Bombay's original name was Mumbai, the name of the ruling goddess. Now that the British no longer rule India, that western port city is called Mumbai again. The port of Calcutta is called "Kolkata" again and the ruling demon is "Kali," the ugly Hindu goddess of death. In Ephesus, Turkey, where the Apostle Paul preached, the ruling goddess was "Artemis" (Diana under the Greeks). The Greek "goddesses" are beautifully carved, in the graceful artistry the Greeks were famous for, but their goddesses were *not* "nurturing females." They were idols, lovely in appearance *but filled with demons, just like the idols in India.* A Turkish guide who gave us a private tour explained that Artemis' necklace represents men's testicles, to show that "she" has more power than many men. Power to harm or to help, according to the degree of adulation people accorded "her." *The desire of every demon is to be worshipped by humans, to be "god on this earth."* Deceptive devils find spiritual conspirators among foolish and profane humans, usually women, who consider themselves "gods" because demons manifest themselves through them. Sinful and profane, they choose to become homes of devils.

WHEREVER CHRISTIANITY IS OPPOSED, EVIL RISES. Stay close to God and *away* from evil people. At the "end time" before Christ returns there will be a rise of evil that will confuse people who don't have God's Holy Spirit within them to give them warnings. The Bible tells us that many will be deceived by the kind of "lying wonders" that will be done by satan and demons during that time. In Revelation 13 we read about how satan is "the beast" who will oppress the world in the time just before Jesus returns. But Jesus *will* come, gather and protect the people who belong to Him, put down evil and then restore the planet.

The Holy Spirit came to make Jesus real to us, and real *in* us. Ask Him to be real in you. *New Age is a demonic slavery system, similar to what the entire evil realm suffers. Avoid anything "New Age."*

Example #87
TV Cameraman Tracked By Demons

This is a sad case of a man trapped by New Age. We couldn't set him free because he clung to the witchcraft healing he had received.

When Campus Crusade for Christ was based in California at Arrowhead Springs I got a phone call from the front desk of the hotel, asking for Roy. But he was overseas. The receptionist then asked if I (Eleanor) could come to the hotel to talk to a nervous wreck of a man who had come to Crusade headquarters asking for prayer to "stop the spying." I went, and met the poor man. He had been demonically trailed from the time he received a "New Age" healing of a painful leg. To his dismay, afterwards as he traveled to various cities around the U.S. to film sports events, he was *tracked* by New Age witches. Even though he went to great lengths to keep his travel assignments secret, no matter what city he was in, or what hotel, New Age witches in Hollywood would phone his room and tell him *where* he was, what he was wearing, what he was doing, where he was sitting, what he was reading, what he was eating, etc. That amused the witches but completely unnerved the man. Doubtless that was the cruel thing the witches intended, for they laughed as they told him about himself.

How could the New Age witches track him like that? Because witches are conduits for demonic spirit behavior and messages. In *God Wins* we have told you about some of the people involved in witchcraft; fortune tellers are receivers of messages from demons, influenced by demons, and witches are cooperators with demons and senders of demons. But that is not the same thing as being physically inhabited by demons, as New Age witches are and desire to be. The most prized home for a demon is a human body, because a body offers so many possibilities for control of humans and flagrant display of sin. That is what happens in New Age witchcraft as demons invade profane people under the guise of being helpful "spirit guides." Demonic things occur and the people (usually women) foolishly think they are "goddesses." Delusional. The women have become physical homes of demons and the demons cause the paranormal circumstances.

As a cover, such people invariably deny even the existence of demons. They talk about "spirit guides," and that the "power" is their own. Foolish, deceived, profane. What God says awaits them is not going to be good. The Bible tells us that "those who practice magic arts will be in the fiery lake of burning sulfur, along with the devils that used them" (Revelation 21:8). Many New Age witches consider themselves "goddesses" similar to the goddess statues of the Mid-East. They are similar to those stone statue goddesses only in the fact that their power comes from demons resident *in them*, just like demons "live" in stone idols. The demons within the witches display manifestations and profane human cooperators think those manifestations demonstrate their *own* power. To me, their push into "New Age" occultism seems to reflect an arrogant hostility toward God and men and children, a consuming desire to "rule."

At the lowest rung in the demonic realm are the little "tattle tale" demons that report back to whatever higher ranking evil spirits or witches want information. That is what was happening to the TV cameraman. The demons that accompanied the healing of his leg (the bait he willingly took) were then attached to him and he couldn't get rid of them. The presence of the demons, and harassment by them was the price of his healing. In varying degrees, demons can attach to humans when they commit any kind of severe sin, *but involvement with witches is the worst, because witches are such close conspirators with evil that they can send demons to harass people, as they were doing to the cameraman.*

The cameraman was desperate to get the spying stopped. He was so upset and nervous that even as I met with him at Arrowhead Springs he kept wriggling, couldn't sit still. I feared he was on the verge of a nervous breakdown. Sadly, I had to tell him that he could not be rid of the devils unless he renounced the demonic "healing" of his leg that gave devils the legal right, spiritually, to attach to him and transmit their tattle-tail messages to the witches in Hollywood. He wanted me to pray for his healing, but it would not have done any good unless he renounced his willing contact with demons. When Roy returned home he told the man the same thing. The man went away sad, trembling, beside himself with anxiety. We don't know why the New Age witches tormented him. It was cruel. But "cruel" is entertaining to people whose minds and bodies are homes of demons.

Example #**88**
Victory! Roy Frees Teenage Girl From New-Age "Spirit Friends"!

"Oh give thanks to the Lord, call upon His name; make known
His deeds among the nations. Sing to him, sing praise to Him."
(Psalm 105:1, 2a)

In New Age witchcraft, "spirit guides" are assigned to people. Those guides are demonic and invade the person's mind, giving directions, pretending to be friends, telling lies, harassing their life.

Late one night, Roy got a phone call from a desperate woman who was foster-parenting a teenage girl. The girl was a Christian but very troubled. She frequently ran away, couldn't sleep at night, and attempted suicide by slashing her wrists. "Kathy" (not her real name) *heard six voices and regularly talked to all of them.* She said they were "her friends, her only friends" (which is what the voices said in her mind, to isolate her). When Roy went over, the girl told him their names, insisting they were with her "to be her friends." Roy knew they were demons but didn't say that to Kathy because he needed to maintain conversation with her. When he asked if he could tell them to go, she shouted *"No!"* because they were her "only true friends." That's what the voices in her head were telling her. So she wanted to keep the "friends."

Roy silently prayed for wisdom. Then he asked Kathy, "Does Jesus love you? Is He your friend too?" She hesitated a moment, then said, "Yes," she thought so. "Would Jesus ever lie to you?" "No." "Can we ask Jesus if your friends are His friends too?" She hesitated a moment, then nodded. Roy continued, "If they are Jesus' friends, I know He would want you to keep them."

So he began to pray out loud, *"Jesus, you know how Kathy values these friends. We present them to You. The first is Patricia. If she is your friend, too, then we want her to stay. But if she is not your friend, then in the name of the Lord Jesus Christ I command Patricia to leave right now. I break off her relationship with Kathy completely."* Roy then asked Kathy, "Where is Patricia now?" "She's gone," Kathy whimpered. Roy went through the same process, name by name, with each of the five remaining "friends" until finally all were gone. Kathy broke down and cried because "all her friends were gone." Then, in the Name of Jesus Christ, Roy quietly forbade them to *ever* return to Kathy, in the same way or in any other form. It had taken almost two hours and finally Kathy was tired and wanted to sleep. (Being exhausted is typical of someone who has been freed from evil spirits.) Roy prayed the Blood of Christ's protection over her life and his, and left.

The next morning Kathy's foster mother phoned Roy to thank him. She said that for the first time, *Kathy had slept peacefully through the night. She had returned to being the warm, happy personality she was before her mind had been invaded by demonic "spirit guides" pretending to be her "friends."* We never knew for sure what had happened that allowed demonic spirits to harass Kathy, but most likely it was New Age contacts. Sadly, psychiatric wards have many people like Kathy and can't help them. They can only theorize about what mental condition might have caused them to "hear voices." Jesus is the One who can help them. He knows each person's mind and life.

The teenage girl with spirit friends is an example of "ground level" spiritual warfare, which involves casting demons out of individual people. Dr. C. Peter Wagner teaches about casting out devils in his book (*Spiritual Warfare Yesterday, Today, and Tomorrow*). He writes, "To do it, He [God] uses Christians. He lives in them and works through them." Roy adds, "When a Christian wants to send an evil spirit away from a person, it helps if he can learn the name of the spirit. *The name is generally the specific harassment you have noted.* For instance, a 'spirit of hate.' If you can name it, that demon can't pretend it isn't there. You name it and tell it to leave, in Jesus' Name, and forbid it to return. And you pray the Blood of Christ's protection over yourself and the person you prayed for."

Casting Out Demons

In Matthew 12:29 we are told to *bind the strong man (satan) so we can steal his goods (people he is oppressing).* That is what occurs when we free someone held captive by him.

Roy's General Pattern for Casting Out Demons

1. **Pray for God's help** and the presence of the Holy Spirit to give you wisdom and insight. If possible, work with a second person, who might catch a clue you miss.

2. **Interview the person,** to get as much information and insight about their problem as possible. Inquire what was going on in his or her life *when the problems started* that might have triggered the problem. Had they played with occultic games or gone to a fortune teller or received any objects from someone involved in the occult? Were they heavily involved in hallucinogenic drugs? Were their parents or family in generations past involved in evil? If a person has been molested, it opens the door for satanic harassment, but you must be careful that you *not* plant the idea of sexual harassment in someone's mind who might then falsely accuse someone. Instead, you can ask questions such as, "How did you get along with family members as you were growing up?" Or, "Did anything traumatic happen in your childhood or in your life?" If something is wrong, by that time in the interview the person might remember the problems and speak of them.

3. **Diagnose what the problem is.** If the person has committed or been involved in serious sin, the demon has a right to be there and will not leave until the person sincerely asks God's forgiveness. Then the demon no longer has the "sin" hold on the person. Perhaps the problem is drug related, or the person has participated in witchcraft activities such as séances, or New Age, or is in possession of New Age paraphernalia or a "charm" given by a witch. *The more accurately you can identify the problem, the greater success you will have.*

   Note: If the sin was something committed *against* the person (such as physical abuse), although the *victim is innocent,* the demon of that abuse has to be renounced, so it cannot continue to emotionally harm the victim's life, or allow other spirits such as rage, or depression, or immorality to take root in their lives.

4. **Command satanic harassment or demons to leave, in Jesus' Name and by His Blood.** They are afraid of Him. Then, after you have prayed, have that person speak against satan and his oppression of them, being as specific as possible (basically repeating what you said). This will help *them know what to do if attacked in the future.*

5. **In Jesus' Name forbid any demonic retaliation in any form. Pray the Blood of Christ's protection over the person and yourself.** Satan is annoyed when a Christian helps someone escape some cruel thing he is doing, and we have experienced that he will retaliate against us within 24 hours IF we haven't "prayed the Blood" over our lives. If we have "prayed the Blood" he can't touch us. Also "pray the Blood" of Christ over the other person and your families.

6. **Counsel the person in follow-up.** Encourage him/her to be involved in a church or Bible study and help them arrange that if necessary; don't leave the person spiritually stranded. If possible, help the person to be accountable to a strong Christian. If there was serious sin in their life, remind them evil can come back if the sin resumes. It should be every Christian's desire to lead a clean life; forgiven and pleasing to God.

Three Levels of Spiritual Warfare Praying

In his book *Engaging the Enemy,* Dr. C. Peter Wagner teaches that there are THREE LEVELS of Spiritual Warfare Praying. They are different yet interrelated. All the problems represented by the levels are caused by demonic activity.

- The "FIRST LEVEL" is warfare for a demonized individual, like the teenage girl who was oppressed by demonic "friends," and in Jesus' Name Roy got rid of her demons (Example #88).

- The "SECOND LEVEL" is spiritual warfare against witchcraft groups, New Age, occult organizations, etc. (Example #86).

- The "THIRD LEVEL" is warfare against territorial spirits that hold communities and religious and political systems in bondage. (An account of victory over territorial spirits is Chapter 6, Example #27.) In that situation Roy and the Thai Campus Crusade for Christ Director were able to break the power of regional territorial spirits in northern Thailand. Then the people in surrounding areas could understand and receive the Gospel.

Dr. Wagner counsels: "Christians are told to 'put on the full armor of God, praying always with all prayer and supplication in the Spirit' (Ephesians 6:18). Prayer is the central activity. Prayer will produce faith and obedience, a 'holiness' that seeks God's purposes on earth. A 'holy' person does the will of God. John 2 sums up the context of spiritual warfare: 'You are strong and the word of God abides in you, and you have overcome the wicked one' (1 John 2:14b). 'The weapons of our warfare are not of the flesh, but mighty through God to the pulling down of strongholds [of evil]' (2 Corinthians 10:4)."

Forbid spirits to be anywhere in your home, bothering your family or any of your equipment. You have Jesus; therefore *you give the orders.* Quietly speak, that if any are hanging around your house, to *get out and stay out, in Jesus' Name, and not come back.* If none are there, you haven't lost anything by speaking that command. But if they are there, they have to leave.

And in Jesus' Name *post angels around your home and property,* in a blanket prayer covering what is important to you. When Roy and I pray that way, in Jesus' Name we forbid any evil spirit to cross over our property line. It has made an amazing difference. Then we are protected from the spirits spoken about by the Apostle Paul, the "huge numbers of wicked spirits in the spirit world" (Ephesians 6:11, 12). You can also forbid the enemy to ever disturb your sleep or the sleep of anyone in your household. Pray the Blood of Christ's protection over your entire household.

CHAPTER SEVENTEEN

CHILD SACRIFICE

Murder of the Innocent:
An "Abomination"

S ATAN IS ALWAYS cruel. To gain favors from him, people of ancient cultures put infants and young children into the fires of pagan altars. God called that practice an "abomination," the strongest word used in the Bible to describe a horrific evil. It meant a situation causing "extreme disgust, hatred, abhorrence, detestation, loathing" (*Webster's*). Not only is killing infants a despicable cruelty, in God's sight it is the *ultimate crime*, because humans are *made in His image*.

History of Child Sacrifice: The Canaanites

In his *Handbook for Spiritual Warfare*, Dr. Ed Murphy writes about the *demonic practice of child sacrifice*: "Child sacrifice was *commonly practiced* not only among the pagan Canaanites, but in all probability among most of the major people groups whose inhabitants worshipped the same or similar demonic gods as the Canaanites. *It was a major demonization of the Canaanites, the people God ordered Joshua to destroy at Jericho.* Some Canaanites escaped to Carthage, North Africa, and became the Phoenicians. Drs. Lawrence E. Stager and Samuel R. Wolff report that a *Phoenician cemetery in Carthage*, dedicated exclusively as the repository of the burnt bones of child and animal sacrifices 'is the *largest cemetery of sacrificed humans ever discovered.*' Stager and Wolff also reported that the cemetery is approximately 60,000 square feet, with as many as 20,000 urns in it. Some contain the burnt bones of up to three young children from the same family, aged from early birth to six years old." Murphy, quoting Stager and Wolff (*Child Sacrifice at Carthage—and in the Bible*) p. 247.

"Thousands of urns were lost when the Romans destroyed the

cemetery in 146 BC because Roman law did not permit human sacrifice. *But the evil practice continued.* The sacrifice of little children into the fires of 'Baal,' the Canaanites' major demonic idol, took place continually for at least 600 years (paraphrased from Murphy's *Handbook of Spiritual Warfare*) pp. 246–248. Tertullian, the great Early Church Father, writes about the horrible practice of child sacrifice continuing even in his day. He calls it "the evil activity of satan causing his servants to sacrifice their own children to him." He then writes that *"satan required that unholy crime…and parents were glad to respond,* and fondled [hugged] their children that they might not be sacrificed in tears" (*Child Sacrifice at Carthage—and in the Bible*) p. 247.

God Forbids Sacrificing Infants and Children

"The LORD said to Moses, 'Give the Israelites these instructions, which apply to those who are Israelites by birth as well as to foreigners living among you. *If any among them devote [give as an act of devotion] their children as burnt offerings to Molech [another idol inhabited by satan], they must be stoned to death…* And if people of the community refuse to execute the guilty parents, then I myself will turn against them and cut them off from the community" (Leviticus 20:1–5). In Deuteronomy 18:10–12 *God said, "Let no one be found among you who sacrifices his son or daughter in the fire* [as the Canaanites and Phoenicians did]."

WHY CHILDREN? Satan is a coward, and cowards attack "easy prey." Anything smaller or weaker is easier to hurt because that person can't defend himself or herself. That is why evil people abuse children, and evil men abuse women. *Satan attacks infants and young children because that offends God the most. Humans are made in His image,* and satan's goal is to mar (destroy) that image. The type of heart God wants all people to have is often best represented by children, who usually are innocent, sincere, and trusting. "Unless you change and become like [have the hearts of] little children, you will never enter the kingdom of heaven. Therefore, whoever humbles himself like this child is the greatest in the kingdom of heaven. And whoever welcomes a little child like this in my name welcomes me" (Matthew 8:3–5). *That is the attitude God wants people to have toward children.*

When people obey God's Word, or even tenets of common decency, infants and children are safe. But when people are hard-hearted and cruel, innocent little children suffer and sometimes die. Developing babies, and then infants and young children, are physically and emotionally very vulnerable. They need the *protection* of caring adults. They are guiltless and helpless, with no power at all, and unless they are protected by caring adults they are prey to bullies, human and demonic. Oppressing infants and children *is the opposite of the way God wants people to treat them.* "He [Jesus] said to them, 'Let the little children come to me, and do not hinder them, for the kingdom of God belongs to such as these. I tell you the truth, anyone who will not receive the kingdom of God like a child will never enter it.' And *he took the children in his arms, put his hands on their heads and blessed them*" (Mark 10:14–16). Likewise, our behavior should be a *blessing* to children, not a danger.

Example #89
God Cares About Unborn Infants

True Story "The Smell of Rain"

Some people think an infant could not remember a pre-birth experience. But a little girl in Texas, born when her mother was only 24 weeks pregnant, *did* have memories from her first days after being born. This can only mean that unborn infants at the same stage of development are *also* capable of acquiring memories. This moving account shows how *God loves even developing babies!* The following is her true story from Dallas, March 10, 1991.

Complications had forced Diana Blessing, only 24 weeks pregnant (5 months), to have an emergency caesarian to deliver Dana, the couple's new daughter. She was 12 inches long and *weighed one pound.* There was only a 10% chance that she could live through the night. If she lived, the doctor said she would never walk, talk, would probably be blind, suffer mental retardation, and more. Dana's underdeveloped nervous system was essentially raw. She lay in an incubator and the parents could not even cradle her against their chests. All they could do was pray that God would stay close to their little girl. Nothing changed immediately, but as the weeks went by, baby Dana slowly gained an ounce of weight here, a bit of strength there.

At last, when Dana was 2 months older, her parents held her for the very first time. Doctors still had no hope for her having a normal life. But five years later, on one blistering afternoon in summer of 1996, near their home in Irving, Dana was talking non-stop with her mother and several adults sitting nearby, when suddenly she fell silent. Hugging her arms across her chest, little Dana asked, "Do you smell that?" Smelling the air and an approaching thunderstorm, Diana replied, "Yes, I think we are about to get wet. It smells like rain."

Still caught in the moment, Dana shook her head, patted her thin shoulders with her small hands and loudly announced, *"No, it smells like Him. It smells like God when you lay your head on His chest."* In the incubator, during those long days and nights of her first months of life, when she couldn't yet see, and her nerves were too sensitive for her parents to touch her, Dana felt God holding her "on His chest." It was His loving scent that she remembers so well (http//activerain.com/blogsview/834930/the-smell-of-rain-true-story-of-dana-lu-blessing).

Child Sacrifice Today: Abortion

In the centuries of child sacrifice into fires, satan had blinded people spiritually (as in Example # 29). They could no longer tell right from wrong. He worked to make evil so socially acceptable that mothers *weren't bothered* by throwing their child/children into fire! Shocking! Today we think that could *never* happen, yet satan is using the *same deceit now*, to blind people as to what is morally right or morally wrong. He makes it socially acceptable to throw thousands of babies into the chemical fire of abortion every day, fires that burn the infants to death!

God says He knew each person before any of us were born on earth. He said, *"I knew you before I formed you* in your mother's womb" (Jeremiah 1:5). That applies not only to you and me, but to *all* babies, in all wombs, in all stages of development, in all eras. So in *God Wins* we refer to an unborn infant as a baby, because God considers the developing infant *a person He knows, just as He knows you and me.*

Satan has caused society's view of "human life" to become so debased that in a pregnancy, the definition "human life" *depends solely* upon whether the expectant mother *wants* it. If she wants it, it is considered a "baby in utero" and the medical community will go to extreme measures to keep the "baby" alive, even giving it prenatal surgery if necessary. But if it is *unwanted*, it is considered merely a "blob of tissue;" a non-person, *and its right to live is deemed void.* So it is mercilessly burned with chemicals, cut up, and discarded or used for vanity products. That is *demonic! It is as bad as what the Canaanites did.* If the mother had any compassion at all for human life, she would have given it up for adoption! But because women who get an abortion are generally told that "It's just a blob of tissue," and they *can't see the cruelty of what is happening, many of them are naïve, many of them lack appropriate alarm and rage and remorse.* And sadly, a percentage of the women who have repeated abortions genuinely don't care how their sexual behavior affects the human beings they conceive. Or care that an infant has a right to live, and be raised in a loving home, with both parents. Women who are casual about sex and infants are today's "Canaanites."

Humans are *created in God's image* (Genesis 1:26). *God holds life as being sacred.* People are meant to live and achieve on earth and then continue living in Heaven, an actual physical world some people have seen (including a friend of ours), a world that is more interesting and beautiful than anything that exists on earth. People were created for that wonderful "forever life" *before they were even born.* The fact that God says He knew you "before I formed you in your mother's womb" represents at least two things:

1. The fact that *every infant is a high creation,* intended by God to live and accomplish on earth, and after that to live forever. God gave humans an amazing advantage: a brain so complex that it has literally *hundreds of billions of nerve cells,* formed and developed throughout fetal life. No other creature has a brain that can compare.

2. The issue of the woman causing pain to something precious to God; a developing infant known to Him since
long BEFORE the baby was even formed in the her womb.

After an abortion, when some women realize what actually happened to their baby, many have to be in grief counseling for months.
At the time, abortion seemed an easy way to be rid of the unwanted
infant. But having destroyed it will always be a pain in her heart. And
the infant was not unwanted! Hundreds of childless couples long to
adopt a baby. The baby could have been given into loving arms; she
didn't have to kill it. It means she had little or no comprehension of
the fact that it was the God of the Universe who "designed" and gave
"life" to the infant she discarded.

Most abortions are done for women's personal reasons. Some
women have difficulties that interfere with the probability that she
could be an effective mother: her profession, her marital status, the
availability of time to devote to a child. Yet most people would agree
that killing infants is a grievous thing. I sympathize with women who
are young and frightened and embarrassed and know their parents
would be angry. Or women who are pregnant from rape or incest.
Sadly, the majority of women who seek abortions weren't using a contraceptive. And in the abortionist's office the woman was probably
told that the developing baby "is just tissue," without brain or feelings,
and that what is done to the infant "won't matter." It *does* matter. And
now that science knows more, honorable doctors acknowledge that
even a 4 month old fetus can gain impressions and feel pain.

If any woman reading this book is pregnant with an unwanted
baby, *please ask God to give you a way to let your baby live.* You are
two people, living in one body, *each of you with a right to exist.* Please
don't be a "Canaanite," and kill your child like the worst possible
"wicked witch" fairytale, in which the infant is confined, is doomed
to die, and has no way to escape. *Killing helpless infants and children
is what demons have gotten hard-hearted people to do for centuries.*
Why? Because demons hate God. And they hate people, because people
are created in God's image. And they are jealous because people who

love God will get to live forever in Heaven while they, the demons and satan, will be cast away.

The in utero infant is gaining the marvelous body he or she will need in order to succeed on earth. Please respect that amazing development. After three months in the womb the fetus has *emerging consciousness and sensitivity to pain*. Above all, don't cause pain. That is the thing devils most like to *do*. And each abortionist is being used by devils as he kills infants. He is a 21st century *Canaanite*, used by the same demons, killing the helpless. To abort a developing infant beyond 3 months, especially from 5 months until day of birth, is *a torture killing*. No anesthetic is used. If the same thing were done to animals, the perpetrators would be arrested and punished. Please do not put your innocent unborn infant through that hell. *Instead, pray to God to lead you in how to help both you and your infant.* He will. He will be pleased that you want to let your baby *live*. There are many churches and organizations that would be happy to help you.

Who Is at Fault?

The greatest fault in murdering unborn infants lies with people who run abortion mills. They encourage abortion, which is very profitable. And unless the abortionists are ignorant or unthinking, they know what happens during abortion. They know that infants beyond 3½ months in the womb suffer terribly as they are being aborted. Abortionists have *seen* women's abdomen's *twist* as the infant writhes in agony when a corrosive (skin destroying) substance is injected into the amniotic fluid and burns him alive. And they know that infants thrash to avoid the knife or scissors if they are being killed that way. I've heard women comment, "But the procedure is so silent." Of course it is silent! The woman is sedated and the baby is submerged in uterine fluid, unable to scream its agony. Have you ever tried to scream underwater? It is impossible. But in the infant's mind he *is* screaming! The dead baby goes back to God, despite what cruel adults have done to it. But the people who did it, and sanctioned it, and profited from it, will be on their way to hell unless they genuinely repent.

About a decade ago, the owner of a large abortion mill lost two of his adult daughters and their husbands and several young grandchildren when their private plane nose-dived straight down into a cemetery, close to a memorial for unwanted infants. Tragic, ironic justice. We wouldn't have wished that grief on anyone, but we also wouldn't have wished agony and death on the thousands of infants the man's abortion business killed and possibly still kills because abortion is so lucrative.

Official Injustice

If a frightened teenager drops her new-born baby into a trash can, she is held for murder. But if the same teenager had gone to an abortionist to have her baby killed, neither the girl nor the abortionist would have been charged with a crime. The effect on the baby would have been the same. Death. But because the girl discarded the baby herself, she is held for murder. The professional baby killer is not. He has probably killed hundreds, perhaps thousands, of infants; and *she is arraigned in court for letting one baby die.* The scales of justice are not balanced.

But the *primary cause of abortions is the blatant, widespread immorality of today's culture.* Unwanted infants didn't ask to be conceived, and they certainly didn't ask to suffer a cruel death. That agony was forced upon them by women who couldn't be bothered to use a contraceptive or who mistakenly thought the infant wouldn't suffer during abortion. And the men involved were not moral enough to avoid fathering a child they didn't want. That doesn't mean God doesn't still love them, but it does mean that the women (and men) are living in a way that demeans the value of life, whether their children remain alive or are doomed to die. *Each child deserves loving parents and a stable home life.*

There Is Forgiveness

God's anger about abortion does not mean that He doesn't still love the women who have had abortions. He does still love them, and if they genuinely repent and ask His forgiveness, He will forgive them.

But the babies they aborted are still dead. That part of the tragedy cannot be undone.

I know of a woman who met her aborted son in Heaven. For years this woman had secretly grieved over the baby she had aborted. Then she asked Jesus to please forgive her and come into her life. He did. Not long afterward, *He gave her a very vivid dream in which she was in Heaven, and she met the child she had aborted, a boy.* He was about twelve years old by then, but *she knew him immediately,* and was thrilled that he knew her too, and was happy to see her. The woman wept as she told about it. *She was so glad for that evidence that his life had continued.* And because she is forgiven, she will be in Heaven someday too, and see her son again. Heaven is a very real place, as real as earth but more wonderful, and in Heaven there will be *no more sorrow.*

In Revelation 21:3–4 we read about Heaven: "Behold...God Himself will be among them, and He will wipe away every tear from their eyes; and there will no longer be any mourning, or crying, or pain...they have passed away. Behold, I [God] am making all things new."

Stages in Fetal Development

1 month (4 weeks) Using electron microscopes and fiber-optic devices, Lennart Nilsson, famed Swedish researcher and photographer of pre-birth infants has proven that infants *have extremely complex bodies from very early in development.* At just 4 weeks (one month) in the womb, and just ½ inch in size, the embryo has a heart that is pumping blood to its liver and aorta.

1½ months (6 weeks) The embryo would still feel no pain. That ½ inch body is scarcely visible, but in that tiny body *100,000 new nerve cells are created every minute!* By the time of birth there will be some 100 billion new nerve cells. Nilsson (*A Child Is Born*) p. 90.

2 months (7 weeks–almost 2 months) The embryo has been transformed from a single cell into many millions, all precisely programmed for their specific tasks. By two months (8 weeks) the embryo is only 1½ inches long from top of head to rump, but *everything to be found in a fully grown human being has already been formed* (*A Child Is Born*) p. 78.

A Crucial Time

3 months (12 weeks) Prior to three and a half months, the developing fetus is asleep, as though under anesthesia in a hospital. *But at three and a half months the infant's mind and nerves begin to awaken. They desperately try to avoid the knife.* To America's shame and the world's horror, the U.S. government legalized killing unborn infants at *any stage in their development, including the day of their birth (called partial-birth abortion).* No mercy, no anesthetic. It is torture killing. The women (and men) who pushed for that shocking law, and the politicians who caved to those demands, are modern day "Canaanites," just as guilty as ancient Canaanites who threw their young children into fire. *What a horrific black mark that is on America, a nation that used to be known for Christian mercy.* Any abortion beyond 3 months is a violation of the most basic rule of decency: Do not cause pain. I beg all people reading this book to *please have respect for developing infants.* They *have no way to protect themselves.* If you are pregnant and don't want to be, please *let the baby live and give it into loving arms.* And in the future, if you don't want an infant, please prevent conception. The infant should not have to suffer because the woman was careless or uncaring.

4 months (16 weeks) The baby's *brain* and nervous system are *awake.* The tiny infant is only about *4 inches long, but can feel fear and pain* (*A Child Is Born*) p. 110. Nilsson said he was surprised at how soon in development an infant is *fully human.* In the 3rd and 4th months *it can grasp with its hands and kick with its feet.*

4½ months (18 weeks) The baby's body just needs refinements like eyelashes and fingernails and size and fully developed organs.

5 months (20 weeks) Evidence persuaded Dr. Anand that fetuses can feel pain by 20 weeks gestation [5 months] and possibly earlier (*NY Times*, 2008/02/10).

5–6 months (20–24 weeks) The infant's growth within the mother becomes noticeable. *All major systems are in place* in the baby, but refinements continue.

7 months (28 weeks) The infant's *eyes are open* and it will use its hands to shield its eyes from the light if a fetoscope with a light attached to it is inserted into the uterus (*A Child Is Born*), p. 112.

At 7 months the baby can also see a rosy glow through the thinned uterus and *hear sounds and music and voices* (*A Child Is Born*) p. 114. Can babies in the womb hear voices and form attachments? A mother who enjoyed classical music often held music tapes to her abdomen as her baby was developing. Her son became a musical prodigy, playing his violin in Carnegie Hall when he was only 19 (*San Bernardino Sun*), June 18, 2010.

Jesus said, "See that you do not despise one of these little ones, for I say unto you that their angels in Heaven continually see the face of My Father who is in Heaven" (Matthew 17:10).

CHAPTER EIGHTEEN

SATAN AND DEMONS

T HE SCRIPTURES CLEARLY teach that there are three orders of spirit beings that are part of our world—namely, *Deity, angels, and human beings* and that *these three orders are in constant, functioning contact"* Warner (*Spiritual Warfare*) pp. 26, 27. "Deity" means God the Father, Jesus, and the Holy Spirit. *Angels* means God's holy angels, *and* evil angels known as satan and demons. Some people call demons the "dark angels."

How Did Satan Get Here?

We also read about satan's fall in Revelation 12:7-9. "And there was war in heaven, Michael and his angels waging war with the dragon [satan]. The dragon and his angels [demons] waged war and they were not strong enough, and there was no longer a place found for them in heaven. And the great *dragon* was thrown down, the *serpent* of old who is called the devil and satan, *who deceives the whole world;* he was thrown down to the earth, and his angels [demons] were thrown down with him" (Revelation 12:9). For many centuries pagan peoples have realized that "dragons" and "serpents" and ugly-faced carvings represent demonic power: dragons in China, cobras in India, and ugly carvings in Africa and South America and elsewhere. Many people in those areas honor the demons represented by those reptiles.

Background

"The accuser of our brethren has been thrown down, who accuses them before our God day and night" (Revelation 12:10). When satan and the other fallen angels were expelled from Heaven, doubtless they were bitter. As Dr. Warner expressed it, "They became like disgruntled employees who throw sand into the gears of the machines they operate in order to sabotage operations and 'get' the boss. *The fallen* angels now use their delegated power in the material realm to create alienation and to pervert God's good creation. Human suffering and the destructive forces in nature were not part of what God pronounced 'very good' [Genesis 1:31]. This is the work of an enemy. They operate, as it were, on a leash—outside of which God retains His absolute sovereignty. Satan and his forces have tried, whenever possible, to mar the reflection of God's glory in nature by *introducing enmity, perversion, and even catastrophe* into this realm. [That certainly suggests demonic influence in political centers of the world.] 'For the creation was subjected to frustration, not by its own choice, *but by the will of the one who subjected it*' (Romans 8:19–21). Satan was the one who subjected it" Warner (*Spiritual Warfare*) pp. 30–32.

"The power of gods [devils] to assist or resist Yahweh [God] in war, to hinder answers to prayers, to *influence* 'natural' disasters, to inflict diseases on people, to deceive people, and so forth, *is assumed throughout the Bible*" Gregory A. Boyd (*God at War*) p. 118. Are illnesses and catastrophes just a "normal" part of living on this earth? Perhaps not. Mankind has virulent enemies in the unseen. "*The 'world in between'* [the invisible spiritual world] *is characterized by warfare, and earth is its battleground*" (Gregory A. Boyd).

What Do Satan and Demons Do?
Lie, Oppress, Harm, Deceive, Torment

Prior to being thrown down to earth Lucifer had become proud, jealous, selfish, rebellious, unsuitable for Heaven. Being expelled from Heaven and cast down to earth was not the "throne above the stars" that he had envisioned for himself. It was a literal "put down." Even his name was changed. He became "satan" and seemingly took about a third of the other angels with him in his rebellion (Revelation 12:4, 5). Those angels became known as "demons" and are his army.

Demons don't "love" satan; there *is no love in that realm*. Separated from God, who alone is love, *neither satan nor demons are capable of love*. It is probable that they even hate each other. Unlike the freedom of self-determination that they enjoyed under God's authority, under satan's rule the demons are locked into a system of servitude, in which every demon has to obey larger, higher-ranking demons or be punished. A friend of ours who cast a demon out of a man asked the demon where it wanted to be sent. "Should I send you to satan?" "Nooo," the demon begged fearfully. "Couldn't you just send me to Jesus?" How sad. Too late. He made his choice when he rebelled in Heaven.

Demons are satan's unwilling, but "locked-into-service" army. Cast out of Heaven along with satan because they, too, were puffed with pride, they *each* seemed to hope to "be God." That's why demons seek worship from witches and their followers. Adulation from humans is their *one way of getting to "be God"*—to at least somebody. But instead of being fully able to enjoy that status, each demon is also enslaved to satan, who is the personification of "hate." Demons are without God and therefore *without love*, so everything they do is bitter, with evil motive and evil consequence.

Demons have names that represent their destructive assignments against mankind: "spirit of fear," "spirit of hatred," "spirit of violence," "spirit of lying," "spirit of greed," "spirit of pride," "spirit of murder," "spirit of addiction," "spirit of sloth," "spirit of lust," "spirit of rage," and many more. *Involving people in sin is the "work" that demons do.* For every destructive human behavior you can name, there are vast numbers of evil spirits, with the specific assignment of involving people in that particular sin. Roy has found when counseling people harassed by demons that the closer he can get to *identifying the name of each demon,* commanding them *by name* to leave, the better success he has in getting rid of them.

Avoid Cruelty: It Is Demonic

Satan's attitudes are the opposite of God's. God operates a realm of love; satan operates a realm of hate. And Satan and demons hate people, and people deeply influenced by demons hate other people. Especially avoid any religion or individuals or groups in which you note "hate" and violent mistreatment of others. It invariably manifests itself in "high control," the submerging of the individual into group dogma, and even violence or the threat of violence toward people who hold different views. Those are attitudes of people who do *not* have God in their lives. Cruelty expresses satan's mind, his diabolical delight in inflicting pain. Through the bloody violence he initiated and sustained over the centuries, satan mercilessly sacrificed many millions of lives. From the holocaust to the over 40 million abortions annually worldwide, satan has been the "god of death," working through cruel political and religious and criminal organizations. The killing of innocent people is still going on everywhere in the world. In North Africa, adherents of Islam fall upon African villages at night and kill tribespeople, especially Christians like the Dinkas. *Religions of violence are demonic.*

People who are cruel know their minds churn with thoughts of hatred and violence, self-importance, and hunger for power over others. What they might not know is that their sadistic thoughts and their desire to harm others are *caused* by demons. Or, if they suspect that, they don't seem to care. Every person is responsible before God for what he enjoys dwelling upon mentally, and he is also responsible for what he does to other people. *There is no such thing as loving God and being cruel.* Those are *opposites*. People who claim they are doing evil things "for the honor of their god" or their religion, either have a demonic god or they are willingly deceived. Satan's purpose in giving cruel thoughts is so people will act upon those thoughts and harm other people. In some religious cultures men behave violently and cruelly even to their own sisters and wives. About the viciousness of Saddam Hussein's Iraqi secret police, who torture-killed thousands of prisoners, General Schwartzkopf described the participating Iraqi forces as being "not of the same human race [i.e. demonic, subhuman]" George Otis (*The Last of the Giants; Lifting the Veil on Islam*). pp. 114–115. That sadism, "delight in excessive cruelty" (*Webster's Dictionary*), expresses satan's mind and came also from Hitler and Stalin and the cruel Japanese during WWII. It comes from Muslim treatment of non-Muslims and women they feel free to abuse. And it comes from individuals who torture within the secrecy of their own homes. They are sub-human, the type God was sorry he had created and would have destroyed in the flood if they had lived at that time.

Names of Satan in the Bible

They describe his position, his immoral character, and the punishment that awaits him.

1. Abaddon (Revelation 9:11) Hebrew for "angel (demon) of the abyss," the bottomless pit

2. Accuser (Psalm 109:6; Revelation 12:10)

3. Adversary (Revelation 9)

4. Apollyon (Revelation 9:11) Greek for "angel (demon) of the abyss," the "bottomless pit."

5. Beelzebub (Matthew 10:25; Mark 3:22) the ruler of demons

6. Belial (2 Corinthians 6:15) the devil

7. deceiver of the world (Revelation 12:9)

8. devil (Matthew 4:1, 5; 25:41; John 6:70; 13:2; Ephesians 4:27; 6:11; 1 Timothy 3:6, 7; Hebrews 2:14; 1 Peter 5:8; Revelation 2:10; 20:2, 10) "And the devil, who deceived them, was thrown into the lake of burning sulfur."

9. dragon (Revelation 12:9)

10. enemy (Matthew 13:28, 39)

11. evil one (Matthew 13:19, 38; John 17:15; Ephesians 6:16; Hebrews 2:14; 1 Peter 5:8; Revelation 2:10; 20:2, 10)

12. father of lies (John 8:44)

13. god of this world (2 Corinthians 4:4)

14. liar (John 8:44)

15. murderer (John 8:44)

16. prince of the power of the air (Ephesians 2:2)

17. ruler of demons (Matthew 9:34)

18. ruler of this world (John 12:31; 14:30; 16:11)

19. serpent of old who is called the devil and satan (Revelation 12:9)

Example #90
Demon-Controlled Man in Indonesia

Satan is an oppressor and tormentor. In Indonesia we met one of his victims in 1968 when we were young new missionaries living in Bogor, in the hills above Jakarta. Roy and Mrs. Aswandi, our translator, invited ten church leaders and their wives to our home. Roy explained why we had come to Indonesia and what we hoped to accomplish for Christ in their country. We were seated in a large, elongated circle in our living room and Roy showed visual aids of his evangelism materials and explained their use in helping people learn to know Christ personally. The pastors and their wives seemed pleased, and wanted to pray for Roy. Several of them prayed. I could only understand a few of their phrases: "Bapa kama jang ada disorga" (Our Father who is in Heaven). And "Dalam Nama Jesus" (In the Name of Jesus).

Then an Indonesian man seated about ten feet away from me began "praying" in an oddly aggressive way. God commanded loudly to my mind, *"Stop him!"* I whispered, "satan, in Jesus' Name, stop!" The man immediately became confused and stammered to a stop. He got up and left, not looking at anyone on his way out. The shocked Indonesians told us he had been cursing Roy, cursing the Campus Crusade ministry, cursing our evangelistic booklets, cursing any effort Roy would make to bring Indonesians to Christ. They were afraid to try to stop the man for fear he would curse them, too. Mrs. Aswandi had invited the man to our home because he worked for a Western mission organization (that doubtless didn't know it either!) The pastors and their wives had been aghast at the man's words and wondered what had caused him to stop so abruptly. Through our translator I told them what God had commanded me to do and they were pleased.

We learned that the demonized man lived on the other side of a tall stone wall that separated our homes. (That was the way the Dutch built their homes when they ruled Indonesia for 400 years as the Spice Islands.) Occasionally Roy met the man on our sidewalk as he was going to work, and Roy always greeted him. The man looked away, wouldn't speak, and hurried by. However, Roy is a cheerful and hopeful man and he was determined to try to "love him into the Kingdom."

Church leaders said the man was a professing Christian, but had evil attitudes and conduct so they considered him evil, or at the very least extremely unpleasant and puzzling. We realized the truth of that as we heard him yelling loudly at night and pounding on the walls of his house for *hours,* sometimes for four unbroken hours. We didn't see how anyone could have that much strength! We realized it must be a demonization, but nothing in Roy's seminary training had equipped him to help such a person. We earnestly prayed for him but didn't know what else to do. And the man had not spoken to Roy since he was in our home. So Roy didn't feel free to ask him about the pounding.

But one night at around 11 p.m., in the midst of his yelling and banging, we heard the man cry out loudly, *"Roy! Roy! Come and help me! Please come and help me!"* Over and over. The entire neighborhood could hear him. It was the first time he had spoken to Roy since he was in our home. Roy got an Indonesian Christian to go with him to the distraught man's home and they prayed earnestly for him, *but nothing changed.* It was before Roy and I had any experience in attempting to set a demon-possessed person free. Later, we learned that we needed *tell* the offending demon to get *out* of the person, *leave him alone, in Jesus' Name.* As Christ's ambassadors, instead of pleading with God to get rid of the demon, Roy and his fellow Christian had needed to give a *direct order* against satan, in Jesus' Name. Since that time, we've helped many people. But at that time, as new missionaries, we didn't know what to do to help the man, and neither did any of our fellow missionaries. I am telling it in this book so if you are ever confronted with someone like that man, you will know that instead of pleading with God on behalf of that person, you need to directly "order the demon to leave, in Jesus' Name."

Later we learned the man had been raised on one of the most severely demonized islands in all of Indonesia, an island known to be openly controlled by devils (as in chapters five and seven). Roy was sad that he hadn't been able to help the man, despite pleading with God on his behalf, but at that stage neither we nor any fellow missionaries knew that Christians can "give orders" in Jesus' Name and the enemy has to obey. It was not until we were back in America that we learned what we should have done, and what other missionaries needed to know also. And if the man had brought demonic masks with him from his island, those masks needed to be smashed and burned, to deny the demons a home.

Example #91
Victory! Jesus Rescues Demon-Controlled Guatemalan Youth!

"Sing to the Lord a new song, for He has done marvelous things."
(Psalm 98:1)

Roy's cousin, Dr. Jerold Reed, was long-term director of the Covenant Mission work in Mexico. He wrote to us of a case in Guatemala in which a *teenage Christian youth made a pact with satan* when he was in severe trouble. (We'll call the boy "Jose.") A powerful demon entered Jose and took over his body. It talked through him, put him in rages, threatened to kill him, and went in and out of him. A missionary, Rev. Norman Parish, told the boy to renounce his part of the pact he had made with satan. *The boy did that,* but suddenly another voice came out of his mouth, saying "I'm too late, I'm too late." It was a lengthy battle, with many people praying over a period of weeks, but without permanent success.

Then God gave Norman an idea. Instead of telling the demon to get out of the teenager, in Jesus' Name, he forbade the demon to leave Jose until it renounced its hold on him. And in Jesus' Name Norman forbade the demon to leave until he (Norman) gave it permission to go.

The demon became upset. He didn't want to be restricted. He tried to make deals with the missionary. Speaking from Jose, the demon said, "If you let me go I will close down a [long term] center of witchcraft in Guatemala City." The missionary commanded the demon to shut it down anyway, in Jesus' Name. (A month later the witchcraft center was closed.)

But the missionary still didn't allow the demon to leave Jose, and the demon tried to offer other "deals." (*Note:* The missionary, indwelled by God's Spirit, had authority to give orders and the demon *had to obey.*) The demon was frantic at being confined. It cried out, "Let me go! I have never been confined to one place for so long. *Now I know what it will be like to be confined to hell!*" (No question in the demon's mind that he would be going there.) Finally the spirit said, "I renounce my claim on Jose." Norman commanded the spirit to leave Jose and never return. But he seemingly hadn't known to pray the Blood of Christ's protection over the youth, and forbid the demon to return, (Just as Roy and I didn't know to do that when we tried to help the little Mexican girl in Example #1) The demon convulsed the youth, throwing him to the floor. It left, but then it came back and gave the youth *superhuman* strength, so that several men had to use all their might to restrain him. Rev. Parish commanded, "Spirit, in the Name of Jesus I command you to give me your name and come out of Jose and never return." The spirit answered, "My name is 'Death!'" And it left. At that same hour the witch doctor (male witch) that had been following them and going against them, died. (In witchcraft, if a demon cannot carry out a death curse, that demon will sometimes go back and kill the witch.) Later, an angel made himself known to Rev. Parish, saying he was sent by God to guard over Jose.

Rev. Parish, unconvinced, "had had it" with "voices" and put the supposed angel to the test, asking him, "Why did Jesus come in the flesh?" The angel responded, "To be a ransom for mankind." The angel stayed with Jose, protecting him throughout his teenage years, until he was firmly established in Christ. It had been an extremely bad situation. The boy had been foolish and sinful in what he did, *but God did not abandon him.* His body had been "controlled" by a strong demon, but his spirit was still owned by God and God fought for him.

Example #92
Victory! Demon-Possessed Chinese Woman Set Free!

This is an example of actual demon-possession where someone is *"owned"* by a demon. It is an extreme situation, but not uncommon in cultures where people don't have Christ. And not only does satan oppress people, but he delights in torturing them. Mrs. Filip Malmvaal, of the Swedish Mission in China, reported that there is nothing demons like so much as causing pain. (That applies also to people who are demonized. They are cruel, controlled by demons.) The following true story was reported by Mrs. Malmvaal, a Swedish missionary...

"In Saratsi, North China, a woman was demon-possessed. The demons tied her with ropes and chains and burnt her with hot irons. She had been possessed for two years. *Her family wanted to dedicate her to the devil so she could become a fortune-teller medium [and make money for them].* But on the way to the 'Devil's Temple,' the demon-possessed woman broke away from her family and ran to the gate of the Swedish missionaries and they gave her sanctuary." Mrs. Malmvaal reported, "Now the battle began. Together with co-workers I had prayed for many possessed Chinese, but never had we been in such a battle as this. There were never fewer than two praying and they prayed hour after hour. You cannot for one minute take your thoughts away from the Blood and the Cross or you will lose power; and never have anyone with you who is afraid. *You must take your stand that the enemy has been conquered through the work of Christ.* We would pray...then sing of the blood and the cross.

"After hours of battle, the woman would become rational, *but she would not name the name of Jesus,* and so we knew she had not been freed. This kept on for three weeks...Someone called, 'Come at once; she is very violent.' Miss Freelander and two of our Chinese Bible women went with me. We had not prayed long before the evil spirits *spoke through her* and said, 'I am well now; you can go to bed' [a demon pretending to be the woman herself]. I said, 'In the name of Jesus, we will not leave this woman before you have left her.' We prayed for some time, when the evil spirits said, 'We did not know that you were so determined as all this; we have waited for this evening to make her go out and take her own life.' This was spoken in Chinese through the woman. We prayed on for about half an hour, when *the evil spirits left her and she began to pray, and together with us praise the name of our blessed Lord Jesus Christ.* She was wonderfully saved, and learned to read her Bible and sing hymns" (*Demon Experiences in Many Lands*) p. 74.

Can a Christian be Demon-Possessed?

Is it possible that a person can have Jesus *and* demons in his life? "Yes," as strange as that seems, especially if the demons were there *before* the person received Christ and were not expelled. In the Early Church, so many people came from pagan backgrounds that it was common to have a "rite of exorcism" to expel any demons that might be hanging on to the person's life. Then that person could grow in his relationship with Christ without the hindrance of demonic harassment.

A Christian can be oppressed, even "controlled," inhabited, like the Guatemalan youth, but a *Christian cannot be owned by satan.* Possession implies ownership, but "it would be impossible to be *owned* by satan and Christ at the same time" Warner (*Spiritual Warfare*) p. 80. The demon clearly was *in* the youth, and his own sin of seeking help from satan had allowed it to come in. But the demon did not own him. Jesus owned him—and fought for him—and won. Jesus is the *superior power.*

With his *own* Blood, Jesus redeemed all people who sincerely ask God for forgiveness of sin, the thing that separated them from God. The Apostle Paul wrote, "For it was the Father's [God's] good pleasure for the fullness [of God] to dwell in Him [Christ], *and through Him to reconcile all things to Himself, having made peace through the blood of His cross.* And although you were formerly alienated and hostile in mind, engaged in evil deeds...yet He has now reconciled you in His fleshly body through death, in order to present you before Him [God] holy and blameless beyond reproach" (Colossians 1:19–22). Thankfully the Chinese woman in Saratsi was set free from actual demon possession, transferred from being owned by satan to being owned by Christ.

CHAPTER NINETEEN

ANGELS HAVE GREATER POWER THAN DEMONS

G OD'S ANGELS HAVE broad responsibilities in the physical and spiritual worlds, as well as major responsibility to *assist people who love God or who God knows will love Him in the future*. Angels help in ways that people are often not even aware of, preventing accidents and deflecting harm (Psalms 34:6–7). Dr. Warner writes, "We see angels doing such things as giving guidance to people (Genesis 22:11, 15; 31:11, 12), protecting them from danger (Genesis 32:1; 2 Kings 6:17), delivering them (Daniel 3:28; Acts 5:19; 12:7), destroying enemies (Genesis 19:13; 2 Chronicles 32:21; Acts 12:23), providing food for a weary prophet (1 Kings 19:5, 7), and other acts of ministry to 'those who will inherit salvation'(Hebrews 1:14)" Warner (*Spiritual Warfare*) pp. 29–30.

Angels Are God's Staff to Run the World

"God uses angels to carry out His purposes in the world He created. Far from being an impersonal, material world operating by 'natural law,' the world is functionally upheld by the power of God exercised by His authority through angels. Scripture indicates that they maintain various functions of the earth, such as controlling 'forces of nature,' to inflict plagues on the Israelites (2 Samuel 24:15, 16) and the Egyptians, being involved in the pillar of cloud and pillar of fire that led the Israelites out of Egypt (Exodus 14:19; Numbers 20:16), killing 185,000 of the enemy (Isaiah 37:36), causing a severe earthquake that rolled the stone away from the tomb of Christ (Matthew 28:2). God used angels in the past to punish severe wickedness, and at the 'end of the age' He will use them to 'harm the land and the sea' (Revelation 7:2)" Warner (*Spiritual Warfare*) p. 30.

It might be that some of what are called "natural catastrophes" are actually punishment from God's angels for mankind's wickedness. It is interesting to note that some of the most severe catastrophes of the past few years occurred in places where the people officially blasphemed God, boasted of their sinfulness, trained terrorists, harmed children, or attacked Christians. *Are God's angels powerful? Yes!* And they are present in great numbers where people are earnestly praying, and *in even greater strength where people are fasting and praying.*

God's Angels Work As a Team with Christians.

The angels need Christians to pray, and Christians need angels to act upon their prayers. Remember the "SIDS" baby of Example # 9? Angels were there, but they did not rescue the baby until a Christian told satan to get off the baby's chest, in Jesus' Name. We all need to pray more. It is important to our families, our nation, and the world. Christians are sometimes "asleep at the switch," so to speak, when it comes to praying. They are busy and it is easy to assume that *other* people are praying, so they don't need to. Perhaps sometimes others are praying, but sometimes they are not. When you pray, it is good to have a list to follow, so less important thoughts won't crowd into your mind. And try to pray out loud, if only in a whisper. *Speaking* prayers brings the strongest angelic assistance. Let God impress upon you what He wants you to pray about. Prayer is not an "all or nothing" thing; don't feel discouraged if on some days you have not been able to pray, or have forgotten to pray. You can also talk to God on and off as you go about your day. Think about the fact that He is with you, in you. Prayer will become a treasured time, and angels will bring victories.

Angels' assignment from God is to *help people,* especially people who love God, and they work in tandem with God to accomplish His benevolent purposes. However, there is a logistical problem: *Praying Christians aren't as numerous in the world as people who sin.* So what is obvious is that there is more demonic activity than angelic activity. That is unfortunate, but God allows people free will to pray or not to pray, obey or not obey. And then there are consequences of blessing or lack of blessing. However, when Jesus returns to earth with his vast army of powerful angels and strikes down satan and demons and unrepentant people, it will be obvious to all that God's angels are *vastly more powerful than demons. Demons know that time is coming, and fear it.* When Jesus was on earth demons fearfully asked Him, "Have you come to destroy us?" (Mark 1:24; Luke 4:34). All demons know the time of their destruction is coming and that Jesus is the eternal King.

Opposite Systems

Angels and demons work under opposite systems. Demons operate freely wherever there is sin, or where people are tending toward sin. Angels do not. They generally refrain from intervening until people pray or God gives them an order to bring help or retribution. Power from God's angels is released in response to the obedience and faith and prayers of God's people. That is why it is critical that as individual Christians, and as a moral community and nation, we need to be a prayerful and righteous society. And we need to have courage to protest and reject obvious evils in the society.

Why Satan Attacks Christians

Jealousy

Satan hates God. He wanted to rule the universe but instead got thrown out of heaven. And satan hates people. Humans who are forgiven will live forever, but satan will have neither forgiveness nor life. When the battle is over, *God's heirs will have the kingdom and satan will be bound.*

Attempt to Grieve God…

Satan has no way of harming the great God of Heaven, except by causing Him anger and grief over the damage he wreaks upon humans and the earth. Satan especially wants to immobilize or diminish the effectiveness of people who are already "joint heirs" with Christ, hoping they will become ineffective in getting other people out of satan's kingdom and into Christ's. Satan's major ways of attempting to hurt God are to try to hurt people who love God, and to keep as many people out of Heaven as possible.

In Ephesians the Apostle Paul explains that we have been adopted into God's family, and are "joint heirs" with Jesus Christ. As God's children and heirs, we are His primary representatives here on earth. "God has commissioned us with His authority to invade the territory of the enemy and reclaim it for the Lord" Warner (*Spiritual Warfare*) p. 82. If satan can get us to live at a low level and neutralize the Christian mission to bring more people into the kingdom of Christ, that is the best he can do for himself. Christians meeting in churches are not a threat to him *unless* they are bringing people to Christ. Then satan attempts to interfere. Usually he does that by causing discord. Christians need to be careful to think the best of one another, be on guard against satan's tactics. And Christians need to *pray together,* aware that they have unseen demonic enemies they can defeat if they pray.

Can Demons Read Minds?

Some people think a human mind is inviolate, that no one can know what a person is thinking. But human "psychics" can appear to read minds. How are they doing it? They are getting information from demons, as noted in Chapter 13 under "Witchcraft Mindset." Because spirits have access to human minds and can interject ideas into them, we all *need to be careful not to assume that everything that pops into our mind is our own thought.* What is good, though, is that God's angels also put ideas into people's minds, for their benefit and protection, and your spirit can recognize their beneficial counsel. We need to *forbid any kind of evil spirit access* to our mind, recognizing and discarding ideas immediately that are contrary to God. *To be able to do that, you have to know what God says.* That is a major reason Christians read the Bible and go to church.

Example #93
Occult Harassment Suffered By Eleanor

It is important even for children to avoid occult influences: games, books, movies, etc. I had a strange and troubling experience when I was twelve years old, before I received Christ into my life. I had been invited to participate in a Ouija board game at a distant neighbor's house. I'd never played the game before, but foolishly did so. I was asked to think of something that no one else knew. I did that, and closed my eyes so I couldn't influence where the little open-centered table would go. Whatever occult force was working through the game spelled out *exactly* the answer to my secret question. *It was chilling.* I was sorry I went! *Worse yet, demonic harassment came home with me.* In my bedroom that night, with all the lights off, I saw small, bright-colored, luminescent faces moving around on my ceiling. Not every night, but often enough to be puzzling and disturbing. I tried to think perhaps it was because I'm an artist (or like to think I am), but if so, why did the strange faces appear only after I had used the Ouija board? The situation gave me the creeps.

Then, when I was seventeen, at a church summer camp I asked Jesus to forgive me and come into my life. I wish I could say that suddenly everything in my life became noticeably happier, as I had hoped it would, but that wasn't the case. *Everything got worse.* I was bewildered. I knew Jesus had saved me, but *I could sense that I had an unseen enemy, although I lacked the words to express that bewildering idea.* And I continued to see the strange, glowing faces on my bedroom ceiling at night. Not until much later in my Christian life did I understand that satan was fighting to hang on to the ancestral part of our family line that he considered "his."

After I was married, and the strange glowing faces happened again, I told Roy. He said, "We'll put a stop to that! Satan, in Jesus' Name I *forbid* you to *ever* do that to Eleanor again!" That was the end of the glowing faces. The Ouija board had been a "hook" to fascinate children, get them interested in "special powers," and attach demons to their lives. I had never told anyone but Roy about the strange problem, but recently a young Christian woman who came for counseling told me that as a child she had seen "ugly, glowing faces on the ceiling" of her bedroom at night. (The same thing I saw!) She said it started the night a neighbor next door conducted a séance in her garage. A "séance" is deliberate contact with demons. And that sin brought demons that attacked her too. Demons hate Christians, are jealous that Christians will live forever in a wonderful place, while they, the demons, will be punished.

What Drives Demons Away?

The Name of *Jesus!* The Blood of Jesus, words from God in the Bible, *and avoiding sin.* You give the order against satan in the Name of Jesus, and demons flee. They are afraid of Him.

DEMONS CANNOT BE WHERE CHRISTIANS HAVE FORBIDDEN THEM AND RIGHTEOUSNESS EXCLUDES THEM.

Resist the enemy (satan) who "prowls about like a roaring lion looking for someone to devour. *Resist him, firm in your faith*" (1 Peter 5:8, 9a). Satan will come into eternal condemnation for his crimes. But for now, the pressures he and his demons exert on people force them to make moral and spiritual choices. Dr. Warner writes, "Satan and his demons seek every way possible to keep God's people from doing whatever they do to the glory of God (1 Corinthians 10:31). Their primary tactic is the lies they tell about the character of God and about our relationship to Him. We need to see the secularization of our society as an attack on the very character of God; and we need to see that when we as Christians operate within a secularized worldview, we contribute to that process" (*Spiritual Warfare*) p. 32. Satan knows he will be defeated, and out of spite he works to keep as many people as he can away from God.

"*The principle objective of satan is to render God's servants spiritually ineffective.* One of his very productive tactics has been promoting the move away from a functional belief in demons and demon-caused problems in this world to the assumption that there is a scientific explanation for all such phenomena. With that drift there often seems to be a corresponding tendency to question the supernatural activity of God as well. Spirit causation, whether evil spirits or the Holy Spirit, is too often questioned. [And a person doesn't attempt to defend himself against what he doesn't realize is a threat.] *His* [satan's] *ultimate aim is always to get us to doubt the character of God and to reject His authority in our lives.* This often manifests itself in a questioning of the authority of God's Word" (*Spiritual Warfare*) p. 97. God's angels do the *opposite*. They draw us close to God.

Importance of Having the Holy Spirit's Help

In the Bible, in 2 Peter 1:21 we read, "No prophecy was ever made by an act of human will, but men [who were] moved by the Holy Spirit spoke from God." *The Holy Spirit is the powerhouse of the Trinity:* Father, Son and Holy Spirit. *The Holy Spirit is God in action:* In Roy's gigantic concordance of the all the verses in the Bible, *I found 120 references to activities of the Holy Spirit, from Genesis to Revelation.* In Genesis 1:2 the Holy Spirit moved upon the waters in creation. Speaking about Moses, in Exodus 31:3 God said, "I have filled him with the Spirit of God in wisdom, in understanding, in knowledge. A prophecy about Jesus in Isaiah 61:1, 2 reads: "The *Spirit of the Lord is upon me*...to bind up the brokenhearted, to proclaim liberty to captives...to comfort all who mourn." And there are many more references to the ministries of the Holy Spirit of God, especially in the New Testament, where Jesus was baptized by the Holy Spirit, and by the Spirit's power was able to cast out devils. Matthew 12:28 *"If I cast out devils by the Spirit of God, then the Kingdom of God has come to you."*

Then *Jesus* sent the Holy Spirit to help the Church through all the ages until He returns to earth as King. Romans 8:9 tells us, "If anyone doesn't have the Spirit of God within him, he doesn't belong to Christ." "If the *Spirit of Him* [the Holy Spirit] who raised Christ Jesus from the dead lives in you, He *also* will give life to *your* mortal bodies, through His Spirit who dwells in you" (Romans 8:11). The Holy Spirit is personal, the dynamic part of the Trinity who empowered Jesus and the entire Church Age. To find all the Bible references to the Holy Spirit, google Strong's Exhaustive Concordance of the Bible on your computer. Select "Holy Spirit" to pull up the list.

Where satan has deceived Christians into being afraid of the spiritual gifts that the Holy Spirit gives, or has caused them to think those supernatural gifts are not from God, those people will be vastly less effective spiritually than they could be if they had some gifts from God's Spirit. Those ministry gifts are intended to bring about God's mercies on earth. Earnest Christians will want to cooperate in that.

Satan knows his time on earth is short but he will struggle to hold onto this planet. He and the other rebellious former angels were expelled from Heaven because they got "too big for their britches," so to speak, but *they continue to lie to themselves and struggle for dominance and permanence on earth.* They cling to the vain hope that finally *they* will get to *"rule it all."* Satan was kicked out of Heaven for wanting to "have a throne above the heavens" and rule the universe (Isaiah 14:12–15). He still wants that and tells that lie to New Age occultic groups. They naively think *they* will take over the universe. Not a chance. *The Bible, with a 100% accuracy rate, has prophesied satan's doom and the doom of his followers.*

SECTION FOUR:

THEN JESUS CAME

CHAPTER TWENTY

THEN JESUS CAME TO DESTROY THE WORKS OF THE DEVIL

Hail the heaven-born Prince of Peace!
Hail the Son of Righteousness

Mild He lays His glory by,
Born that man no more may die.
Born to raise the sons of earth
Born to give them second birth

Hark! The Herald Angels Sing,
Glory to the newborn King!
(by Charles Wesley and Felix Mendelssohn)

"The Son of God appeared for this purpose,
to destroy the works of the devil."
(1 John 3:8)

Overview

NONE OF US can know spiritual truth beyond what we learn from Jesus. He did *miracles of mercy* of many kinds by God's power. He made the blind to see, the deaf to hear, the mute to speak, the lame to walk, and raised the dead. He "healed all manner of diseases" (Luke 6:19). He turned water into wine, calmed the raging seas, created food to feed the hungry, and cast out devils.

From the time Jesus appeared on earth, *demons knew who He was and tried to kill him. They knew He had come to earth to overcome them* (1 John 3:8). *But they did not know how Jesus was going to do it.* Satan worked first through King Herod of Jerusalem. When the Wise Men told Herod about the bright star they had seen, they asked the location of the *King* who had been born. (It must have taken them about two years to reach Jerusalem on their camels.) Herod feared for his own position as King, so he ordered the deaths of all baby boys under two years old. Jesus escaped, because in a dream God warned Joseph to flee to Egypt. When Jesus was an adult, satan offered to give him "all the kingdoms of earth if Jesus would fall down and worship him" (Matt. 2–4:10). Jesus refused. *Satan* arranged for proud religious leaders to have Jesus beaten and scourged and crucified. Jesus had warned His disciples that would happen, and told them that "on the third day He would be raised up" (Matt. 20:17–19). When Jesus was put to death, satan and his demons must have thought they had won. But they had not! *Because Jesus had not sinned, death could not hold Him.* Before He went to the cross Jesus knew what His death would accomplish: *the transfer of His eternal Life to whoever believes in Him.*

The verses below are specific to Jesus' ministry of casting out devils. In these situations and in all the stories we have related in *God Wins*, it was *Jesus, through the Holy Spirit's power, who helped the people.* It was *"by His Name" that the wonderful things were accomplished.*

Scripture References to Jesus Casting Out Demons

Some of the verses listed below, and in the list in example #95 are also mentioned in the beginning of the book. I am hoping you will study them again. The Bible is full of wonderful verses from God about many aspects of living life honorably and lovingly, and leading people to Christ. These verses are primarily about Jesus' consistent victory over evil. I abbreviated a few multi-verse references and encourage you to look them up.

Luke 9:1   "When Jesus had called the twelve disciples together, *He gave them power and authority to drive out all demons.*"

Matthew 12:28   Jesus speaking: *"If I drive out demons by the Spirit of God, then the Kingdom of God has come upon you."* (He was able to drive them out, proof that the Kingdom of God had come.)

Matthew 10:1   "Jesus summoned his twelve disciples and gave them authority over unclean spirits [demons], to cast them out"

Mark 3: 11   "Whenever the evil spirits [devils] saw Him [Jesus] they would fall down before Him and shout, '*You are the Son of God!*'"

Example #94
Jesus' Victory Celebration!

When Jesus sent his 70 Disciples out *into* the wider community to heal the sick and cast out devils in His Name, they were thrilled by their success and so was Jesus. He already knew they had been successful, because while they were ministering without Him, He "saw satan fall from heaven like lightning" (instantly!), knocked out of power by ordinary humans speaking orders in Jesus' Name. Scripture tells us that Jesus "*Rejoiced greatly in the Holy Spirit*" (Luke 10:21, NIV). He was ecstatic! He might have been dancing for joy! *It was a victory celebration!*

It was *proof* that His work would carry on! In the power of the Holy Spirit satan had been struck down and would be struck down again and again and again through the ages, in Jesus' Name. His followers would *gain victories for God and for people.* The 70 Disciples healing the sick and casting out devils was a forerunner of "Kingdom of God" power from the Holy Spirit that Jesus promised His followers right before He ascended into Heaven. Before that, only Old Testament Prophets and men of God like Moses were able to challenge satan and win, because they had power from the Holy Spirit resident within them. Now, for the same reason of the Holy Spirit's power, Christians of today also can overthrow satan's oppressions. That is what this book is about.

That ushered in the Christian Age, when for the first time in history, people other than prophets would be able to go up against mankind's ancient enemy and *win!* Jesus is still rejoicing today when any of His team defeats satan. In 1 John 4:2 we read, "*Jesus came in the flesh to destroy the work of satan.*" Everything He did was tied into that goal. When He saved you from sin He destroyed the work of satan in your life, rescuing you for Heaven. When He healed the sick, He destroyed the work of satan that marred God's creation. When He cast out devils, He overthrew the strongholds (strong holds) that satan had on people's lives.

Example #95
More Scripture References to Jesus' Authority Over satan and Demons (Devils)

1 John 4:2	"This is how you can recognize the Spirit of God [in a person]. Every spirit that confesses that Jesus has come in the flesh is from God."
1 John 3:8	Jesus came in the flesh to destroy the works of the devil.
Matthew 4:1	Jesus resisted the devil.
Matthew 9:23	Jesus healed several blind men, then a demon-possessed man.
Matthew 12:22	Jesus healed a blind/mute demon-possessed man; then the man could see and hear.
Mark 1:23	Demons in a man recognized Jesus as the Son of God and were afraid. "Have you come to destroy us? I know who you are—the Holy One of God!"
Ephesians 6:27	"Our struggle is not against flesh and blood, but against the rulers, the authorities, and the powers of this dark world, and against spiritual forces of evil in the heavenly [air around earth] realms."
Mark 1:27	Jesus "commands even the evil spirits and they obey Him."
Mark 1:32	Jesus drove out many demons but (at first) would not let them speak because they knew who He was (and Jesus didn't want that known yet).

Mark 5:3–15	Jesus cast out a "legion" of demons.
Mark 6:7	Jesus gave His twelve disciples authority over demons.
Mark 6:13	Empowered by Jesus, the disciples were casting out many demons.
Mark 9:17–27	When the demon saw Jesus it threw the boy into convulsions. Jesus commanded the demon to get out and not return.
Mark 16:17	Jesus said, *"In my name cast out devils."*
Luke 4:34, 35	The demon cried out, "I know who you are, the Holy One of God."
Acts 8:6, 7 & Luke 6:17–19	Jesus healed all that were oppressed by the devil.
Luke 9:42, 43	The demon threw the boy down in a convulsion, but Jesus rebuked the demon and healed the boy.
Luke 13:11	A demon severely crippled a woman for 18 years. Jesus healed her.
Luke 10:17	"Lord, even the *devils are subject to us in your name.*"
Luke 10:18	"Jesus said, "I beheld satan fall" (Knocked out of power by Jesus' disciples using His name against evil.)
Acts 8:6, 7	Unclean spirits came out and the paralyzed and lame were healed.
Acts 26:18	to open their eyes so they may turn from darkness to light, and from the dominion of satan to God.

Example #96
Miracles in the Book of Acts!

The instances of divine intervention mentioned in the book of Acts are numerous and varied. Many kinds of supernatural manifestations are listed. Following are a list of miracles, occurrences that *transcended the forces of nature.* See Google.com.therealpresence.

org/archives/miracles. Those miracles of mercy are to continue until
Jesus returns to earth as its eternal King. Then they will no longer be
needed. (The following list was obtained from therealpresence.org, a
Catholic website.)

I. Individual Miraculous Phenomena
A. Resuscitations from the Dead
1. Peter raises the disciple Tabitha.
Acts 9:36–42
2. Paul raises the young man Eutychus.
Acts 20:9–12
B. Miraculous Cures and Exorcisms
1. Peter heals the lame man at the Temple gate.
Acts 3:1–16
2. Ananias cures Saul of blindness.
Acts 9:17–18
3. Peter heals the paralytic Aeneas.
Acts 9:33–35
4. Paul cures the lame man of Lystra.
Acts 14:7–9
C. Miraculous Penalties or Afflictions
1. Ananias and Sapphira struck dead at Peter's feet.
Acts 5:1–5
2. Herod suddenly slain by an angel.
Acts 12:23
3. Paul temporarily blinds the sorcerer Elymas.
Acts 13:9–12
D. Nature or Cosmic Miracles
1. Violent wind of the Holy Spirit in *Jerusalem*.
Acts 2:2–6
2. Shaking of the assembly building in Jerusalem.
Acts 4:31
3. Prison doors open for the Apostles.
Acts 5:17–25
4. Philip snatched by the Spirit of the Lord.
Acts 8:39

    5. Peter liberated from prison by an angel.
       Acts 12:5–11
    6. Chains fall from Paul and Silas.
       Acts 16:25–30

II. Collective Miraculous Phenomena

    1. Many signs and wonders done by the Apostles in Jerusalem
       Acts 2:43
    2. Apostles perform signs and wonders among the people
       Acts 5:12
    3. Peter's shadow cures many in the streets
       Acts 5:15
    4. Multitudes from outside Jerusalem are healed
       Acts 5:16
    5. Stephen works great signs and wonders
       Acts 6:8
    6. Philip cures crippled and possessed in Samaria
       Acts 8:6–8, 13
    7. Miracles worked by Paul and Barnabas on mission journey
       Acts 14:3
    8. Great signs and wonders done among the Gentiles
       Acts 15:12
    9. Miracles worked through objects touched by Paul
       Acts 19:11–12
    10. Paul heals all the sick brought to him on Malta
       Acts 28:9

These miracles were done the way Jesus did them and taught His Disciples to do them. He promised that Christians would be empowered by the same Holy Spirit until He returns.

CHAPTER TWENTY-ONE

MIRACLES

Definition: "Miracle or Magic?"

AN INSTANT, RADICAL *change to the cellular structure of a physical object,* or a change that is far beyond the normal range of physical possibility, is called a *"miracle,"* or *"magic," depending upon whether it was God or satan who caused the change.* To differentiate the two spirit powers, satan's miracles are called "magic." That is *not the pretend magic* of a "magician" who entertains people by sleight of hand, pulling a rabbit out of a hat or a string of silk handkerchiefs out of his sleeve. Those are clever tricks, but not actual "magic." Genuine magic is an "abrogation" of natural law, a "setting aside" of physical law as though it didn't exist. A miracle from God does the same thing; *it overrules natural law.*

In the Indian section of Singapore, Roy and I watched a demonstration of Hindu "magic." Several Hindu priests had fasted for several days and prayed to "spirits" (demons) to display their power. They were standing in the street, and several hooks with ropes attached were punctured through the skin on each man's back and attached to medium sized wooden carts. The priests then slowly pulled the carts down the street. The wounds on their backs did not bleed or tear. That was the "magic." Indian spectators watched fearfully. Another demonstration of Hindu magic is to walk on glowing-hot coals without getting burned. That also was an abrogation of natural law. Demons have power to do that, and so do God's angels. Demons do it for show-off, to keep viewers in fear of spirits, so that they remain tied to belief in those spirit powers. *God's angels do miracles to help people, never for "show-off."*

Down through the ages, Jesus' followers have continued the miracles of His Kingdom, demonstrating the "powers of the world to come" that Jesus said would occur when the Holy Spirit was "poured out upon them" (Acts 1:5). That outpouring happened at Pentecost and has happened to every Christian since then who *asked God* to fill him with His Spirit and use Him for God's glory. Why don't we see more miracles? They seem to occur primarily among people who love God and *ask God's Spirit to be working among them and through them.*

Example #97
Three Old Testament Miracles

Moses leading the Israelites across the Red Sea on "dry land" and the water rushing back and drowning pursuing Egyptian chariots was a great miracle (Exodus 14). Egypt was never powerful again. Another miracle was the "manna," the nutritious wafers from Heaven that fed the Israelites in the desert. A third miracle was *the fall of Jericho.* Ancient Jericho had walls so thick that houses and a street ran along the top of them. For Joshua and the Israelites to give a great shout and the thick walls fall down *flat* and *inward* was a *very great miracle* (Joshua 6:20). Archaeologists have found sections of those thick walls that fell inward (History channel).

In Joshua 5:13 we read that before the fall of Jericho, a man was standing opposite Joshua with *his drawn sword in his hand.* Joshua went to him and asked, "Are you for us or for our adversaries?" The man responded, "No; rather I indeed come now as *captain of the host of the Lord.*" And Joshua fell on his face to the earth, and bowed down, and said to him, "What has my Lord to say to his servant?" The captain of the Lord's host said to Joshua, "Remove your sandals from your feet, for the place where you are standing is holy." And Joshua did so. The "man" probably was Jesus, in pre-birth to earth form, because it is God's presence that makes something "holy." Joshua knelt before Him. The "man" had come to fight the Canaanites with Joshua, assuring victory. God was *very angry with all the people in the land of Canaan because they worshipped satanic idols and sacrificed their little children into the fire of those idols.*

Miracles in Today's World

Example #**98**
Victory! Angelic Tanks!

"He has remembered His love and faithfulness to the house of Israel."
(Psalm 98:2)

Angels fought for Israel in the "Six Day War" of 1967 when Arab nations attacked it. *A great miracle took place in the Sinai Desert.* The Jews, recently immigrated to Israel, were woefully short of military equipment. They had only one tank patrolling the Sinai Desert when an Egyptian force of more than fifty tanks crossed the Red Sea and landed on the Sinai. The Jews in the lone Israeli tank were sure they were "done for." But suddenly, the leading Egyptian tank ran up a white flag and the commander surrendered all his tanks. Why? The Egyptian said they couldn't possibly fight the *100 Israeli tanks that surrounded them.* But the Israelis had only *one tank!* What had the Egyptians seen? God must have caused the Egyptians to see *the army of the Lord; angelic warriors appearing as Israeli soldiers in tanks.* The Egyptian surrender supplied the Israelis with much-needed tanks, and Israel amazed the world (and themselves) when they *won the war in six days.* There were other miracles also, as God fought for Israel. TBN film [Turner Broadcasting Network] of angelic miracles in modern day Israel. The film can be ordered.

It was similar to the appearance of angelic warriors that the prophet Elisha reported in 2 Kings 6:17-22. When enemy horses and chariots from Aram surrounded their city, Elisha's servant was very afraid. Elisha prayed, "O Lord, open his eyes so he may see." Then the Lord "opened the servant's eyes," and *"he looked and saw the hills full of horses and chariots of fire all around Elisha."* As the enemy came toward them, Elisha asked God to strike them with blindness, and He did. Then, instead of killing them, under Elisha's instruction the Israelite king led the blind soldiers to a place where the Israelites fed them "a great feast" and then sent them away. That ended Aram raids into Israel. (The 100 angelic "tanks" in the Sinai were a modern-day version of the same rescue by God.)

The miracles that God's angels perform are *never for "show off."* Their miracles are to help God's people in crisis or to punish extreme wickedness.

Example #99
Victory! A Moat of Blood!

"Do not touch my anointed ones; do my prophets no harm."
(Psalm 105:15)

A number of years ago a Campus Crusade friend who worked in Senegal, Africa for many years told us about an amazing miracle that occurred there. A small Christian tribe that had been threatened by a large tribe *prayed for God's protection.* When the many men of the strong tribe ran to attack, they turned and fled in fear. What had happened? Word came back that the enemy tribe *saw a "river of blood," a "moat" of blood surrounding the village of* the weaker tribe. It scared them so badly that they never again attempted to harm the smaller tribe.

Example #100
Victory! Stopping Wind and Rain!

"Shout for joy to the Lord all the earth, Burst into jubilant song!"
(Psalm 98:4)

A missionary friend in Indonesia told us about being with Octavianos, an Indonesian evangelist, when *Octavianos stopped the wind and rain, just as Jesus did.* During Octavianos' evangelistic meetings for about 200 people out in a clearing in East Java, an unseasonably heavy wind began to blow. It rocked the bamboo podium and buffeted the people so severely that they could not have stayed. Octavianos asked our friend to pray. Bill began, "Father if it be Your will..." and Octavianos interrupted him, "Brother, that's not the way to pray!" Octavianos lifted his hand to the sky and commanded, "Wind, in the Name of the Lord Jesus Christ, *stop!" And the wind stopped!* The people stayed and heard the Gospel. The next evening heavy rain began to fall even though it wasn't yet monsoon season. Again Octavianos asked Bill, "Pray, brother." Bill answered, "No, you pray." Octavianos did, in the same way. He reached his arm to the sky and said, "Rain, in the Name of the Lord Jesus Christ, STOP!" And the rain stopped.

I was intrigued, and wanted to talk to a man who could do the kinds of things Jesus did; stop wind and rain in His Name. So I made an appointment to meet with Octavianos in Jakarta. He explained to me, "When you *know* what God wants to do, your praying is over; you just *tell* it to happen, in Jesus' Name." He continued, "I knew God wanted those people to hear the Gospel, so I told the wind and the rain to stop, in Jesus' Name, and they had to obey. You use your voice because Jesus is in you; *it is a command to His angels to make the thing happen."* It was what we had been learning, but we had never applied it to inanimate things like weather. Then Octavianos looked puzzled and asked, "Don't they learn anything in seminary in America?"

Example #**101**
Victory! Stopping the "Big Fire" in 2003!

"Give thanks to the Lord, call upon His Name: make
known among the nations what He has done."
(Psalm 105:1)

A huge miracle stopped the raging fires surrounding Lake Arrowhead in 2003, seen on TV all over the United States. *A fire chaplain did the same thing Octavianos did.* It was 90 degrees *hot,* and wind-driven fires swirled on three sides of the Lake Arrowhead area. The Fire Marshall told the Fire/Police Chaplain that if the wind didn't change within 20 minutes he would have to pull his men off the fire, to save their lives, and let the homes at Lake Arrowhead burn. The Chaplain standing with him yelled at the fire: *"Fire, in the name of the Lord Jesus Christ, Go Back!"* And *"Satan, in Jesus' Name I forbid you to destroy Lake Arrowhead!"*

Within about fifteen minutes a *whirlwind descended from the sky over Lake Arrowhead, putting out all three fires at once! It was the only kind of wind that could have accomplished that.* A wind from one direction would have blown one fire back on itself and put it out, but it would have enlarged the other two fires. In response to the command given in Jesus' Name, angels sent *exactly the right kind of wind to extinguish all three fires at once.* Then the temperature dropped from *90 degrees to 30 degrees in that one day* and it began to *rain and then snow,* snuffing the embers! Another miracle! *God saved the mountain!* The "voice" of a Christian, commanding in the Name of the Lord Jesus Christ, gave angels the right to *intervene.* What a glorious thing! Thousands of homes and beautiful trees were saved, including ours. It was a miracle! Residents had been praying for God's intervention for days. But not until a Christian gave a *command* in Jesus' Name did the situation change.

Example #102
Victory! Turning the Wind!

"Tell of His glory among the nations, His
wonderful deeds among all people."
(Psalm 96:3)

About ten years ago, five days and nights of continual east-to-west wind drove an earlier forest fire about 10 miles from Running Springs to Lake Arrowhead, threatening the hospital and hundreds of homes. A Fire Marshall came into the church on Sunday morning and ordered the congregation to leave. Out on the steps I whispered to Roy, "Let's do what Octavianos would do; *tell* the fire to go back!" We turned our heads so other people couldn't hear us and I whispered, "Wind, in the Name of the Lord Jesus Christ, *turn,* go the other way! Fire, go back on yourself! Satan, in Jesus' Name I forbid you to destroy the hospital or any homes in Lake Arrowhead!" The wind began to die back, then changed direction and *within 10 minutes was blowing exactly the opposite way* (west to east). That put the fire back onto the blackened area, putting itself out. Praise God! Outside the church, and later in town, I overheard people say, "Wasn't that wonderful! And strange, the way the wind suddenly changed direction!" I didn't say anything. It didn't need to be said and they wouldn't have understood; we haven't been taught those things in America, or at least Roy and I hadn't been. We thank God for Octavianos and what we learned from him in Indonesia. There is no point in learning something if we don't apply it. We are telling it now so *if you ever need it, you'll know what to do.* You don't have to yell, but you must *speak* Jesus' Name against the problem. And then pray the Blood of Christ's protection over yourself.

Example #103
Victory! The Tsunami Miracle!

"He is my refuge and my fortress, my God, in Him will I trust."
(Psalm 91:2)

This is the *amazing story* of the *miraculous way God saved the 26 children and caretakers of a Christian orphanage from the massive tsunami that struck the Bengal Bay the day after Christmas, 2004.* In America it was reported on national TV. The orphanage was at Navalaji Beach, a peninsula of the beach in Sri Lanka, (formerly Ceylon), on the shore of the entrance to the immense Bengal Bay. People on the western side of Sri Lanka and in the mountains of that beautiful island were safe, but the tsunami totally destroyed lower level areas along the bay, including the orphanage. This event is paraphrased from the first hand report given through multiple media outlets.

The story: Pastor Dayalan Sanders, Director of the orphanage and often called "Father" by many of the villagers, had gotten up before dawn to pray for the orphanage and individual children. Then he went back to sleep. He awakened at about 5 AM to prepare his Sunday sermon, and at about 7:30 when he looked out at the sea it was calm, "like a sheet of glass." A little later his wife ran into the room, terrified, "Come look, the sea's coming in!"

"I had never seen her look so frightened. I said, "Keep calm, God is with us and no harm will come to us unless it is our time" (to go to

Heaven). I casually walked out on our 4 acre grounds in a palm tree grove, with buildings for our chapel and the boys' dorm and a girls' dorm. I turned and looked at the sea, at the beach, and I just couldn't believe what I saw.

Words defy description. It was a massive 30-foot high wall of sea, black in color, stretching from one end of the beach to the other end, rushing toward us like a thousand freight trains. That thunderous roar itself petrified you with fear. I did not even have a moment to think out a plan...I had got to get the children out. I knew we just had a few seconds before we could get to the other side of our premises...I shouted "Drop everything you've got in your hands and get to the boat!" They came...I ran...I carried...I just threw them over the fence to the boat. This was the *first* time they had ever left the little motor on the boat, and it was the *first* time that Stefan, the boat man, was able to get the motor going on the first try. In one pull it started.

"I called upon my God, I prayed and my God answered my prayer. There was no power on earth that could resist the force that was behind that body of water, *so the only safe place was right on top of it. I was determined I was going to get on top of that.* With 32 people, 26 of them children in his small boat, Father Sanders ordered Stefan to head the overloaded launch (long boat) with its 15 horsepower motor straight at the wave. The craft sped forward, a bright green boat flag emblazed only with the words, "Jesus is Lord" flapping from a pole at its bow. The wave was coming and *immediately* with it. *Immediately a scripture was popped into my mind: When the enemy comes in like a flood, the spirit of the Lord shall raise up a standard against it"* (a war banner). And from there I got the courage, I just stood up in the small boat and I lifted both my hands and I said, *"I command you in the name of Jesus Christ on the strength of the scriptures, to stand still!"* And I thought I was imagining at the time that the *massive wall of water, it stood!* I am not one given to exaggeration, I saw as if something was holding it back, some invisible force or hand...*it just stood.* A miracle!"

That was confirmed later by surviving villagers who had climbed up palm trees and coconut trees to survive the onslaught. They told him that when the water got close to their boat, it just stood still, slowed down and gave them the chance to get the boat up. They wondered how that could be. I said, "There is no power on earth that could have held it back, but the power of God." I said, "I called upon God and *I commanded it in the name of Jesus,* who, 2000 years ago commanded the waves and they obeyed, He commanded the sea and they obeyed, and this is the very same God, He did the same to us and *He gave us those precious few seconds that we needed to start."* (At the first yank on the starter rope, the engine just sputtered into life.)

An hour-and-a-half later, the group, exhausted and dripping wet, but with everyone on board still alive, floated into the town of Batticaloa. The orphanage buildings were swept away as though by a giant broom. "Now half the children (of the village) are not here. Half the people are not here (were drowned)." But the people of the *orphanage were safe! They felt they had been led up over the wave by God's angels!* I praise God for that, and for the *brave obedience of the Director!* (700 Club television report) and verified by many reputable reporters. A CNN interview of the orphanage Director can be seen at http://www.godtube.com/watch/?v=7YDWNNNX.

The surge of the tsunami wiped out child-molestation beaches on Thailand's west coast. In dying in the tsunami, at least those children *escaped their tormentors* and went straight to Heaven. The tsunami also devastated Aceh (Ah'chay), at the far northern tip of Sumatra, Indonesia's largest island. *Aceh is the major Al Qaida terrorist training base in South-East Asia,* where the Bali Beach bombers were trained. In Meulaboh, a northern Sumatran city on the coast of the Bengal Bay about 110 miles south of Aceh, about 400 Indonesian Christians lived among thousands of Muslims. It was reported by several sources that before Christmastime, Muslim officials in Meulaboh told the Christians not to celebrate Christmas in their homes, but to go elsewhere, perhaps climb a mountain. The Christians did that. They camped on a mountain for several days and enjoyed Christmas together. *And that is where they were when the earthquake and tsunami struck the day after Christmas.* They felt the earthquake, but they were safe, high above the flood waters of the tsunami. And on the Indian side of the Bengal Bay, hundreds of Hindus lost their lives. Hindus in that area had burned the homes of hundreds of Christians. The total tsunami death toll around the entire Bay of Bengal at that time was estimated at about 300,000.

Was the tsunami a retribution? Possibly. Certainly situations in some areas around the Bengal Bay were evil: cruel to children, hostile to Christians, and a breeding ground for violence. The Bible makes it clear that God's angels and "fallen angels" (demons) have power over forces of the earth. Could God's avenging angels have caused the sea-floor to split and the tsunami flood in? They have the power, but whether they caused it, I don't know. Certainly catastrophes happen, but it was a strange coincidence, and very sobering. We praise God for the miracle of tsunami "standing still" at the word of the Lord, allowing the boatload of orphans and their Christian caretakers to survive. A Campus Crusade missionary friend in Asia reported that *thirty new Christian churches* now exist in villages along Thai coasts damaged by the tsunami.

Example #104
Victory! The Invisible Bus!

"He will command his angels concerning you, to
guard you in all you in all your ways."
(Psalm 91:11)

Another great miracle is how Winnie Bartel, a women's conference speaker, got to the air terminal she needed. Winnie represented an International Women's group that worked to better the conditions for women in some Third-World countries. *She has spoken to our U. S. Congress* about the needs of those women. After speaking at a women's conference in Jamaica, Winnie's return flight to New York was delayed. She didn't arrive at Kennedy Airport until long past midnight. The terminal from which she was to catch her morning flight to Los Angeles was at least a mile away, much too far for her to walk at night, and ground transportation was closed. It was also dangerous outside the terminal, with drunks hanging around. She didn't know how she could get to the terminal she needed. She was cold; it was February and her jacket was in her luggage.

Winnie told me about the following experience and has also related it to women's groups she has spoken to. She prayed, and soon a very kind, ordinary-looking man approached her and asked if she needed help. "Yes." He told her she could catch a little bus over by a diner, and he would take her there. He told her to walk close to him. He was very warm, which helped her. The man smiled as they approached the diner and he told her not to be put off by the way the little bus looked. It had brightly painted flowers all over it! Winnie said the man boarded the colorful mini-bus with her, and a cheerful driver drove her to the entrance of the terminal she needed. The bus stopped in front of the door and Winnie stepped down with her carry-on bag and turned to thank the men. *But no one was there.* No man, no bus, no driver. Nor had there been the sound of a bus driving away. She was "just there," at the right terminal, transported in an amazing way. She is still amazed. God's Word tells us there is just a *"thin veil"* between this world and the world we can't yet see. So we are never without help. God's angels are always with us. Please remember that. If you are a Christian, you are *never without help.*

Example #**105**
Victory! Back From the Dead!

For the Lord is righteous. He loves justice;
upright men will see His face."
(Psalm 11:7)

Paul Eshleman, the former Director of Campus Crusade's worldwide JESUS Film ministry, documented an amazing miracle. Bill Bright, founder of Campus Crusade passed it on to friends. The story: In northeast India, inland from the port city of Calcutta, (high up on the northeast side of India along the Bengal Bay) are Malto tribes, where devils are worshipped and witchcraft is practiced. The Malto people had been very hostile to the Gospel. When the JESUS film team tried to show it in the Malto area they were turned away. A few days later, a

16 year old Malto girl died. The family was about to bury her when she suddenly, miraculously, woke up. The people said to her, "Then you weren't dead!" "Yes, I *was* dead," she exclaimed. "I went to the place of the dead. But God has given me seven days to tell you about the real God, the true God."

The next day she sought out and found the film team near another Malto village, and told them her story, and that God had told her she was to go with them. For the next seven days they showed the JESUS film to the now-receptive Malto villagers. Before every crowd she fearlessly proclaimed, "I was dead but God has sent me back to tell you that this film is about the true and living God. He has given me seven days to tell you. You need to believe in Him." Then, after the seventh day, although physically she appeared fine, she collapsed and died, just as she said she would. Paul Eshleman explained that as a result of this, hundreds of people who were bound by the chains of satan turned to the living Christ. *At least six churches were established in the Malto area.*

Example #106
Victory! The Swarming Bees!

"Sing to the Lord a new song, for He has done marvelous things."
(Psalm 98:1)

Roy is extremely allergic to bee venom. Three or four stings could kill him. One warm spring day in the San Joaquin Valley of California, as Roy was on his cleat tractor, disking up a field of tall weeds in preparation for planting cotton, he accidentally ran over a nest of swarming bees (bees with a queen bee, resting on their way to find a place to build a new hive). Hundreds of angry bees swarmed up from the weeds and buzzed around Roy's head. *The situation could not have been worse.* Roy was alone in an unpopulated area, he was far from his truck, and the bees were frenzied. It was the "triple play" of what makes bees angry: 1) Roy had disturbed them; 2) It was the hottest time of day; and 3) He was "sweaty"—a smell bees hate. Roy desperately needed to be able to reach his truck quickly, but in the weed-choked field his tractor could only move slowly, in low gear; *low and slow*. To make matters worse, his truck was parked at the far end of the long field. It was a life-threatening situation.

With hundreds of angry bees roaring around his head, Roy whispered, "Jesus, Jesus, Jesus, Jesus, Jesus," the whole long, slow, way back to his truck. He got off the tractor very, very slowly, bees still buzzing angrily around him, and opened the truck door slowly. "Jesus, Jesus, Jesus, Jesus, Jesus, Jesus." He slowly got into the truck and slowly closed the door. To his amazement, *not one bee had stung him and not one bee had even gotten into his truck*. It was *miraculous!* When he got home he was pale and shaken. (Being Norwegian and English Roy's skin is very light anyway, but when he got home from escaping those bees he was *white*.) He said it was the most afraid he had ever been. He was very grateful to God for saving his life. Roy had called on *Jesus*, and was protected. *It was a miracle.*

Example #**107**
Victory! Miracle of the Watermelon Seeds!

On our farm we grew not only cotton, but citrus and watermelons. One spring, Roy planted 20 acres of watermelons in a rented field of "white ash" soil, to be irrigated by furrows. That soil is wonderfully rich, but farmers know it is risky to plant in, because if white ash gets rained on before the seeds sprout, the *sprouts can't come up. Water on white ash soil forms a crust that is almost as hard as concrete. You lose your potential crop*. That's what happened to Roy's watermelon field two days after he planted it. Rain. Roy tried everything possible to break the crust that had formed over the seeds, but *every tool he pulled behind his tractor bounced off the hard crust just like it was going down a highway*. In the middle of the field Roy knelt beside his tractor and asked God to enable the watermelon seeds to break through the crust. He couldn't replant or he would miss the prime time of the watermelon market, which is the 4th of July, and we needed the income. *Every day, Roy prayed for those seeds to come up*. After 4 days he saw cracks begin to form in the concrete-like crust, and little green watermelon plants peeked up. *It seemed like a miracle! Roy praised God.*

Example #108
Victory! God Heals Roy's Back!

"Break forth and sing for joy, and sing praises!"
(Psalm 98:4)

Roy's words: While I was in my third year of seminary, still farming also, I ruptured a disk in my back lifting heavy farm equipment. The continual pain made it very difficult to sit for hours on the hard chairs at seminary, but I didn't want to take the pillow Eleanor offered because I didn't want anyone to know I was injured. I intended to be a missionary, and I knew that no mission board would accept a candidate with a bad back. At home I sometimes hung by my legs on the metal T-bar of our clothesline to get some relief. As standard procedure, the mission board kept asking me to get a physical, and I kept stalling. They kept asking. I went to three different doctors, hoping one of them *wouldn't* detect my problem. But the last test was always hitting my knee for reflex. There was none. Finally, after being shot full of purple dye, the slipped disc was confirmed by X-ray and an operation scheduled. As I was wheeled into the X-ray room I was able to share the Four Spiritual Laws with the male nurse and he received Christ.

In the meantime, on a day trip up to the Sequoias, I met a man in ministry and told him about my problem. He anointed me with oil and prayed for me. I also felt confirmation from the scriptures that God would heal me. The minister had told me to *thank God in advance for my healing because "time is nothing to God; your faith is what is important to Him."* I tried to do that, but the pain increased to the point that I often stood in my seminary classes to ease the pain. Several months went by and my back only got worse.

One night I couldn't sleep because of the pain, so I walked up and down our dark driveway in the vineyard to get some relief. I wanted to believe God for healing, but the pain was so intense and had gone on so long that I felt desperate. I looked up into the night sky and said, "God, if you really intend to heal my back, just drop a star in the sky to show me you plan to heal me." Immediately, a huge falling star streaked above me. I went inside and told Eleanor, and then went to bed. *In the morning the pain was gone completely.* It took a couple of days to stretch the muscles in my back so I could tie my shoes. I have not been bothered by back pain since that time, even though I began "back-breaking" work for a cement contractor, pouring concrete, working it into driveways, while I raised support to join Campus Crusade. *My back didn't hurt at all.* It was truly a wonderful miracle to be suddenly healed, and not need surgery. I have marveled at the 'falling star,' the streaking meteorite. God had prepared it long before the night I asked Him for it.

Example #**109**
Victory! Jesus Saves Karen's Life in Indonesia!

"The Lord has made known His salvation."
(Psalm 93:2)

The crisis began the day before Roy was to return from ministering in Thailand. It was a hot day, and our daughter Karen, 11, was sitting out under a huge shade tree, happily visiting with two Indonesian girlfriends who were sitting "Indian style" picking at grass as they talked. Karen was leaning back on her hands, her arms outstretched. Her hands rested on the damp, gigantic fallen leaves. She unknowingly was stung by offended giant millipedes she had disturbed. We knew some giant millipedes lived under the big leaves but didn't know they are poisonous. We thought they were like the small millipedes in America; ugly but harmless. And in Indonesia we almost never saw one. Karen left her friends for a little while in order to go to town with me to get some things for Roy's return. (To make an "apple pie" for him from some unripe mangos. Not exactly the same, but close.) On the way to the village market Karen showed me her left hand and said it hurt. I checked carefully but couldn't see any cut or puncture or even a scratch. As we were buying some things she said "Now my other hand hurts, too." A puzzle. And especially so because Karen was never a child to complain. When we got home she went down to the lawn again to join her girlfriends. But around noon when the three girls came up to the house, Karen was fighting tears. "Mom, look at my legs! They hurt and are all swollen!" My heart froze. Karen's knees looked as though they were covered by inch thick foam rubber. We needed a doctor! We had no phone and no car at home, so my Indonesian helper ran to get Ron Thurman, our fellow Campus Crusade missionary. He came in his VW bug and drove us to the doctor's office. By the time we got there, Karen could no longer walk. Ron had to carry her in. Dr. Budi quietly called me aside and urgently said, "This is very serious. She has either rheumatic fever or rheumatoid arthritis; I don't know which, but take her home, put her flat on her back *and don't give her anything.* I'll check my medical books and be at your house in an hour. By then it was night, and very dark. Ron drove us home and helped me get Karen into bed and then prayed for her and left to go home. My two younger children, Mike and Robin, were asleep. I felt alone in the crisis.

I sat beside Karen's bed, quietly praying for her and trying to reassure her that everything would be all right; Dr. Budi would "come soon and know what to do." But about 30 minutes after getting her to bed Karen mumbled, "Mom, something's wrong with my tongue" and opened her mouth to show me. The left side of her tongue was *badly swollen, (the same side as the first hand she showed me).* Then I was immediately afraid that the other side of her tongue would swell also, *and then her throat.* She might suffocate! I turned away so Karen couldn't see my fear and whispered a desperate, *"Oh Jesus, tell me what to do!"* In a strong voice to my mind *He* commanded: *"Eleanor, give her Roy's bee sting medicine!"* (I knew Roy's mother had sent a small bottle of something with him when we went to the mission field in case he got a bee sting, but I didn't know what the medicine was. Those many years ago I'd never heard of "anti-histamine.") But I ran to Roy's office to get whatever it was, ran back to Karen and gave her three of the little pills. Then I held her hand and smiled at her and told her she was going to be fine! Jesus had told me what to do! The swelling in Karen's tongue began to recede and in ten minutes was completely gone. In a half hour more the swelling on her knees was gone. I didn't know what caused the problem, but Karen would live! *I will love Jesus forever for telling me what to do.* The doctor didn't arrive until two hours later, and still had no idea what had been wrong.

Not until many years later did we find out. A small news article in National Geographic reported that the giant millipedes of Indonesia are poisonous and inject the poison through their front feet if they are disturbed. As Karen leaned her hands back on the leaves, there must have been a couple of disturbed millipedes. Tiny injections, no marks, but *potent poison.* If Jesus hadn't told me what to do, we probably would have lost our beloved Karen. Our family will thank God forever for saving her life. Later, as Roy trained missionaries, he gave them a list of medicines to take with them overseas, including antihistamine and antibiotics. They might not find them where they were going, or they might not have time to get them, or there might not be a doctor available.

Example #110
Victory! Steering Wheel Unlocked!

"As high as the heavens are above the earth, so great
is His love for those who fear [reverence] Him."
(Psalm 103:11)

Most Moslem countries allow little or no freedom of religion. In some of those countries it is even dangerous to have a Bible. A brave Iranian Christian with a trunk full of Bibles was driving in the semi-desolate mountains of Kurdistan, hoping to give some Bibles to Muslim Kurds. On the high road his steering wheel suddenly locked. He slowed to a stop. With no town or village in view he wondered how he could possibly get his steering mechanism fixed. Suddenly he saw three Kurdish men climb a rise and approach his car. One of them asked, "Do you have the books?" "What books?" "In our village we three men had been praying together to know the true God. Then we each had the same dream—that if we would come up to this road, on this day, at this time, someone would bring us books that tell how to know God. We have collected money to buy them. Do you have the books?" "Yes!" beamed the Iranian Christian. The Kurds loaded up with Bibles and walked down their narrow pathway on the side of the mountain.

When the Iranian Christian got back in his car he found that his steering wheel was no longer locked. God clearly had assigned an angel to lock the steering wheel at the exact place where the three men had been told they would get "the books." Many Kurds became Christians as they read the Bibles, and churches were started. This event was told to Roy by a close friend of the man who delivered the Bibles. (For his safety, the man's name cannot be known. In fact to protect his family he changed his name and moved to a different city.)

CHAPTER TWENTY-TWO

HEAVEN IS REAL

Can People on Earth Be Contacted
By Loved Ones in Heaven?

ANY PEOPLE WONDER whether loved ones in Heaven know what is happening to their family on earth. There are reasons to think they *do* know, and can give encouragement if needed. Dr. Billy Graham and Dr. Norman Vincent Peale are two reliable examples of people who have been encouraged by departed loved ones. But *any communication with people who have left this world is to be initiated only by those in Heaven, not by people on earth* (Deuteronomy 18:12–24). Below are their accounts, and also two stories illustrating personal relationships with loved ones continuing between the realms of heaven and earth.

Victory! Evangelist **DR. BILLY GRAHAM** reported *hearing* his mother's voice when he was wrestling with a problem he couldn't solve. His mother had passed away years before, but he *heard her voice* give him the right answer. She couldn't have done that unless she was aware of his problem. This true story and the following two are from *Guideposts Magazine, a publication that has blessed our family for many years.*

Victory! **DR. NORMAN VINCENT PEALE** reported that on a Sunday morning as he was preaching in his Marble Collegiate Church in New York City, he suddenly *saw his father* (his father's spirit) standing in an aisle amidst the congregation, dressed in clothing of his by-gone era. His father beamed at him and waved, calling out, *"Carry on for Christ!"* And then the father vanished. It was a wonderful encouragement for Dr. Peale.

Victory! A BOY WHO MET HIS FATHER! A young boy had never known his father, a soldier who died in battle before the boy was born. The mother kept all photos of her dead husband hidden away, not wanting her son to long for the father he could never know. Then there was some kind of accident or illness and the young boy died in the hospital. Doctors fought to bring him back to life and finally were successful. When he was awake, the boy told his mother he had been in Heaven and met his Daddy, and his Daddy was happy to see him. But then his Daddy told him he had to "go back" and grow up and "take care of Mommy." The mother was skeptical, thinking it must have been a dream or a subconscious longing. When they were home, she took out her long photo of the father's regiment and showed it to her son. The *boy smiled and pointed directly to his father.*

Note: The father was in Heaven, yet he *knew* his son who was on earth. And he must have known of the son's illness and when he would arrive in Heaven, because he was there to greet him. That indicates that the father (the departed loved one) had knowledge of what was happening on earth, and that even though they had not been able to be together he loved his son.

Victory! A BOY IN HEAVEN! *"Faith Like Potatoes"* is the true story of a South African potato farmer who learns to trust God. In it, a much-loved young boy is run over by a tractor and dies. Everyone is heartbroken. But a few weeks later, the boy's father has a vivid dream of being in Heaven, and his little boy runs toward him across a beautiful grassy field, beaming, and throws himself into his father's arms. The father clutches him tight. "Oh, son, do you want to come home?" "No, Daddy, I want you to come *here!*" The father awoke rejoicing and comforted. We loaned our copy to neighbors and they liked it so much they immediately ordered six copies of the DVD for family members.

Example #111
Victory! The Welcoming Committee!

"We are His people, and the sheep of His pasture."
(Psalm 100:3b)

My mother had died about ten years before my father, and as he was dying I felt her presence beside me in the hospital room. That morning God had wakened me with, "Comfort the dying." So I hurried to Dad's convalescent hospital even though he wasn't expected to die. But I could see that he was very weak, and because of what God had said, I knew he was going to die. I felt a "sacred atmosphere" in the room as I held Dad's hand and talked gently to him about asking Jesus to forgive him, the way we all have to do. His eyes were closed, but he nodded. I sensed Mom's presence beside me, and that Dad's mother and sister Anna were there too. They had died in Germany many years before. I felt that Dad's angel was also there. I couldn't see him, but he seemed to be standing to the left, at the head of Dad's bed. I have heard that even through closed eyes, dying people can "see both worlds," the material world of earth, and the spirit realm we can't normally see. They are aware of the living people in their room, and their loved ones from long ago who are there to greet them and escort them to Heaven. Dad was probably aware of both worlds. He died completely peacefully. I marvel that the people in Heaven *must have known what was happening to their loved one on earth*, because *they knew when to come.*

Dad had told me that when his sister Anna died in Germany, her fiancé and all of Dad's family were gathered around her bed, weeping. But right before she died, Anna sat up and *beamed at something only she could see.* "Oh, it is so beautiful! Don't keep me here!" And she lay back and was gone. They felt sure she had glimpsed Heaven.

Example #112
Victory! "I've Got a Pulse!"

"I will sing praises to my God as long as I live."
(Psalm 104:33)

The EMT mentioned earlier was on duty in a hospital emergency room when a Christian woman was rushed in by some friends, not breathing. She had suffered a severe allergic reaction. Doctors worked on her for half an hour, but couldn't get a heartbeat or pulse. "She's gone," they said. "We can't help her." And they walked down the hall. A young nurse remained. As soon as the doctors were out of earshot, the EMT, who knew about the "SIDS" baby (Example #9), whispered, "satan, if you're on this woman's chest, get off! *In Jesus' Name, get off!"* The nurse suddenly exclaimed, "I've got a pulse!" Doctors rushed back. The woman was alive. Prolonged oxygen deprivation had severely damaged her brain, but doctors kept her alive for several days, long enough for her family to gather around her and tell her they loved her and say good-bye, "until Heaven."

Example #113
Victory! Dr. Bravo Was in Heaven!

"Praise the Lord, O my soul, and all my
inmost being, praise His holy name."
(Psalm 103:1)

In Chapter 9, #44, we told you about Dr. Norman Bravo, the former Director of Mountains Community Hospital at Lake Arrowhead, who came back from the dead. But there is more to tell. He died from allergic suffocation. He was hiking in the forest with his son when something in the air caused him to have difficulty breathing. His inhalator had run out, so his son ran to get help. But it was more than half an hour before paramedics were able to reach Dr. Bravo and get him to the hospital. Doctors put him on life support but knew he was dead. He had no brain waves, his hands had curled up, and there were other clinical signs of death. They told Dr. Bravo's wife Heidi, "We're sorry, but he's gone," and asked her permission to take him off life support. Heidi refused, and kept praying. After three days, Dr. Bravo woke up. Lack of oxygen had harmed him, so he couldn't speak, or walk, but when he was able, he told Heidi that *he had traveled by himself through the stratosphere to reach Heaven,* without any sense of fear, and time didn't seem to exist. When he arrived at Heaven, *an actual physical place,* he saw the luminous "Holy City" the Bible tells about in Revelation 21. He said it is a *beautiful,* immense, one-mile square cube of *translucent gold, filled with light from inside.* The Bible says the building will descend to Jerusalem at the proper time, *unhindered by gravity, just as angels are unhindered by gravity and Dr. Bravo himself was unhindered by gravity.* From it, Jesus will rule the earth in righteousness forever.

The immense building Dr. Bravo saw in Heaven will be Jesus' head-quarters in Jerusalem when He reigns on earth as its eternal *King.* "And the kings of the earth will bring the glory of their nations to it" (Revelation 21:26). Dr. Bravo said he didn't see inside the glowing building, but all around the long foundation he saw the layers of the beautiful gemstones the Bible speaks of in Revelation 21:18–20. He said he also saw two colors that don't exist on earth, but had no way to describe them because they don't relate to any colors in earth's light spectrum.

After Jesus was resurrected, He remained on earth for forty days (Acts 1:3) and appeared to more than 500 people (1 Corinthians 15:3–6). Then, as His Disciples watched, he ascended into Heaven, unhindered by gravity. "Two angels in white stood by as the Disciples watched Jesus go up, and said, "Why are you men standing around looking up at the sky? This same Jesus is *going to descend the same way you see Him going up"* (Acts 1:11). 1 Thessalonians 4:16–17 tells us what will happen when Jesus returns to earth to destroy evil and bring His reign of peace. *"The Lord Himself will descend from Heaven with a shout,* and with the voice of the Archangel Michael and with the trumpet call of God, *and the dead in Christ will rise first,* brought back to life. After that, we who are still alive will be caught up with them in the clouds, to *meet the Lord in the air.*" In Matthew 24:36 the Bible says only God knows the day and the hour of Christ's return. He gave signs, which tie to Israel becoming a nation again after 2000 years away from Jerusalem, but no one knows the actual moment. He said it will happen "in the twinkling of an eye" (1 Corinthians 15:52). We all want to be ready!

Example #114
Victory! Johanna Meets Her Twin Sister in Heaven!

"For you make me glad by your deeds, O Lord;
I sing for joy at the works of your hands."
(Psalm 92:4)

Our red-headed friend Johanna Olson was an identical twin whose sister died when they were infants. Her parents had never told Johanna about her twin because they didn't want her to feel sad. Yet she *was* sad, and no one knew why. When she was in kindergarten, the principal commented to her mother, "If I didn't know better, I'd think Johanna is a twin missing her twin." "She *is* a twin," whispered her mother, surprised. "Her sister died in infancy." Still nothing was said to Johanna about her twin. Then, about a year later, a house was on fire across the street one night, and Johanna was so frightened that she might die and not go to Heaven that she jumped out of bed, knelt down and prayed, "Dear Jesus, please come into my heart." Then she jumped back up into bed and pulled the covers up and went to sleep. She had a *vivid dream.* In it, *a little red-headed girl who looked just like her* ran across the grass and threw her arms around Johanna, laughing and beaming with happiness. *Her twin!* Johanna had met her twin! She was thrilled! And Johanna wasn't sad any more.

Example #115
Victory! Seeing Mom in Her "New Body!"

(This verse makes me think of both God's
love, and my mother's love toward me.)

*"Because he [God, and my mother] loves me," says the
Lord, "I will be with her in trouble, I will deliver her
and honor her and show her my salvation."
(Psalm 91:14–16)*

My mother came to America from Germany right after she and my father were married. Mom told me that at first she was very lonely here. She longed for her family and friends and the beauty of southern Germany, where the Danube River first flows out of the mountains of the Black Forest. Then she received a letter from a German friend, telling her that he had received Jesus into his life. But he didn't tell her "how." Mom wanted to know Jesus too! She was raised in the Lutheran Church, and yes, she loved and honored God, but *know Him personally?* No, she couldn't say that she did. *But she wanted to.* She fasted and prayed for three days, and grieved over having spoken impatiently to the milkman a few days before. On the third morning, as she was dusting in her living room, *the whole room filled with light and Jesus appeared to her, His arms outstretched.* She knew He had received her. Mom loved Him all her life.

I had an extraordinary experience with Mom when Roy and I were overseas. I was worried about her because before we left America she had begun to suffer from what seemed to be Alzheimer's. The few letters I received from her were phrased alarmingly repetitiously. I loved Mom very much. Her love was the only love I had known as a child, and I couldn't bear for her to be suffering or to no longer know me. I was in a hospital in Singapore, thinking about her, when I heard a soft knock at the door and looked up to see it open and *Mom* came in! Only she was *young!* About 28, *younger than when I was born!* Yet I knew her instantly! It was Mom! She was beautiful again, with shining honey-gold hair and wearing a green print silk dress (her favorite color) with a lovely emerald jeweled pin that my Brother Ralph had given her. She looked happy and completely peaceful and unrushed—so different from what her busy life had been like on earth. Mom walked over to a window and looked out at the palm trees, then came over to my bed and smiled at me and gently said, "Dear Ellen, what is there to worry about for you or for me?" And then she was gone.

I thought God was telling me that Mom had died, comforting me by letting me see her as she is now, in Heaven. But then I learned that Mom was still living. It was a "time warp," or a vision of what Mom would be in Heaven. I'm not sure which, *but God let me see Mom as she would be, so I could let her go when the time came.* The next life is our *real life,* and Mom is there now. By the time she left this earth I was glad she could escape her body, which had become a prison. I had seen her as she is now, in Heaven! (And I have the emerald pin she left behind when she died. Mine is slightly tarnished, but the one I saw her wearing was beautiful and shining.) I have read from people who have "been there and back" that in Heaven people have things they loved on earth; homes they love, in colors and furnishings that just suit them. So Mom is happily visiting with people there, and Dad is playing his grand piano, perhaps even with Beethoven, whose piano concertos Dad played every night. The *best of what man has created transfers; the trash will be destroyed.*

During all my growing-up years my gentle, happy mother talked to whoever she could about Jesus, often leaving evangelistic tracts here and there, praying people would take them and understand that they could know God personally and live forever. "I have to do this," she said. "Jesus died for me and I want other people to know Him too!" The following is what Mom would tell you: "Be sorry for your sin. Ask Jesus to forgive you and come into your life. *He will. When you have Him, you have life forever.*" Talk to Him, let Him talk to your heart. Learn to know Him better and better. *"He loves you and will be your help, even forever."* (German phrasing).

At the end of *God Wins,* in the Appendix is more information about how you can know God personally. Imagine! You can call on Him any time of the day or night and He will hear you and "commune" with you and help you. Imagine! Access to the King of the Universe any time *you* want to talk to Him. It's amazing, but *true.*

Heaven Is an Actual Place
Your future is yours to choose.

As Gregory A Boyd stated, "Humans have freedom to progress in what they accomplish *physically* by faithful work, and what they accomplish *spiritually*, through prayer and kind treatment of others. Those who love God will progress in both those areas of effort as an outgrowth of their relationship to Him." But what if people don't want to follow either God or satan? Actually, there is no such thing. If people aren't following God, they are already deceived. The Apostle Paul said, "If our Gospel is hid, it is hid from those who are perishing, in whom the *god of this world [satan] has blinded the minds of them that don't believe,* lest the light of the glorious gospel of the Lord Jesus Christ, who is the image of God, shine in unto them and they be converted" (2 Cor. 4:4). They need to turn their thinking around while there is still time. None of us know when our time is "over." If you are a deceived person, please get on your knees before God and ask Him to forgive you and drive off the "deceiving spirits." You don't want to go where they'll be going. God loves people, and I think He will grieve over the people who reject His love. But what happens to humans eternally is their choice to make.

God would like all people to be able to enter Heaven. But their sin has to be forgiven. God won't permit satan's evil to enter Heaven. That doesn't mean you never sin again, and God knows that, but it does mean you are on the "right track." You have the promise of life forever and His help in living your life on earth. God gives freedom to choose, but *you have to make that choice while you are alive. "Neither is there salvation in any other: for there is no other name under Heaven given among men whereby we must be saved"* (Acts 4:12 Thompson Reference Bible). Satan hates you and wants you to be destroyed. Jesus *loves you,* and wants you to live forever.

A well-known theologian was asked to tell the most important truth he had ever learned. He answered with these words from a Sunday school song:

Jesus Loves Me, This I Know
For the Bible Tells Me So.

Jesus Loves Me, He Who Died,
Heaven's Gates to Open Wide.

"The person who has the Son of God has *life* forever" (1 John 5:12).

CHAPTER TWENTY-THREE

THE EARLY CHURCH

*"Lord, who may dwell in your sanctuary? He who speaks the
truth from his heart and has no slander on his tongue."*
(Psalm 15:1, 2)

Early Church Fathers Had Power From God

UNTIL JESUS CAME, only the Old Testament Prophets or other
especially anointed people could contend with evil *directly.*
Then, when Jesus came to earth, satan was even more afraid
of *Him.* Satan is still afraid of Jesus today, and anyone in whom He
dwells, *if* that person knows how to cooperate with God to get rid of
evil. Otherwise, demons play the same roles they have always played:
"liar," "bully," "robber," "murderer," "tempter," "trouble-maker," "pretend they don't exist," and more.

Among all people, only Christians have the ability to directly get
rid of evil. As you know from our examples, witchcraft can employ
strong demons to get rid of lesser demons. But *only Christians can get
rid of all demons.* That's because Jesus is the ultimate power, and He
has chosen to work through His people. He said, *"If I drive out devils
by the Spirit of God* [and He did] *then the Kingdom of God has come
upon you"* (Matthew 12:28). That meant devils are *real,* and Jesus was
able to cast them out by the power of the Spirit of God. Jesus ushered
in *"The Kingdom Age"* When Christians believed what Jesus said, did,
and told them to do, they were able to work almost the same miracles
that He worked, *striking down evil.* No one could do it as consistently
as Jesus, but their general ability to strike down evil was *evidence that
Jesus was in them and operating through them.* And the Church grew.

Example #116
Victory! St. Patrick, Apostle to Ireland!

I *thank God for St. Patrick* and what God accomplished through him in Ireland. He was a brave and powerful and godly man, led by the Holy Spirit.

St. Patrick ministered to the Irish 400 years after Jesus was on earth. His real name was Patricius Magonus Sucatus (AD 389–446), and he was the son of well-educated evangelical Roman Christians who had fled to England to escape the persecution of Christians in Rome. At age 16, Patricius and about 1,000 other English were captured by Irish slave-raiding pirates in Bannavem, on the Severn Estuary and he was sold to a cruel Druid chieftain named Milchu, who renamed him "Patrick." Milchu was a religious leader of the pagan Irish.

Patrick was put out on a lonely hillside to tend pigs and forage for his own food, which was extremely difficult. He was hungry and afraid, and in his distress he remembered portions of scripture his parents had required him to memorize. He began to pray. Jesus made Himself real to Patrick, and Patrick felt comforted. After six years of slavery, in a miraculous way Jesus helped Patrick escape, even without money, and he was taken aboard a ship back to England.

In England, Patrick had a dream that repeated three times: "Patrick, Patrick, come back and tell us about Jesus." It was the Irish, calling to him, over and over. After his extremely difficult experience there, *Patrick did not want to go back to Ireland.* But he recognized God's call and prepared himself. *God filled Patrick with His Holy Spirit and Patrick became a mighty missionary to the Irish.* He converted virtually the entire population of then-pagan Ireland; healing the sick, casting out devils, teaching the Bible and sending Bible story tellers into villages to carry the Gospel to people who couldn't read. The few converts who could read and write were assigned to make copies of the Bible *so it could be broadly taught to the Irish.* Patrick blessed the Irish with the gospel of Christ and scripture.

Earlier, Patrick had challenged Druid witchcraft. Prior to gaining complete liberty to preach the Gospel all over Ireland he had gone to Northern Ireland to challenge the Druid King. On the one night during the year when, on penalty of death, all fires had to be extinguished, and only the King could light the first fire, *Patrick deliberately built a bonfire in sight of the King.* Dragged before the King as he intended, Patrick loudly proclaimed, "Jesus is the light of the world! Those who know Him do not walk in darkness!" And he preached the Gospel of salvation in Christ. The King's brother became a Christian and because of him Patrick was given liberty to preach all over Ireland. He was so successful that about Patrick it was said that "He found Ireland all pagan and left it all Christian."

Was it really true? Did St. Patrick really convert the Irish? A proof is that a century later it was *descendants of St. Patrick's Irish converts who took the Gospel to Europe* Thomas Cahill, (*How the Irish Saved Civilization*), St. Patrick's (*Confessions*), and (*Encyclopedia Britannica*).

Earlier Church Fathers
In chronological order, they span four centuries.

Example #117
Victory! Justin Martyr!

(AD 100–165)

Justin Martyr had studied all the great philosophies of his day. In his *Second Apology* (his explanation c.a. 153) Martyr wrote about exorcisms and healings. "For numberless demoniacs throughout the whole [known] world, and in your city many of our Christian men exorcising them in the name of Jesus Christ, who was crucified under Pontius Pilate have healed and do heal, rendering helpless and driving the possessing devils out of the men, though they could not be cured by other exorcists, and those who used incantations and drugs" John Wimber (*Power Evangelism*) p. 157, cf. Coxe vol. 6:190.

Example #118
Victory! Irenaeus!

(AD 140–203)

In his books *Against Heresies,* which are devoted to the heresy of Gnosticism, (thinking "knowledge saves,") Irenaeus, Bishop of Lyons, wrote about the gifts from the Holy Spirit. He reported: "For some do certainly and truly drive out devils, so that those who have thus been cleansed from evil spirits frequently join themselves to the Church. Others have foreknowledge of things to come; they see visions, and utter prophetic expressions. Others still, heal the sick by laying their hands upon them, and they are made whole. Yea, moreover, as I have said, the dead even have been raised up, and remained among us for many years. And what shall I more say? It is not possible to name the number of gifts which the Church (scattered throughout the whole [known] world), has received from God in the name of Jesus Christ" Wimber (*Power Evangelism*) p. 158.

Example #119
Victory! Tertullian!

(AD 160–220)

In his book *To Scapula,* chapter 6, Tertullian gives this account of expelling demons and healing: "All this might be officially under your notice, and by the very advocates, who are themselves also under obligations to us, although in court they give their voice as it suits them. The clerk of one of them who was liable to be thrown upon the ground by an evil spirit, was set free from his affliction: as was also the relative of another, and the little boy of a third. How many men of rank (to say nothing of the common people) have been delivered from devils, and healed of diseases! Even Severus himself, the father of Antonine, was graciously mindful of the Christians; for He sought out the Christian Proculus, surnamed Torpacion, the steward of Euhodias, and in gratitude for his having once cured him by anointing, he kept him in his palace till the day of his death" Wimber, (*Power Evangelism*) p. 159; cf. Coxe vol. 3:107.

Example #**120**
Victory! Antony!

(ca. AD 1251–356)

Antony, spoken of in his biography by Athanasius, had dealings with the supernatural, especially in dealing with demons. He reported: "Once, a very tall demon appeared with a procession of evil spirits and said boldly: 'I am the power of God, I am his providence. What do you wish that I grant you?' I then blew my breath at him, calling on the name of Christ, and I tried to strike him. I seemed to have succeeded, for immediately, vast as he was, he and all his demons disappeared at the name of Christ" Wimber, (*Power Evangelism*) p. 159.

Please note: It is *not common* for Christians to see demons, but many people have been frightened by them in nightmares. You can defend yourself. While awake, in Jesus' Name forbid satan to *ever* trouble your sleep or the sleep of any member of your family. Do it out loud, if only a whisper. And speak the protection of the Blood of Christ over your sleep and the sleep of your family.

Example #**121**
Victory! Jerome!

(ca. AD 291–371)

"In his book *Life of Saint Hilarion,* Jerome tells of many miracles, healings, and expulsions of demons that occurred during his ministry" Wimber, (*Power Evangelism*).

When Jesus was on earth, He recognized evil, and demons could not operate freely. "When the evil spirits saw Jesus, they fell down before him, 'You are the Son of God'" (Mark 3:11). They knew—and still know—that they are condemned. "Calling the twelve [disciples] to Him, Jesus sent them out two by two *and gave them authority over unclean [evil] spirits* [to cast them out]" (Mark 6:7). People who have Jesus in their lives today have that same authority. Jesus told them, "And these signs will accompany those who believe: *In My name they will cast out devils*" (Mark 16:17). That was the pattern of victory of the

Early Church Fathers through Jerome and is to continue until Jesus returns to earth to establish His Kingdom. He will banish satan and all demons.

<h1 style="text-align:center">Example #122
Augustine!</h1>

(AD 354–430)

In his famous and beloved book, *The City of God,* Augustine affirmed the miraculous. "He wrote, 'It is a simple fact, that there is no lack of miracles even in our day, and the God who works the miracles we read of in the scriptures uses any means and manner he chooses.' Augustine asserted that the ones that happened and were recorded in the New Testament are 'absolutely trustworthy' and tells of the miracles that happened in Augustine's own day: a blind man's sight was restored, breast cancer healed, gout healed, a girl was delivered from demons, a priest brought back from the dead, and many more" Wimber, (*Defferari 1947: vol. 24*) pp. 433–445. (Yet except for the healing of a young woman, there isn't record that Augustine participated in gaining miracles such as he wrote about.) His own doctrine, different from that of the other Early Church Fathers, was that God was "far off" in heaven. Augustine influenced people to accept whatever occurred in their lives, trusting that it came directly from the hand of God, for God's great benefit and perhaps theirs, also. That theology is still strong in many churches today.

Early Church Theology

The theology we have from Jesus and His Disciples and the other Early Church Fathers whose records we have is that God is *personal.* In the person of the Holy Spirit, God is the "Comforter" who in the name of Jesus can help people change their circumstances; miracles can take place and difficulties be overcome. Even during Augustine's time, those Christians who had the Spirit of Jesus living within them were able to continue the merciful things Jesus had accomplished while on earth. "Heal the sick, cast out devils, raise the dead, etc." And as St.

Patrick and other Early Church Fathers and lay Christians had experienced, God was not "far off." He lived within them and used them to help others.

A major spiritual consideration of both theologies was the question of God's "distance" and how He relates to people. *Is He far away? Or is He close? Or is He both?* People tend to "place" God where they have felt His presence, or not felt it, but the Bible teaches that God is not limited to "place." He is everywhere. His Spirit created the universe, yet He knows even the number of hairs on each person's head (Matthew 10:30). *Jesus instructed His followers that God is close to them, helping them.* And *He promised that there would be even more help when the mighty Holy (completely pure) Spirit of God descended upon their lives.* He told them to "*wait* for the gift my Father promised, which you have heard me speak about. For John baptized with water, but in a few days *you will be baptized with the Holy Spirit—You will receive power when the Holy Spirit comes on you*, and you will be my witnesses in Jerusalem [near], and in all Judea and Samaria [farther away] and to the uttermost parts of the earth" (Acts 1:3–8). It was through the power of the Holy Spirit that Early Church Fathers were able to accomplish mighty works of God. Throughout the ages, God's Holy Spirit has ministered on earth and used anyone who humbly asked to be used by Him.

Example #**123**
Victory! St. Boniface!
Missionary to Germanic Tribes!

St. Boniface (680–754) was a celebrated English missionary. Because England had a king, rather than a pope, *Boniface had been free to read the Bible.* He gained genuine faith in the Lord Jesus Christ. In 718 (300 years after the Early Church Fathers) Pope Gregory II called on Boniface to preach the word of God to the pagan Germanic tribes that lived in northern Europe.

The Germanic tribes from Scandinavia had migrated from the Netherlands (lands far away) into areas of northern Europe and Russia approximately a thousand years before Christ. (The tribes were called

"Germanic" and the lands of their origin were later called Norway, Sweden, Denmark and Holland.) In AD 200 some of the Germanic tribes settled along the Rhine, for its better climate, and by AD 400 some of them moved farther south to Rome. (They were so blond and tall that the shorter, dark-haired southern Europeans at first thought the Germanic peoples must be "angels." But the pagan behavior of those tribes dispelled that idea.) Hence Boniface was sent to work among them.

St. Boniface's labors among the Germanic peoples earned him the title of *"Apostle to Germany"* (*World Book Encyclopedia*). When some of his converts slipped back into paganism, in 723 Boniface went up into Friesland (modern Holland) to literally "root out the problem." The Germanic tribes had continued to worship the pagan god, Thor, conducting their worship at a huge oak tree called "Jupiter's oak" in northern Hesse (*Wikipedia.org/wiki/Saint Boniface*). It was said, but not verified, that the tree was the home of a powerful demonic spirit that wanted a blood sacrifice. When Boniface and his men arrived, he told the Germanic tribesmen that he was going to chop the tree down, and called out a loud challenge to their "god" [a demon] to kill him if the oak tree had power! The pagans expected him to die, but instead, Boniface and his men chopped at the tree. *A tremendous wind came up and blew the tree over. It split into four parts.* Boniface called out to the Germans, *"How stands your mighty god! My God is stronger!"* They were amazed, and converted to Christianity. The oak was used to build a cathedral in Hesse that is still standing. (*Wikipedia.org/wiki/ Saint Boniface*) and (*World Book Encyclopedia*).

Boniface was courageous and strong-willed but kind. Later in his life he allowed himself to be killed by robbers who thought he and his fellow priests were carrying gold, when what they were carrying were bags of books. Boniface and his companions carried weapons with which to defend themselves against wild animals in the forests they walked through, but he urged his fellow priests not to use their weapons against the robbers. Why? I think it was because Boniface knew that he and all his fellow priests would immediately be in the presence of Christ, but the unsaved robbers would not be, if they were killed.

That was the opposite of the behavior of many (not all) of the later priests who tortured and killed people if they had even a scrap of scripture in their possession. People in Europe wanted to be able to read scripture, just as St. Patrick had been able to read it and St. Boniface had been able to read the Bible in England. But the Church hierarchy in Europe feared loss of control over the people if they allowed them to read the Bible (which very few priests even read). So for 300 long years the official Church persecuted, and/or put to death, anyone who was found with even a scrap of scripture in their possession. It was monstrous, a terrible time and a terrible crime. St. Patrick and St. Boniface were men with Christ's love within them, mighty men of God who helped people, but sadly, many other priests of the Church were self-serving, concerned only about maintaining their own power, and the prestige of the Church.

The **APOSTLE PETER**, considered by Catholics to be the earthly cornerstone of the Church, gave this order: "To sum up: *All of you* be harmonious, sympathetic, brotherly, kindhearted, and humble in spirit; not returning evil for evil or insult for insult, *but giving a blessing instead...* For the one who desires life, to love and see good days, must keep his tongue from evil and his lips from speaking deceit. He must turn away from evil and do good; he must seek peace and pursue it. For the eyes of the Lord are toward the righteous, and His ears attend to their prayer, but *the face of the Lord is against those who do evil*" (1 Peter 3:8–12). Unfortunately, unlike St. Boniface and St. Patrick, many Church leaders in the Middle Ages didn't read the Bible, so they didn't know what Peter and Jesus taught or did. *If they had read the New Testament, and obeyed it, the history of the Middle Ages would have been very different.* As it was, it was hundreds of years of injustice and cruelty, perpetrated by men who claimed to represent God. It was demonic.

The Reformers: Three Brave Men

Example #124
Victory! Wycliffe!
(1328–1384)

John Wycliffe was an Englishman; reformer, Christian scholar, and Doctor of Divinity at Oxford. He translated the *New Testament from Greek into English in 1382*. Six years later, the entire Bible in English was issued. He could do it because England was controlled by a king rather than the Church. Wycliffe held that "the Bible was the highest source of truth and that it contained all that was necessary for man's salvation" (*World Book Encyclopedia*). He argued against some of the doctrines and land-holding and corruption in the Church, wanting Churchmen to be humble people, like Christ's disciples. That angered Church powers and Wycliffe was imprisoned and accused of heresy. Fortunately for him, Wycliffe died a natural death before they could burn him at the stake (*wikipedia*). The Church later exhumed Wycliffe's bones and burnt them anyway. But Wycliffe was safe in Heaven.

About a hundred years later, *Johannes Gutenberg*, (1398–1468), a German from an aristocratic family, *invented the printing press*. That made it possible to *print pages of the Bible* and other books. It had alphabet letter-type that could be repositioned to form any words and sentences required. The typesetter had to be very skilled, able to read in reverse and set letters in reverse, from right to left. Then, when the type was inked and pressed onto paper, the words flowed from left to right, the way they are read. By 1450 the press was in operation.

Example #125
Victory! Tyndale!
(1494–1536)

William Tyndale was an Englishman who lived a hundred years after Gutenberg. Tyndale was a brilliant biblical translator and scholar who *spoke eight languages fluently. He translated the first New Testament that was printed in common English*. It was the first Bible printed on

Gutenberg's moveable-type printing press. When a priest ridiculed Tyndale's efforts, saying "We are better to be without God's laws than the Pope's," Tyndale angrily replied, "I defy the Pope and all his laws. *If God spares my life ere many years, I will cause the boy that drives the plow to know more of the scriptures than you!*" He secretly translated many books of the Old Testament and wrote compositions about the Christian life. Tyndale was betrayed by a friend who acted as a secret agent of the Church or the King, and he was imprisoned in horrible conditions for over 500 days. He was put on trial for heresy and treason in what viewers described as "a ridiculously unfair trial" and convicted. Tyndale was then strangled and burnt at the stake in the prison yard. His last words were *'Lord, open the King of England's eyes.'* Three years later King Henry VIII published the 1537 English "Great Bible" (*greatsite.com*).

Example #**126**
Victory! Luther!
(1483–1546)

Martin Luther was a German Catholic priest and university professor. He was just eleven years older than Tyndale, and like Tyndale, Luther believed God's words in the Bible: "*The entrance of Thy Word gives light* [to hearts and minds]" (Psalm 119:130). Luther secretly translated the Old Testament from Latin into German, and later he translated the New Testament. He wanted people to see that *their faith needed to be in Jesus,* rather than in the practices of any church. The Bible verse he is known for is Romans 5:1, "*The just shall live by faith* [in Jesus]," rather than having to fear that the Church is continually counting up people's "works" to decide whether they should be allowed into Heaven. "Luther came to believe that God, through Christ, is constantly trying to save mankind" (*World Book Encyclopedia*).

In a public debate, Luther denied the supreme power of the Pope, citing what the Bible says about the priesthood of Believers, that God calls every person who has Christ in his life "a priest" (1 Peter 2:9), meaning every believer is indwelled by God and should minister His love to other people. Luther was excommunicated and put on trial before German princes, nobles, clergy and a new Emperor, who demanded that he retract his teachings. Luther refused, saying, "Unless I am refuted and convicted by testimonies of the Scriptures or by clear arguments...my conscience is bound in the Word of God. I cannot and will not recant anything." Luther was condemned as a "heretic," a "non-believer" because he wanted Germans to be able to read the Bible. He had defied the Church doctrine forbidding it. That meant death, but a powerful friend, Frederick of Saxony, sent a band of masked horsemen to seize Luther and hide him in Frederick's castle. During the ten months he was there, Luther used his time to translate the New Testament from Greek into German (*World Book Encyclopedia*).

The furor died down and Luther began teaching the Bible to some of his university students, who also protested some of the excesses of the Church. The group became known as "protestors," the Protest'ant church, or "Protestant" church. *Luther preached transformation by faith in Christ,* so people would understand that it is *not "good works" that saves them, but faith in Christ.* Then, with God's Spirit *in* them, from their heart they *want to do good works.*

Luther wrote a list of 95 Church practices he considered morally wrong, and in 1517 he made them public by nailing the list to a church door in Wittenberg, Germany. Gutenberg's printing press carried the "Ninety-Five Theses" all over Europe, fanning the Protestant Reformation.

To have God's words in the hands and hearts of the people is what Wycliffe and Tyndale and Luther sacrificed their lives to achieve. Now the New Testament of the Bible is in 1,223 languages and the entire Bible is in 471 languages. In Heaven the three men must be rejoicing. And so are the multiplied thousands of converts who read those scriptures, and the hundreds of Bible translators who have put God's words into languages that people around the world can understand.

CHAPTER TWENTY-FOUR

POWER FOR MINISTRY

"May the words of my mouth and the meditation of my heart be
pleasing in your sight, O Lord my Rock and my Redeemer."
(Psalm 19:14)

The Holy Spirit Is the Power

JESUS PROMISED THAT the *Holy Spirit* would be the *power* of the Church Age: from the time He ascended into Heaven until the time He returns. Acts 1:8 records that right before Jesus was taken up into Heaven He said, "But *you will receive power when the Holy Spirit comes upon you;* and you will be my witnesses in Jerusalem, and in all Judea and Samaria and to the ends of the earth." He told them, "Anyone who has faith in me will do what I have been doing. He will do even greater things than these, because I am going to my Father. You may ask anything in my name and I will do it" (John 14:12, 13b). Wherever the Church demonstrated "power from God" by giving the Gospel and gaining miraculous answers to prayer, the Church grew.

God uses any Christians willing to be used by Him. *He wants them to be able to help themselves and others.* Sometimes that involves a "gift of faith" or a "gift of a word of knowledge," or a "gift of prophecy," and sometimes it involves war against demonic oppressions. *The Holy Spirit is the real power in any "power" you see a Christian have;* power to help. "Holy Spirit" means the *"morally pure, all-powerful Spirit of God."* A few seminaries in the U.S. teach that the gifts of the Holy Spirit are still for today, but unfortunately many others teach that the world no longer needs the gifts of the Spirit "because we have the Bible and doctors." So they teach what are called the "service gifts;" teaching, preaching, mercy, giving, helps, and so forth. Those are important, but they can be accomplished by dedicated *human* effort.

We can be sure though, that if those people are "lifting up Christ," working to make Him known, God is helping them.

For hundreds of years, people in many kinds of (Augustinian type) Christian churches have heard that "the time of the Holy Spirit's help is past." If they don't know any better, their faith has been squashed. But in recent years there has been a spiritual awakening, and many churches are now praying for the sick, with good results, and doing other works of the Holy Spirit. Christians are completely dependent upon the Holy Spirit for guidance and power to minister to people and to gain insights and healing and other help. For instance, when Roy teaches spiritual warfare, he points out the importance of the "gift of discernment" from God's Spirit, by which Christians can sense when there is a demonic oppression. It's a special wisdom from the Holy Spirit that a Christian would not have without that gift. God instructs Christians to value the spiritual gifts.

Two Girls Miraculously Healed

Example #127
Victory! Twisted Spine Healed!

Some friends we met at a church here in the mountains years ago have a daughter who had a severely twisted spine. Doctors couldn't help. The mother had heard that in Los Angeles a visiting evangelist had a gift of healing, and that sometimes people were healed. Perhaps not all, but some. So the mother and daughter went to a huge auditorium, not knowing what to expect and scarcely daring to hope for a healing amidst those thousands of people. They were able to get seats in the midsection, walked down the long row to the middle and sat down. The row quickly filled around them. Kathryn Kuhlman, the visiting evangelist, came on stage when the auditorium was full. During the service she stopped and said, "God has told me that someone here has a badly twisted spine. He wants to heal you." (That is a "word of knowledge" from the Holy Spirit, revealing something the person had no human way of knowing.)

The girl did *not* stand up. Then a woman at the end of the row, who had come in *after* our friends were seated (meaning she didn't see the twisted spine), stood up and pointed directly at the girl, saying, "She means *you*." (Another "word of knowledge") So our friend's daughter went forward, up onto the stage, and stood quietly in front of the evangelist. Ms. Kuhlman smiled at her and reached out her hand and the girl fell backward, like on a cloud. She said she felt nothing except the sound of a little crackling in her spine. *But when she stood up, her spine was straight.* No human could have accomplished that. It was the *Lord!* The evangelist clearly had gifts of "healing" and "miracles" from God's Holy Spirit, like St. Patrick had. She cooperated with God by quietly telling the miracle to happen, in Jesus' Name, and He made it happen. The strong Presence of God's Holy Spirit of *mercy* was in that place!

Example #128
Victory! Malformed Face Healed!

A second miracle was told to Roy by a couple who attend our church when they are on vacation. The husband is retired and the wife teaches at Azusa Pacific University. They told Roy that years ago the baby girl of an acquaintance of her husband was born with a cruelly twisted face, a face so deformed that the mother kept her baby hidden at home. In desperate hope, she took the baby to one of Ms. Kuhlman's meetings. Ms. Kuhlman prayed for the baby, and *her little face instantly untwisted and was normal.* What a *mercy!* It was the *Lord Himself,* through the ministry of the Holy Spirit, who did it. Wouldn't we have felt like dancing for joy!

There are "supernatural" gifts from the Holy Spirit; "super" meaning "above" what could be accomplished by even the most well-meaning natural efforts of Christians. Many people are taught that those special ministry gifts don't exist today, but were only to encourage Christians when the Church was young. Those mighty deeds certainly did encourage them! But people of today have problems too, and need special help. Nowhere in scripture is there any indication that those powerful works of God would stop. And *the fact that God's miracles are still happening today is proof that they haven't stopped.* They will not stop until Jesus returns to earth and the need for those gifts no longer exists because sickness and demonic oppression will be things of the past.

The spiritual gifts equip Christians in ways that are impossible without them, as when the pastor had a "word of knowledge" about the child molester (Chapter 4 #19). The gifts are meant to protect the Church, meet people's needs, and draw the surrounding community to Christ. Let us humble ourselves before God and ask Him to give us whatever gifts He wants us to have, so that we can be of maximum help in this wounded world.

God's power is transmitted by His Holy Spirit, the powerful force of God that worked the creation of the earth (Genesis 1:1) and doubtless the heavens. Jesus said the *Holy Spirit* would be the *power of the Church Age.* The "Church Age" was from the time Jesus ascended into Heaven until the time He returns. So we are still in the "Church Age." But sadly, if the Holy Spirit of God removed Himself from most church ministries in the world today, many would go on operating just as they are now and not know the difference. That is how far churches have drifted away from the power of the Holy Spirit, the driving force of Christianity. However, there are still some groups of Christians who look to God's Spirit to accomplish the same kinds of miracles that the Early Church Fathers experienced. Those are churches that are growing, and some of them are experiencing dramatic growth.

Over the centuries, wherever Christians heard what was being accomplished by God's Spirit, and their faith had not been destroyed or watered down by false doctrines or unbelief, they believed God, and He did mighty works for them and through them. Recently I came upon a used book that is a treasure: Guidepost's *God Can Do it Again.* (Amazon and Barnes and Noble carry it.) It records fascinating, amazing, charming, inspiring true stories from various people who experienced miracles of healing at Ms. Kuhlman's gatherings, *healings of hopeless conditions.* In all the meetings, various reputable medical doctors are on hand to verify and document the miracles. Ms. Kuhlman insisted that she had no ministry gifts at all. But what she clearly did have were gifts of *"faith" and "miracles" and "healing" from* the Holy Spirit, the same Spirit of God who empowered St. Patrick. The joy in the congregation was because people could feel that God was in their midst, helping them.

Sometimes people from conventional churches disparage the enthusiasm seen in a setting like that, or comment on what they consider "flaws" in the evangelist's personality because she was so exuberant. She was enjoying what God was doing, just as the people in the audience were enjoying it. To worship differently than what we are used to in our more formal churches is not a "flaw." Consider the results! And if there are actual "flaws" in people in ministry, please remember that no person except Jesus has no flaws. *Pray* for people in ministry. Satan focuses on them, creating misunderstandings and pressures in his attempt to discredit their ministry and deny people their help. We want to give God honor for what He accomplishes through any of His people, whether minister or church member or simply a kind, loving Christian. We don't want to be mired down like Pharisees, thinking we are always religiously "right," discerning "right," worshipping "right," and so on. Remember when Jesus entered Jerusalem and the people were cheering? The Pharisees were annoyed and wanted Jesus to stop the cheering. He answered, *"I tell you, if they keep quiet, the stones will cry out"* (Luke 19:40). The Pharisees had not even comprehended that the promised Messiah was *in their midst*.

How Can You Know What Is Genuine?

A major thing to look for is *who* is getting the glory? The glory and praise should be going to Jesus. Some preachers claim to have special "gifts," such as a "gift of healing." And some I've seen on TV have tended to be theatrical or talk a lot about money. Are all professions of spiritual "gifts" believable? I don't know. But it has seemed to me that there are some "show-off" types of ministers whose excited words seem to whip the congregation into an emotional frenzy, and then I feel uneasy about both the minister and the congregation. But perhaps they are aware of something wonderful that I can't see. And there are godly ministers and fellow Christians who have gained wonderful results, similar to the miracles accompanying the JESUS film. The *crowds that followed Jesus* into Jerusalem *were cheering Him*. Perhaps when people are cheering in services today, they are actually cheering for Jesus! We want to be careful not to be like proud, judgmental Pharisees.

Even though all of us who have asked for forgiveness of sins, and received Jesus into our lives are marked by the Holy Spirit as *belonging to God*, we also know that "belonging to God" is not the same thing as being *empowered* by Him. That special empowering is called "being filled with the Holy Spirit" and enables the Christian to be a *conduit for God's miraculous, merciful help*, such as the fire chaplain turning back the fire at Lake Arrowhead and Ms. Kuhlman giving healing to the two girls. Both had specific "gifts" from the Holy Spirit and it was *the Holy Spirit Himself doing acts of mercy through them. The difference between them and other Christians is not salvation, which all Christians have. The difference is an empowering for service.* Both the chaplain and Ms. Kuhlman must have asked God for that empowering (Acts 2:38). Appendix B tells how to be filled with the Holy Spirit.

Sending the Holy Spirit!

When God works through people to gain miracles, it is because the power of the Holy Spirit is *in* them. But many people don't realize *who* the Holy Spirit is. If people have heard the words the "Holy Spirit," many of them either have no idea what that means, or satan deceives them into thinking it is some extremist wing of the Christian church. People might associate it with excessive exuberance or lack of sufficient pastoral control in the church, making some people feel insecure in that setting. Humans are imperfect, and I'm sure those problems sometimes arise. But it is well to keep a high view, remembering that the Holy Spirit who caused the miracles in this book is the *same* mighty Holy Spirit who was active in the creation of earth.

The *Holy Spirit* is the third person of the trinity; *the Power* of God. The Bible tells us that the "Spirit of God moved upon the waters" in creation, forming the earth and the things on it (Genesis 1:2). The same mighty *Holy Spirit* is the active force in the universe. The Holy

Spirit is the *God of power,* sometimes "take-your-breath-away power," as He affects situations on earth.

After Jesus' death and resurrection, He stayed on earth for 40 days, showing Himself to His Disciples, giving them convincing proofs that He really was alive (Acts 1:1–3). He told them to wait in Jerusalem for what the Father [God] had promised: "You will be baptized with the Holy Spirit" (verse 5). "You will receive *power when the Holy Spirit has come upon you; and you shall be My witnesses*" (verse 8). A corresponding verse is Luke 24:49, where Jesus told His Disciples to wait in the city [Jerusalem] until they were "clothed with power from on high" [the mighty Holy Spirit]. They waited, and the Holy Spirit came! The *mighty Spirit of God* doesn't usually tip-toe in. He comes with more power than some people can cope with. "When the day of Pentecost had come, they [Jesus' disciples] were all gathered in one place. And *suddenly there came from heaven a noise like a violent rushing wind.* And it filled the whole house where they were sitting. And there appeared to them tongues as of fire, distributing themselves, and they rested on each one of them. And they were all filled with the Holy Spirit and began to speak in other languages, as the Spirit was giving them the words" (Acts 2:1–4).

What language does the Holy Spirit speak? *All languages!* Plus a code language that satan can't understand and therefore cannot interfere with. "Tongue" is the historic synonym for "language" because speaking requires the use of a person's tongue. So it was a commonly used term, as in "Do you speak the tongue of the Greeks?" Occasionally, to help someone, the Holy Spirit has even enabled a Christian with a "gift of tongues" to speak a human language that he doesn't know in order to help someone from a different country. I've heard of Him doing that in today's world, to the amazement of the person who has that "gift of tongues," and the gratefulness of the listener, whose heart was moved by a personal message from God.

That is what happened when the Holy Spirit was "poured out" on the Disciples in Jerusalem (Acts 2:1–18). "Now there were Jews living in Jerusalem, devout men from every nation [in that region]. And when this sound occurred [like a "mighty rushing wind"], the crowd came together, and *were bewildered because each one of them was hearing them speak in his own language.* They were amazed and astonished, saying, 'Why, aren't all these who are speaking Galileans? How is it that we each hear them in our own language? Parthians and Medes and Elamites, residents of Mesopotamia, Judea and Cappadocia, Pontus and Asia, Phrygia and Pamphylia, Egypt and the districts of Libya around Cyrene, and visitors from Rome, both Jews and proselytes, Cretans and Arabs—we hear them in our *own tongues* [languages] *speaking of the mighty deeds of God.'* And they continued in amazement and great perplexity, saying to one another, 'What does this mean?' But others were mocking, and saying, 'They are full of sweet wine.'

"Peter, taking his stand with the eleven, raised his voice and declared to them: 'Men of Judea...and all others...heed my words. These men are not drunk, as you suppose, for it is still morning; but this is what was spoken of through the prophet Joel: "I will pour out My Spirit on all mankind; and your sons and your daughters shall prophesy, and your young men shall see visions, and your old men shall dream dreams; even on My bondslaves, both men and women, I will pour forth My Spirit, and they shall prophesy."'" That supernatural phenomenon is what happened to the Early Church Fathers and has continued through the 2000 years since then and will continue until Jesus returns.

What Are the Spiritual Gifts?

Many churches throughout the years, and especially today, have the same gifts from the Holy Spirit that the Early Church Fathers had. They have been called "charismatic" churches, because the Greek word "charis" means "gift." The dictionary defines "charismatic" as "a special divine grace, fitting a person for the life, work, or office to which he was called; a grace, as a miraculously given power of healing or of speaking in the unknown language, or prophesying, etc., 'attributed to some of the early Christians'" (*Webster's New International Dictionary*).

In 1 Corinthians 12, chapters 12–14, the Apostle Paul teaches about spiritual gifts: "Now there are varieties of gifts, but the same Spirit [Holy Spirit]. And there are varieties of ministries, but the same Lord...To each person is given the manifestation of the Spirit *for the common good.* To one is given the *word of wisdom* [told them by the Spirit], and to another the *word of knowledge* according to the same Spirit; to another *faith* by the same Spirit, and to another *gifts of healing* by the one Spirit, and to another the effecting of *miracles,* and to another *prophecy,* and to another *the distinguishing of spirits* [discernment]. To another *various kinds of tongues* [several languages], and to another the *interpretation of tongues* [knowing what the words mean]. But one and the same Spirit works all these things, distributing to each one individually just as He wills...For by one Spirit we were all baptized [spiritually] into one body [Christ] and have *one Spirit* [the Holy Spirit of God]."

God doesn't usually give any one person all the spiritual gifts, because Christians are not meant to be self-sufficient. We are to function as a church "body," needing the benefit of the gifts others in the church have, "for the equipping of the saints, for the work of service, to the building up of the body of Christ" (Ephesians 4:12). Only in that way are we "complete." We need power for service that is *beyond* what is humanly possible. Jesus promised, "You will receive *power* when the Holy Spirit comes upon you [power to help that is beyond human ability] and you shall be my witnesses in Jerusalem, and in all Judea and Samaria, and even to the remotest part of the earth" (Acts 1:8). That is what the Jesus film teams are experiencing as they present the message of salvation in Christ to distant peoples.

The Apostle Paul's Warning About "Tongues"

The Apostle Paul gave *a semi-scolding to the church* about undisciplined use of "tongues" (the unknown language) in church services. Expressed in the common language of the people, his words would have been something like, "Listen guys, I speak tongues (languages) *more than you all!* But in the church *I would rather speak five words that people can understand,* so that I may instruct them, rather than 10,000 words in a 'tongue' they can't understand! Whether it is spoken in the language of God's Spirit or an earthly language, it is useless if the man can't understand it!" And in that chapter Paul goes on to teach specifics about the appropriate use of the spiritual gift of "tongues" (1 Corinthians 14). In a church service, no more than three people are to give messages in "tongues," and *only* if someone is present who has the gift of interpretation, so the congregation will know *what was said* in the unknown language. Otherwise, the person with "tongues" is to keep quiet (verse 28) *"or visitors in the church will think you are all crazy!"* In some undisciplined church services even today, that is the unfortunate impression that is sometimes given.

In a women's class I taught at church, we were gathered in a prayer circle when a woman new to the group loudly began to speak in "tongues." I excused myself and called her aside and quietly asked, "Did you bring an interpreter?" She looked puzzled. "The Bible says if you do not have an interpreter you are to keep silent in the church." She appeared stunned. I'm sure she meant well, but she was "out of order." Neither she nor any of the other women could understand what she was saying in "tongues." So it was a disturbance, a distracting "noise," like having a foreigner speaking loudly in your group. That is what the Apostle Paul said must *not* be done. Restricting it doesn't diminish the importance of the gift; it just keeps the use of it orderly.

My understanding of "tongues," the "unknown language" is that except for an occasional prophecy in church, it is primarily a gift for personal prayer, bypassing the person's mind and softly praying *what God knows the need is, even if the person speaking it does not know.* Many times in life a person does not really know what to pray in a situation. With the "unknown" language, God reaches over the person's conscious mind to give help. So even if the person is speaking quietly in the language he can't understand, something important is being prayed. Sometimes a person with the spiritual gift of tongues also has a *"gift of interpretation."* A friend of mine has both those gifts. She told God she didn't want the gift of tongues unless He would also give her the gift of "interpretation of tongues," so she could know what the prayer concerns are. God gave her both gifts, so as she prays in the unknown language she also gains the interpretation. Her words have proven true, and she has helped many people. The Holy Spirit *always knows what needs to be prayed*. But all should be done "decently and in order," as scripture commands. "For God is not a God of confusion but of peace" (1 Corinthians 14:33).

Example #129
Victory! The Holy Spirit on Timor, Indonesia!

In 1968 an outpouring of God's Holy Spirit came upon a small church on a small island in Indonesia. It was a modern-day fulfillment of Jesus' promise to the Church: "You shall receive power after the Holy Spirit has come upon you" (Acts 1:8). That meant power far beyond human ability. The outpouring of God's Spirit in the mountain town of Soe ("Soy") on the island of Timor ("TEEmor") resulted in many healings and miracles. And the Holy Spirit did *such dramatic works of mercy and power that a great turning to Christ took place.*

If you have a map, the Indonesian island of Timor looks like a little hat that sits on top of Australia. Years ago, Roy and Ais ("ice") Pormes, the Indonesian Director of the fledgling Campus Crusade ministry in that country, flew into Timor's capital city of Kopang to meet with an agricultural official about a possible rice-growing project to fund the new ministry. Ais tried to telephone the official's home but couldn't get through, so Roy and Ais hired a jeep to take them the 60 bumpy miles (96 kilometers) to the man's home. The driver had to go so slowly that it was midnight before they arrived at the agricultural official's home.

Roy and Ais were astonished that *a prayer meeting was going on in the man's home* at that late hour! It couldn't have been contrived, because the agricultural official didn't even know that Roy and Ais were coming. And neither the official nor Ais knew that the other was a Christian! The official told Roy and Ais that God had done dramatic and wonderful things in their midst, and that *many people in Soe had trusted in Christ because of those miracles. The child of a church member had been raised from the dead, water had been changed into wine for communion, people were healed, and from the outside of the church, townspeople had seen "flames" inside the church* (just as were recorded when the Holy Spirit was "poured out" on the Church at Pentecost). Those phenomena caused scores of Indonesians to want to be right with God. They asked His forgiveness and received Jesus as their savior.

Those were the same kinds of phenomena the Disciples saw, and Christians in other eras saw, as the Holy Spirit of God came into their midst.

Why did God do those New Testament marvels in an out-of-the-way place like Soe? Probably some earnest Indonesian Christians there had fasted and prayed for an outpouring of God's Holy Spirit upon them. And God manifesting His power on Timor is another proof that the Holy Spirit's ministry was *not limited to the Early Church Age.* I think we are in what Dr. C. Peter Wagner calls "the third wave of the Holy Spirit." Those miracles, as well as miracles in other places, are *proof* that the time for miracles is *not* past. They can occur again anywhere that Christians meet God's requirements. What are they? A clean heart, the desire to be used by God, and the indwelling presence of His Holy Spirit. Let us be careful not to be 21st century Pharisees, doubting or second-guessing the moving of God's Spirit. Rather, let's say, "Please do it for my church too, Lord, and for me."

Wherever churches or individual Christians had gifts from the Holy Spirit to help people, the church grew. In today's "Third Wave of the Holy Spirit" many churches are experiencing the same kinds of supernatural blessings as the Christians of the Early Church experienced. Those are the churches that are growing. Roy and I have just read a wonderful book, *Riding the Wave,* about things God is doing in this "third wave of the Holy Spirit's power upon earth." There are sixteen true stories of God's amazing love and reality and miracles. Compiled and edited by Kevin Springer, published by Marshall Pickering in England, Amazon.com has a few used copies. The book is a *treasure!*

Example #**130**
Victory! Internet Evangelism!

A major Christian emphasis in today's world is *evangelism and discipleship*. Now, in this computer age, we have *Global Media Outreach,* (GMO) *a media outreach ministry through which individuals anywhere in the world can talk to a Christian online about their spiritual questions.* Several thousand Christians are available to respond to E-mail inquiries. From 2010 through 2012, *195 million* people worldwide visited the computer site and *over 25 million of them indicated commitments to Christ. That is almost equivalent to the entire population of the state of Texas!* (pop. 26,000,000)

What a tremendous reach of the Gospel as computers are used for ministry! Now almost anyone in the world can find God. The way it works is that an inquirer "googles" a need, such as "I want to know God," or "I need help with my marriage," or "Who is Jesus?" Various websites pop up, among them *looktoJesus* and other sites that have the word "Jesus" in them. 5,500 Campus Crusade workers and church laymen in America and other countries answer E-mails. Via his computer, Roy talks to at least one person by E-mail every day or every few days, no matter where he is in the world. He has corresponded with 426 people about all kinds of questions, and 121 have received Christ.

Roy has communicated with people from countries that are open to the Gospel *and from countries that he, as a missionary, could never get into:* Iran, Saudi Arabia, Algeria, Tunisia, and others. Of the callers who wanted to hear the entire presentation of the Gospel, *about half of them received Christ.* Roy guides them to discipleship material online and to verses in the Bible that he knows will help them. The goal is to help those who contact him find Christ and then help them grow in their Christian faith in a church or a home fellowship group if one exists. Through avenues like this, evangelism ministry to the world has multiplied exponentially. These are some of the "greater things" Jesus said would be possible.

Example #131
Victory! The Apostle Paul!

The Apostle Paul was a great example of a man filled with the Holy Spirit of God. He evangelized and taught in many areas of the Middle East and then in Rome, and his letters to the early Christian churches became the text of much of the New Testament. As he was imprisoned in Rome, awaiting execution for preaching that salvation is in Christ, he wrote a last letter to his disciple Timothy: "Endure hardship, do the work of an evangelist, fulfill your ministry. For I am already being poured out as drink offering, and the time of my departure has come. I have fought the good fight, I have finished the course, I have kept the faith; in the future there is laid up for me a crown of righteousness, which the Lord, the righteous Judge, will award to me on that day; and not only to me, but to all who have loved His appearing" (2 Timothy 4:5–8).

Paul was a very brave man! In Ephesus (Turkey), Roy and I saw the amphitheater where he preached. It is *huge, carved out of stone, and* seats 20,000! The silver merchants of Ephesus, who sold statues of the "goddess" Artemis, were angry that Paul was preaching about a *higher* God. Conversions to Christ doubtless cut into their profits. They wanted to kill him. No one likes to suffer, but Paul was not afraid of what people could do to him. *He had seen in brilliant light the resurrected presence of Jesus alive, and heard Him speak! Paul knew there is a world beyond this one and he would be in it* (Acts 9). His heart and mind were set on doing the work the Lord Jesus Christ had for him to accomplish.

Our daughter Karen took me into the magnificent entrance rotunda of the Library of Congress. The names of the most noble contributors to the literature of civilization are carved in large letters around the top of the rotunda. *Among those few honored names is "The Apostle Paul."* It gave me tears in my eyes to see it. *Paul's writings civilized whatever part of the world read them, received Christ, and obeyed.* The United States was founded upon the New Testament of the Bible, much of which was written by Paul. When Paul died in Rome, he *knew it was for the truth, and he was not afraid.* He knew he would immediately be in the world that Jesus is King of, the world that will never end.

The Holy Spirit of Mercy

The Holy Spirit of miracles is also the God of mercy. The Apostle Paul wrote: "Though I speak the languages of men and of angels, if I don't have love I am nothing" (1 Corinthians 13:1). *Jesus inspires Christians to meet needs, and the Holy Spirit gives them power to do it.*

"Holy Spirit" means the *"morally pure, all-powerful Spirit of God."* He does miracles, especially through Christians who have a "gift of miracles," and through many people praying, or fasting and praying. And sometimes He does miracles for no discernible reason. *The Holy Spirit is the real power in any "power" you see a Christian have.* But more frequently than accomplishing miracles, *the Holy Spirit inspires mercy,* which is shown through *kind deeds of concerned people.* Helpless infants and orphans are taken care of, children are adopted into caring homes, the poor and the sick and the dying are cared for. *Mercy expresses God's heart.* The Bible calls it a "gift of mercy" from the Holy Spirit. In many countries there weren't even hospitals until Christian missionaries built and staffed them. Then non-Christian governments felt shamed and built government hospitals. Many people of those countries say they prefer Christian Mission hospitals because the "quality of mercy" is there. (In Singapore I was in a government hospital, "un-tended" by an extremely uncaring nurse, so I understand why the nationals prefer mission hospitals.)

Example #132
Victory! Mother Teresa!

"Blessed are the merciful, for they shall obtain mercy."
(Matthew 5:7)

In India, Roy and I visited Mother Teresa's headquarters in Calcutta. Cleanliness and *peace* and an atmosphere of love are inside and outside her building. In contrast, not far from their ministry of mercy is a tall, hideous statue of "Kali," the Hindu "goddess of death." Dirty, red paint "blood" runs down toothy fangs to pool around a filthy base. Indian women present offerings to "Kali" in hopes she (the demons in the idol) won't harm them or their children during childbirth. At least that is what an Indian woman told me when I asked her. Possibly not all Indian women take the threat of Kali seriously, but that is the fearsome thing the idol represents. Not love, fear. Intrinsic in Hinduism is *fear*. That ugly idol is the opposite of the peaceful, loving atmosphere of dear Mother Teresa's hospital. Her *ministry of mercy* demonstrated *God's love*. If dying people couldn't be brought to her hospital, Mother Teresa walked around the streets of Calcutta to comfort them. Why? Because *God's Love was within her*. She said, "No one should have to leave this earth without feeling loved." Her expanded ministry cared for 10,000 dying lepers. *Mercy and love come from God*. Where people worship idols and practice witchcraft, mercy and generosity are scarce.

Example #133
VICTORY! Food for Orphans!

"I was hungry, and you gave me to eat; I was thirsty, and you
gave me something to drink; I was a stranger, and you invited
me in; I was naked, and you clothed me; I was sick and you
visited me; I was without a home and you came to me."
(Matthew 25:35, 36)

In answer to *George Müller's* earnest prayers, *God provided food daily for more than 2000 orphans in the five orphanages he established in England.* Every day, Müller spent several hours praying for supplies for the orphanages, and every day people brought food and other supplies. Sometimes the food arrived as Müller and his orphans were praying. He kept careful daily records and issued receipts. Over his lifetime, his non-profit organization *cared for 10,024 orphans* and educated them in *117 schools* that people in the community helped him establish. He rejected any kind of government assistance because he wanted to prove God's faithfulness. Müller had eventually *trained 120,000 children for every kind of advanced employment* so they would have a good start in life and not have to beg or dig ditches. And the children learned to trust God and know that He loves them and answers prayer.

In addition to providing food and care and Christian education for orphans, *Müller also distributed 285,407 Bibles and 1,459,506 New Testaments.* It was a complete change from what his own childhood had been. As a 10-year-old boy, Müller was lying and stealing and gambling. *Then someone led him to Christ and his life changed. He became devoted to mercy and the Bible and to proving that God is faithful to answer prayer.* Müller's careful records showed that his organization distributed to needy children what amounts in today's terms to about *90 million dollars' worth of food, supplies, schools, and education.* All of this is a record of history in England. For further details, Google: "George Müller."

Example #134
Victory! "Dream Centers!"

America's Christian organizations minister to this country and the world. In Los Angeles, an extraordinary city ministry began fifteen years ago. Eighteen Christians met for prayer, desiring to extend mercy to needy people. *That ministry now helps 30,000 people.* It feeds and houses several thousand, shelters abused women and children and others who are homeless, provides counseling, medical help, Bible classes, schooling, job training and help in placement. The people themselves named the church: *"Dream Center." Crime has dropped 65% in the area* and local government officials can't understand it. *There are now eight "Dream Centers"* operating in various big cities of the U.S., ministering the Gospel and *practical mercy* to needy people, transforming lives. *The young pastor said Jesus gave them the vision for doing it.*

Example #135
Victory! Widespread Mercy!

Many other Christian groups also minister to needy people, supported by Christians with hearts of mercy: Doctors and dentists fly to provide aid to people who lack medical care. Missionary pilots fly mercy missions in difficult jungle areas. Engineers build clean water wells. Individual Christians with hearts of loving concern do ministries of many kinds as they see needs. *In thousands of ways, in thousands of places, Jesus ministers mercy through people in whom His Spirit dwells.* The Apostle Paul wrote, "Be imitators of God, therefore, as dearly loved children, and live a life of love, just as Christ loved us and gave himself up for us" (Ephesians 5:1).

Gaining forgiveness and life forever are God's gifts to us; helping others find God is our gift to Him. Pray that His angels will lead you to people you can help; people who are hungry or ill or discouraged and/or want to know God personally. If you encounter someone who is hostile toward God, please be patient and kind and pray for God's *light* to come to that person's mind. He or she might come from a family line that has been spiritually blind for generations. A spiritual curse might have been set against the family. The Apostle Paul said, "The god of this world [satan] has blinded the minds of those who don't believe, lest the glorious gospel of the Lord Jesus Christ shine in unto them [their hearts and minds] and they be converted" (2 Corinthians 4:4). "Converted" means turned around in their thinking, so they will seek God. What can we do to help such a person? Pray, and in Jesus' name quietly "speak against" spiritual blindness so God's mercy can come to those people. You might be the only person praying for them. Out loud, if only in a whisper, tell any "spirits of spiritual blindness" to leave that person's mind alone, and pray protection over them so they can "hear and understand" the truth of life in Christ. Praying Christians can ask God's angels to "cast down imaginations, and every high thing that exalts itself against the knowledge of God, and bring into captivity every thought to the obedience of Christ" (2 Corinthians 10:5).

"THE SPIRIT OF A MAN IS THE CANDLE OF THE LORD"

I love that little phrase. The human spirit is *alive* because it is *God's own "light" in each person.* We need to respect that. And we want our life to glow with *Christ's* light and bring others to Him. Those people who love Him will live forever in a marvelous, interesting place of beauty and progress, where there will never again be sorrow or pain or crying or death. Evil will be gone. Until you get there, seek to lift Jesus *up* in people's thinking, and put satan *down*. That is the "spiritual war" every Christian is called to be a part of. Take as many people to Heaven with you as possible!

GOD BLESS YOU!

PERSEVERE, DO GOOD, LEAD OTHERS TO CHRIST!

APPENDIX A

How to Know Jesus Personally

GOD *LOVES* YOU and created you to know him personally. The Bible teaches us that "God so loved the world, that He gave His only Son, that whoever believes in Him will not perish, but have everlasting life" (John 3:16).

Man is separated from God by sin. "All have sinned" (Romans 3:23). "The wages of sin is death" (Romans 6:23). "God demonstrated His love for us, in that while we were yet sinners, Christ died for us" (Romans 5:8). Jesus said, "I am the way, the truth, and the life. No man comes to the Father, except through me" (John 14:6).

We must individually *receive* Jesus Christ as Savior and Lord. Then we can know God personally and experience His love. "As many as received Him, to them He gave the right to become children of God, even to those who believe on His name" (John 1:12).

How to Be Filled With the Holy Spirit

Jesus promised the abundant and fruitful life as the result of being filled (controlled and empowered) by the Holy Spirit. The Spirit-filled life means Jesus has freedom to live His life in us and through us, by the power of the Holy Spirit (John 1:5). *All Christians are indwelt by the Holy Spirit, but not all Christians are empowered by the Holy Spirit.*

"You shall receive power when the Holy Spirit has come upon you; and you shall be my witnesses both in Jerusalem, and in all Judea and Samaria, and even to the remotest part of the earth" (Acts 1:8). Someone who has the Holy Spirit empowering his life is Christ-centered, he wants to help others find Christ. He has an effective prayer life, and reads and understands God's Word. He trusts God, feels close to Him, and endeavors to obey Him.

To seek that filling from God, we tell God we love Him and ask Him to cleanse us of sin and fill us with His Spirit. You can appropriate the filling of the Holy Spirit right now if you sincerely desire to be controlled and empowered by the Holy Spirit (Matthew 5:6; John 7:37–39). Confess your sins. Thank God that He has forgiven all of your sins—past, present, and future, because Christ died for you. (Colossians 2:13–15; 1 John 1, 2:1–3; Hebrews 10:1–17).

HUMBLY ASK GOD TO FILL YOU WITH HIS HOLY SPIRIT.

How to "Walk" in the Spirit

Have faith in God and His promises. You will experience more of God's closeness and power as you talk to others about Him. Maintain a sensitive heart attitude. If you sin, in your heart run to the Father, not away from Him. Confess your sin to Him and there is no barrier. He always loves you, but sin puts up a barrier. Keep that barrier down.

To enable you to experience God's closeness,

1. Confess any sin to God and turn away from it.

2. Mentally "breathe in" the confidence of God's love for you and the Holy Spirit's presence in you. Bask in His love. You can talk to Him at any time. God is always with you, loving you. If you experience persistent discouragement in spite of your desire to please God and walk with Him, get prayer help from a Christian you trust.

Help Others Find Jesus

An easy way to talk to people about Jesus is to share a little booklet. My favorite is what I call the little green booklet, *"Would you like to Know God Personally?"* I smile at the person and ask if I can share with them *the most wonderful thing I ever found out in my whole life! No one yet has refused it.* Or, if time is limited, I offer it to the person. People smile back at me and take the booklet. Most people have never had anyone talk to them personally about God. It is as though no one cared about them or their soul or their eternal destiny. Be someone who does care.

It is almost comical how the devil will try to keep you from opening your mouth to talk about Jesus. He will whisper that your hair isn't combed and you don't look right and you don't have time and the other person doesn't have time and you are dumb and no one is interested. But *as soon as you open your mouth and speak up for Jesus you feel a flood of God's blessing wash over you* (but not until then). It's like a test, and God is smiling. Always let the person have the booklet.

APPENDIX B

Bible Prophecies Fulfilled By Christ

J ESUS IS CENTRAL in Bible prophecy, with 332 distinct prophecies about Him.

The following table is from Science Speaks, by mathematician Dr. Peter Stoner. It contains 53 of the many prophesies that have already been fulfilled!

In order to fulfill only 8 prophecies through one man the odds are 1 in 10 to the 17th power. That would be 1 in 100,000,000,000,000,000. The chance for only 16 prophecies about Christ to come true in Jesus' life are 1 in 10 to the 45th power. For 48 prophecies the chances are an even more amazing 1 in 10 to the 157th power. It is almost impossible to conceive how large a figure this really is. Jesus' fulfillment of these prophecies it irrefutable evidence that He is indeed the Son of God.

JESUS WILL DESTROY EVIL, RESTORE THE
EARTH, AND REIGN ON EARTH FOREVER.

This list would make an excellent and fascinating Bible Study.

	PROPHECIES ABOUT JESUS	RECORDED IN THE OLD TESTAMENT	FULFILLED IN THE NEW TESTAMENT
1.	Born of the seed of woman	Genesis 3:15	Galatians 4:4 John 16:28 Matthew 1:20
2.	Born of a virgin	Isaiah 7:14	Luke 1:26–27 Matthew 1:18, 24, 25
3.	Descendent of Abraham	Genesis 12:3; 22:18	Galatians 3:16 Matthew 1:1

	PROPHECIES ABOUT JESUS	RECORDED IN THE OLD TESTAMENT	FULFILLED IN THE NEW TESTAMENT
4.	Descendent of Isaac	Genesis 17:19; 21:12	Luke 3:34 Matthew 1:2
5.	Descendent of Jacob	Numbers 24:17	Matthew 1:2 Luke 3:34
6.	Tribe of Judah	Genesis 49:10	Luke 3:33 Hebrews 7:14
7.	Family line of Jesse	Isaiah 11:1	Luke 3:32 Matthew 1:6
8.	Heir to the throne of David	Isaiah 9:7 Jeremiah 23:5	Luke 1:32–33 Acts 13:22–23
9.	Born in Bethlehem of Judea	Micah 5:2	Matthew 2:1, 4–6 Luke 2:4–5, 7
10.	Killing of male children	Jeremiah 31:15	Matthew 2:14–16
11.	Shall be Immanuel (*God with us*)	Isaiah 7:14	Matthew 1:23 Luke 7:16
12.	Out of Egypt I called My Son	Hosea 11:1	Matthew 2:14, 15
13.	Preceded by messenger (*John*)	Isaiah 40:3–5 Malachi 3:1	Luke 3:3–6; 7:24, 27 Matthew 3:3
14.	Special anointing of the Holy Spirit	Isaiah 11:2; 42:1	Matthew 3:16–17 John 1:32
15.	His pre-existence	Micah 5:2 Isaiah 9:6–7	Colossians 1:17 John 1:1, 2; 8:58
16.	Declared to be the Son of God	Psalm 2:7	Matthew 3:17; 16:16
17.	Ministry to begin in Galilee	Isaiah 9:1	Matthew 4:12–17

	PROPHECIES ABOUT JESUS	RECORDED IN THE OLD TESTAMENT	FULFILLED IN THE NEW TESTAMENT
18.	He spoke in parables	Psalms 78:1–4	Matthew 13:34–35
19.	He shall be a Prophet	Deuteronomy 18:15, 18	Acts 3:20–22 Matthew 21:11
20.	He shall be a King	Psalm 2:6	Matthew 27:37; 18:37
21.	He shall be a Judge	Isaiah 33:22	John 5:30
22.	He shall be Lord	Psalm 110:1 Jeremiah 23:6	Luke 2:11 Matthew 22:43–45
23.	He healed the broken hearted	Isaiah 61:1–2	Luke 4:18–19
24.	He had a ministry of miracles	Isaiah 35:5–6	Matthew 9:35; 11:4–6
25.	Messiah will be rejected by own people	Isaiah 53:1–3	John 1:11; 12:37–38 Luke 23:18
26.	He is a Priest after order of Melchizedek	Psalm 110:4	Hebrews 5:5, 6
27.	Triumphal entry into Jerusalem	Zechariah 9:9	Mark 11:7, 9, 11 Luke 19:35–37
28.	He showed zeal for God	Psalm 69:9; 119:139	John 2:15–17
29.	He was to enter the Temple	Malachi 3:1	Matthew 21:12
30.	A "stone of stumbling to the Jews	Psalms 118:22 Isaiah 8:14	1 Peter 2:17 Romans 9:32, 33

	PROPHECIES ABOUT JESUS	RECORDED IN THE OLD TESTAMENT	FULFILLED IN THE NEW TESTAMENT
31.	A "light to the gentiles"	Isaiah 60:3; 49:6	Acts 13:47, 48 Matthew 10:4; 26:50
32.	Betrayed by His friend	Psalms 41:9; 55:12–14	Luke 22:47–48; 26:23; 28:28
33.	Sold for 30 pieces of silver	Zechariah 11:12	Matthew 26:14–15; 27:3
34.	Money thrown into God's House	Zechariah 11:13	Matthew 27:5
35.	Price given for potter's field	Zechariah 11:13	Matthew 27:7
36.	Forsaken by His disciples	Zechariah 13:7	Mark 14:50 Matthew 26:31
37.	Accused by false witnesses	Psalm 35:11	Matthew 26:59–60
38.	Silent before His accusers	Isaiah 53:17	Matthew 27:12 Mark 15:4–5
39.	Wounded and bruised	Isaiah 53:5 Zechariah 13:6	Matthew 27:26
40.	Spat upon and struck	Isaiah 50:6 Micah 5:1	Matthew 26:67 Luke 22:63
41.	A vicarious sacrifice	Isaiah 53:5	Romans 5:6, 7
42.	Hands and feet pierced	Psalm 22:16 Zechariah 12:10	Luke 23:33 John 20:25–27
43.	Crucified with sinners	Isaiah 53:12	Matthew 27:38 Mark 15:27, 28
44.	Prayed for His persecutors	Isaiah 53:12	Matthew 27:38 Mark 15:27–28

	PROPHECIES ABOUT JESUS	RECORDED IN THE OLD TESTAMENT	FULFILLED IN THE NEW TESTAMENT
45.	Soldiers gambled for His clothing	Psalms 22:17–18	Matthew 27:35–36 John 19:23, 24
46.	Vinegar offered Him	Psalm 69:21	Matthew 27:34 John 19:28–29
47.	Forsaken by God	Psalm 22:1	Matthew 27:46
48.	Bones not broken	Psalm 34:20	John 19:32–36
49.	His side pierced	Zechariah 12:10	John 19:34
50.	Darkness over the land	Amos 8:9	Matthew 27:45
51.	Buried in rich man's tomb	Isaiah 53:9	Matthew 27:57–60
52.	Resurrected from the dead	Psalm 16:10	Acts 2:31 Mark 16:6–7
53.	Ascension to God the Father	Psalm 68:18	Acts 1:9 Mark 16:19 Ephesians 4:8

Dr. Stoner's mathematical odds as recorded in *"Science Speaks"* are staggering. *The prophecies were meant by God to prepare people for coming of Christ and to convince them that Christ will destroy evil and be the eternal King of earth, reigning in righteousness.*

APPENDIX C

Bibliography
References From Selected Authors

Copyright permission received where requested.

Boyd, Gregory A. *God at War: The Bible and Spiritual Conflict.* (Copyright © 1997 by Gregory A. Boyd. Used by permission of InterVarsity Press, PO Box 1400 Downers Grove, Il. 60515) pp. 21, 22, 45, 118, 119, 231, 232 ivpress.com.

Boyd, Gregory A. *Satan and the Problem of Evil: Constructing a Trinitarian Warfare Theododicy.* (Copyright © 2001 by Gregory A. Boyd, Used by permission of InterVarsity Press PO Box 1400 Downers Grove, IL 60515) pp. 118, 119, 228, 229, 231, 232, 233, 235.

Carlsson-Paige, Nancy. *Taking Back Childhood.* (Copyright © 2003 by Nancy Carlsson-Paige, Penguin Group USA Inc., 375 Hudson St, New York, NY 10014) pp. 13, 15, 17, 19, 20, 21.

Compilation of spiritual warfare experiences from many missionary authors. *Demon Experiences in Many Lands.* (Copyright © 1960 Moody Press, Chicago, IL) p. 87, 88.

Eshleman, Paul. *I Just Saw Jesus.* (The Jesus Project. Campus Crusade for Christ, San Bernardino, California, now Orlando, FL) pp. 113, 115.

Green, Jim. *The Power of Jesus.* (Copyright © 2007 The Jesus Film Project. Campus Crusade for Christ, Orlando, FL).

Grubb, Norman. *Rees Howell's, Intercessor.* (Copyright © 1952 Christian Literature Crusade, Fort Washington, PA) pp. 217–257.

Hillis, Dick, a story in *Demon Experiences in Many Lands.* (Copyright © 1960 Moody Press, Chicago, IL).

Lea, Larry. *The Weapons of Your Warfare* (Copyright © 1989 by Larry Lea, Creation House, Lake Mary, FL 32746).

Michaelsen, Johanna. *Spirit Wars* (Copyright © 1982 Harvest House Publishers, Eugene, OR, 97402) p. 27.

Montgomery, Warwick. *Demon Possession. Demonology in Anthropological Perspective.* (Copyright © 1976 by Bethany Fellowship Inc. Minneapolis, MN) pp. 180, 181.

Moody Bible Institute, *Demon Possession in Many Lands, a Compilation* (Copyright © 1960 The Moody Bible Institute of Chicago, IL).

Murphy, Ed. *Handbook for Spiritual Warfare.* (Copyright © 1992 by Edward F. Murphy. Thomas Nelson Publishers, Nashville, TN) pp. 21, 147–249.

Nilsson, Lennart, and Hamburger, Lars. *A Child Is Born.* (Copyright © 1990 Delacorte Press/Seymour Lawrence, Bantam Doubleday Dell Publishing Group, New York, NY).

Otis, George. *Last of the Giants: Lifting the Veil on Islam.* (Copyright © 1991 by George Otis Jr. Published by Fleming H. Revell, Grand Rapids, MI) pp. 114, 115.

Pentecost, J. Dwight. *Your Adversary the Devil.* (Copyright © 1969 by Zondervan Publishing House, Grand Rapids, MI) p. 174.

Peterson, Robert. *Are Demons for Real?* (Copyright © 1974 by Moody Press, Chicago, IL) p. 8.

Polo, Marco. *The Travels of Marco Polo.* (Orion Press, New York, distributed by Crown Publishers, Inc. Transcribed approximately AD 1280).

Rommen, Edward. *Spiritual Power and Missions: Raising the Issues* (Copyright © 1995 by Evangelical Missiological Society. Published by William Carey Library, Pasadena, CA 91114).

Strong, James. *Strong's Exhaustive Concordance of the Bible.* (Copyright © 1890 by James Strong, Madison, N.J. Abingdon Press. New York, NY, Nashville, TN).

Unger, Merrill F. *Biblical Demonology.* (Copyright © 1952 by Van Kampen Press, Inc. Wheaton, IL) p. 84.

Wagner, C. Peter. *Engaging the Enemy.* (Copyright © 1991 by Regal Books, A Division of Gospel Light, Ventura, CA) pp. 7–15.

Wagner, C. Peter. *Warfare Prayer.* (Copyright © 1992 by Regal Books, A Division of Gospel Light, Ventura, CA) p. 64–65, 81–83.

Warner, Timothy M. *Spiritual Warfare.* (Copyright © 1991 by Crossways Books, a division of Good News Publishers, Wheaton, IL) pp. 7–11, 25, 26, 28–32, 40, 41, 69–71, 72, 77–89, 90–92, 94, 95, 96, 97, 99, 109, 129, 132.

Wilkinson, Tracy. *The Vatican's Exorcists.* (Copyright © 2007 by Tracy Wilkinson, published by Warner Books, Hatchette Book Group, USA, 1271 Avenue of the Americas, New York, NY 10020) p. 30.

Wimber, John. *Power Evangelism.* (Copyright © 1986 by Harper and Row Publishers, San Francisco, CA).

ABOUT THE AUTHORS

D R. ROY AND Eleanor Rosedale have been in ministry with Campus Crusade for Christ for 46 years. They started the Campus Crusade evangelism and discipleship ministry in Indonesia, which now has approximately 500 Indonesians on various major islands of that nation, teaching other Indonesians how to lead people to Christ and how to train yet other Indonesians to do the same thing. Dr. Rosedale holds a Doctorate in Missions from Fuller Seminary School of World Mission and was Professor of World Missions at the International School of Theology. For many years he has taught Missions overseas and he helped establish seven graduate schools: in Manila, Singapore, Nairobi, Zimbabwe, Nigeria, Congo, and Burundi. Dr. Rosedale has taught spiritual warfare classes in those schools and in seminaries and churches in many countries. Eleanor was a primary school teacher and designed and engineered their home, which the family built together. She loves to garden and is an artist and writer. Eleanor travels and teaches with Roy whenever possible.